GLOBAL CHRISTIANITY

D0881857

This is No. 43 of Studies in World Christianity and Interreligious Relations. The Studies are a continuation of the Church and Theology in Context series.

The Studies are published by the Foundation for Studies in World Christianity and Interreligious Relations in collaboration with the Nijmegen Institute for Mission Studies and the Chair of World Christianity and Interreligious Relations at Radboud University Nijmegen, The Netherlands.

The aim of the Studies is to publish scholarly works on Christianity and other religions, from the perspective of interactions within them and between them.

General editor:
Frans Wijsen, Nijmegen, The Netherlands.

Editorial board:
Michael Amaladoss, Chennai, India.
Francis Clooney, Cambridge, United States of America.
Diego Irarrazaval, Santiago, Chile.
Viggo Mortensen, Aarhus, Denmark.
Robert Schreiter, Chicago, United States of America.
Abdulkader Tayob, Cape Town, South Africa.
Gerard Wiegers, Nijmegen, The Netherlands.

Manuscripts for consideration can be sent to Frans Wijsen, Radboud University Nijmegen, P.O. Box 9103, 6500 HD Nijmegen, The Netherlands.

GLOBAL CHRISTIANITY

CONTESTED CLAIMS

EDITED BY
FRANS WIJSEN
AND
ROBERT SCHREITER

Amsterdam - New York, NY 2007

The paper on which this book is printed meets the requirements of "ISO 9706:1994, Information and documentation - Paper for documents - Requirements for permanence".

ISBN: 978-90-420-2192-1
©Editions Rodopi B.V., Amsterdam - New York, NY 2007
Printed in the Netherlands

Table of contents

Frans Wijsen

Introduction

In his book *The Coming of the Third Church*,[1] the Swiss missiologist Walbert Bühlmann (1978, p.20, 143) predicted that the centre of gravity of Christianity would shift from the northern to the southern hemisphere and that the percentage of Christians in the world population would decrease from 31% in 1955 to 16% in 2000.[2] His main argument for this likely decrease was the population growth in the non-Christian—especially Asian—countries.[3] Bühlmann's book was compulsory reading for most missiology students in Western Europe in the 1970s and it influenced the theology and spirituality of many missionary workers. They were trained to do away with the last remnants of Christian triumphalism and to acknowledge that soon they would belong to a religious minority group.

Now, at the beginning of the 21st century we know—thanks to the statistical calculations of David Barrett (2001) and his co-workers and others—that Bühlmann's second prediction did not come true. Even if Barrett is not free from triumphalism (Jongeneel 2001), it is generally accepted that the percentage of Christians in the world's population did not decrease but has remained stable. Barrett even sees a growth to 33.6% by 2025. Likewise, in the 1970s, who could have dared to dream about the fall of the Berlin Wall, the explosion of Pentecostal and Charismatic churches or even the expansion of Christianity in China, at present one of the richest mission fields? But Bühlmann's first prediction did come true. The centre of gravity of Christianity has shifted overwhelmingly to the southern hemisphere (Robert 2000).

The Next Christendom

This rise of southern Christianity has been documented by the American historian and scholar of religion Philip Jenkins in his book *The Next Christendom* (2002). Over the past half century the centre of gravity of the Christian world

---

1   The book was originally published in German and entitled: *Wo der Glaube lebt* [Where the faith flourishes]. For ecclesiastical reasons, the German publisher did not accept 90 pages of the manuscript for publication. The English translation, however, has the complete text.

2   Bühlmann (1978, p.20, 143) assumed that the trends that he saw in his time would continue and that in the intervening period there would not be an unforeseen world catastrophe or extraordinary change in religious attitudes.

3   Interestingly, Bühlmann (1978, p.143 n.12) follows the Swiss theologian Hans Ruedi Weber who bases himself on the Dutch missiologist Johan Hoekendijk.

has moved decisively to the global South, says Jenkins. Within a few decades European and Euro-American Christians will have become a small fragment of world Christianity. By that time Christianity in Europe and North America will to a large extent consist of Southern-derived immigrant communities. Southern churches will fulfil neither the Liberation Dream nor the Conservative Dream of the North, but will seek their own solutions to their particular problems.

Jenkins' book evoked strong reactions—a bit to his own surprise—as the book contained little new.[4] In the United States of America, the prospect of a more biblical Christianity caused reactions of alarm in liberal circles. In contrast, conservatives were delighted by the same prospect. In Europe the book landed in the middle of the debate on Europe as an exceptional case.[5] It was detested by those who stick to the theory of ongoing and irreversible secularisation and welcomed by those who see a resurgence of religion in Europe.

In the present volume, scholars of religion and theologians assess the global trends in World Christianity as described in Philip Jenkins' book. It is the outcome of an international conference on Southern Christianity and its relation to Christianity in the North, held in the Conference Centre of Radboud University Nijmegen, the Netherlands. In view of this conference, a call for papers was sent to some five hundred colleagues all over the world. Philip Jenkins was asked to give the keynote address. The papers of Werner Ustorf, Sebastian Kim, John Chesworth and Ben Knighton were selected to be presented at the conference.[6] The other chapters were not presented at the conference, but written after the conference in response to Jenkins' paper.

Mission Studies in Nijmegen

The international conference was organized on the occasion of the 75th anniversary of the Chair of Missiology at the Radboud University Nijmegen, one of the first chairs in this discipline in a Catholic university in Europe or in the world for that matter (Verstraelen, 1995, p.430–431). Undoubtedly the perspective of missiology as an independent discipline and its place in the university

---

4   See Jenkins 2004, p.20. As early as the 1970s, the German missiologist Hans Margull spoke about the 'tertiarity' of the Church.

5   Scholars such as Peter Berger and Grace Davie (2002) have proposed that the pattern of secularisation in Europe looks increasingly to be a "special case" rather than the vanguard of the future for the rest of the world.

6   The organisers of the conference received 19 replies to the call for papers, 2 of them written by women. The papers to be read at the conference were selected by an international panel with a representative from Europe, United States of America, Africa, Asia and Latin America.

has changed considerably in the course of the past 75 years. In the early 1930s, Mission Studies started as a discipline at the service of propagating the faith and the planting of churches. It was practice-oriented, focused on the training of missionaries. During the 1960s, mission studies became more dialogical and theoretical. It reflected upon the communication between Christians and non-Christians, and upon the communication between Christians in the North and Christians in the Southern parts of the world. It was known under labels such as "theology of religions" and "third world theology".

The institutional setting has also changed over the years. From 1930 to 1948 the chair was directly under the board of governors of the university. Then came its integration into the Missiological Institute, which offered introductions to mission history, mission theology and mission law, together with auxiliary disciplines such as comparative religion, Islamic studies and Arabic, anthropology and general linguistics. In 1966 the institute was integrated into the Faculty of Theology and renamed Institute for Missiology and the History of Religions.[7] Thereafter came the establishment of departments in the Faculty of Theology in the 1980s. The chair of missiology was placed in the department of systematic theology and science of religion; in 1995, science of religion became a department of its own. In 2001, after his appointment to the chair, the present professor of missiology moved the chair to the department of empirical–practical theology, in harmony with its long tradition of missionary anthropology and the empirical study of mission in Nijmegen.[8]

Intercultural Theology Instead of Missiology?

It goes without saying that Western Europe—Germany and The Netherlands in particular—has had a rich tradition in mission studies. In the 1980s still, The Netherlands had chairs for Mission Studies in seven universities. But it is also clear that mission studies has suffered from erosion. Already in 1978, the Münster-based pastoral theologian Adolf Exeler proposed the development of comparative theology instead of missiology. He argued that the end of political colonialism meant there was no longer room for a paternalistic missiology that was at

---

7   In 1964, anthropology became an independent discipline and was integrated in the newly established Faculty of Social Sciences (Meurkens, 2002, p.496–499). General linguistics was integrated into the Faculty of Literature. What remained was mission studies and comparative religion.

8   Already in 1972, the then professor of missiology, Arnulf Camps, proposed a more empirical missiology. It was practiced by his colleague Jan van Engelen (1996). The empirical orientation, basing theory formation on case studies, is seen as a distinctive feature of missiology in Nijmegen (Verstraelen, 1995, p.431).

home only in the North Atlantic region.[9] The Second Vatican Council, moreover, said clearly that mission should be a dimension of all theological disciplines and that local churches should develop their own theologies. To the extent that both of these precepts of the Second Vatican Council were realised, missiology became a doubtful enterprise and comparative theology should work on "the issue that is at stake in missiology" (Exeler, 1978, p.199).

As we view the situation today we need to ask: has the mission of missiology in Western Europe become an impossible mission? Should its concerns be taken over by other disciplines, or should they be taken over by colleagues in Eastern Europe or the southern parts of the world, where chairs and institutes for missiology are mushrooming? Should missiology at European universities be renamed, replaced by another discipline or removed altogether? Is the mission of missiology in Europe completed? However interesting these questions may be, the practice went faster than the theory. In the Netherlands, four of the seven chairs for missiology have been closed or replaced by other disciplines and two have been renamed intercultural or cross-cultural theology. In Germany, the situation is not much different.[10]

A group of missiologists gathering in Lund in 1990 supported the idea of "missiology as an independent academic discipline". However, "this discipline has won its emancipation from theology and locates itself within the larger area of religious studies rather than within the field of theology". This discipline has "a strong empirical orientation" and "deals with the dynamic change" as result of the "interaction between religion and society" and "the interaction between this larger community and the religious bodies". Its academic location is "outside theology, perhaps within a department of religious studies" (Ustorf, 2001, p.74–76).

World Christianity and Interreligious Relations

The international conference that was organised on the occasion of the 75th anniversary of the Chair for Missiology at Radboud University Nijmegen was held shortly after the board of governors of this university had decided to open a new faculty, the Faculty of Religious Studies, next to but clearly separated

---

9   The presuppositions that missiology is 'paternalistic' and 'only at home in the North-Atlantic region' emerge throughout the article, although the author is aware that at the time he wrote the article missiology had already become missiology on "six continents" (Exeler, 1978, p.208).

10   In Britain and the Scandinavian countries there are one or two chairs. The same applies to Southern Europe (Küster 2002).

from the Faculty of Theology. Decreasing church affiliation among young people on the one hand, but also their increasing interest in religion and spirituality on the other hand, were the main reasons for opening this new faculty, as well as ambiguous relations between theologians and church officials and the debated place of theology in a university setting.

In harmony with the suggestions made during the Lund gathering (Ustorf 2001) the Chair of Mission Studies has been placed in the Faculty of Religious Studies since 1 January 2007, and renamed on that occasion. Whereas missiologists in other Dutch universities opted for 'Intercultural Theology' and 'Comparative Theology', as natural successors of 'Third World Theology' and 'Theology of Religions', the missiologists in Nijmegen opted for the name 'Studies in World Christianity and Interreligious Relations', to show unambiguously that the chair has a multi-perspective and poly-methodical approach, theology being one of them. From a post-modern and post-colonial perspective, the classical disciplines with clear-cut boundaries between them had lost their relevance anyway.[11]

The missiologists' teaching assignment in the Faculty of Theology remains. The missiologists' practice in the Faculty of Religious Studies is new and not new at the same time. It is not new because since 1948 missiology in Nijmegen has been practiced in conjunction with anthropology, history and phenomenology of religion, and linguistics. For a long time, mission studies and comparative religion were combined, as is still the case in some German universities. It is new because mission studies in the new faculty is no longer determined by theological concerns, which does not imply that theological concerns are not taken into account.

From Contextual to Inter-contextual Studies

The new chair has as its charge *comparative-empirical studies of Christianity and other religions, from the perspective of intercultural religious communication*. It studies interactions between Christians from various cultural backgrounds, and between Christians and believers of other faiths. It starts from the assumption that in our present-day world, no culture or religion can impose its worldview or lifestyle upon others; it is especially interested in existing power relations in intercultural intra- and inter-religious communication. Mission and (neo)colonialism remain important issues to be dealt with within this broader context.

---

11   Instead of multi-, inter- or intra-disciplinary, we perceive our studies as trans-disciplinary. From a non-Western perspective distinctions between philosophy, theology and religious studies are extremely fluid.

Besides empirical and comparative, the studies will be normative and strategic. The chair not only studies how communication takes place in fact, but also
how communication should take place in view of emancipation and liberation.

From 1989 onwards, the series in which this volume is published has been
called *Church and Theology in Context*. It produced 42 volumes in this spirit of
contextualization. The term contextualization first emerged in response to the
need to train church personnel in the Southern churches locally.[12] Later it
embraced currents of localization, indigenisation and inculturation. However
useful this has been in the later part of the 20th century, in the beginning of the
21st century scholars of religion and theologians see more clearly the interconnectedness of cultures and religions.[13] Therefore the board of editors decided
to rename the series to become *Studies in World Christianity and Interreligious
Relations*. However, we will continue with the subsequent number 43 to show
unambiguously that there is continuity in this change.

The series hopes to integrate the cross-cultural and comparative expertise
of the Chair of Missions Studies, whose 75th anniversary we celebrate with
this volume, the new Chair for World Christianity and Interreligious Relations,
the Nijmegen Institute for Mission Studies and the Church and Theology in
Context Foundation, which will take the name of the series and continue to
facilitate it. The editors are confident that the series remains a valuable means
for exchange of scholarly studies of intercultural religious communication,
within World Christianity and between Christianity and other religions, in collaboration with scholars of intercultural religious communication outside classical disciplines as theology and religious studies, and with partners in other
part of the world.

The Structure of the Book

The present volume reflects the new focus on intercultural studies in theology
and religion. It opens with a contribution written by Philip Jenkins in which he
elaborates on the central thesis of his book *The Next Christendom*. Jenkins' contribution is followed by five clusters of two chapters. In the first cluster, Werner
Ustorf and Ben Knighton interpret Jenkins' work against the background of
the United States of America's geo-politics, comparable to Huntington's *The

---

12   Widely used in Roman Catholic circles were the studies of Schreiter (1985) on methods for
     constructing contextual theologies and Bevans (1992) on models of contextual theology.
13   The new direction is visible in studies of David Krieger on The New Universalism (1991)
     and of Robert Schreiter on The New Catholicity (1998).

Clash of Civilizations. Whereas Ustorf sees Jenkins suggesting an alliance between the United States of America leaders and Southern Christianity, knowing that Christianity is rapidly losing ground in Europe which is also facing, Knighton thinks that Jenkins sees Southern Christianity as a threat to the United States of America's (and Jenkins' own) liberal and democratic values that are foundational for the new world order.

In the second cluster, Sebastian Kim and Frans Verstraelen criticize Jenkins from the perspective of religious statistics. Jenkins looks too much at tables and not enough at contents. Whether or not Christianity has an impact is not dependent on its numbers, but on its integrity. Both authors have a case study approach. Kim writes about Korea, India and Europe; Verstraelen writes about Europe, and The Netherlands in particular. Thereafter there are two chapters that look at Christianity in the context of religious plurality, John Chesworth in Africa and Karel Steenbrink in Indonesia. Chesworth seems to endorse Jenkins' clash of civilizations scenario, while Steenbrink does not. Chesworth sees growing competition between Muslim and Christians in Africa, without knowing who is going to win. For Steenbrink there is a clash in Indonesia, but it is not between religions but is rather within them.

The fourth cluster contains two contributions from a Latin America perspective. Joop Vernooij writes about creolisation, and Henri Gooren about Pentecostalism. However different these contributions may be, they nuance Jenkins' perspective on Christian growth by showing the complexity of religion on the one hand, and the mobility of believers on the other. In Latin America, Christianity is not only mixed with other beliefs, but also people there easily switch from one religious affiliation to another and even from religious affiliation to no religious affiliation at all. One cannot simply equate affiliation with conversion, as Jenkins seems to do. It is mixed with indigenous beliefs and people can easily switch from one religious tradition to another.

The final cluster contains two contributions from women's perspective. Martha Frederiks writes about African women constructing their own theologies without copying Western feminist theologies; Gemma Cruz writes about the Filipina domestic workers in Hong Kong, struggling to earn their own living and creating their own religiosity. Both seem to endorse Jenkins statements that Southern Christians will fulfill neither the Liberation Dream nor the Conservative Dream, but go their own way.

The shape of global Christianity is changing and with it the disciplines that study this development. It is hoped that the contributions presented in this volume will help illuminate the points of contestation both within Christianity and between Christianity and other traditions, as well as illustrate how those changes are being studied by scholars of global Christianity today. In closing the editors wish to express their gratitude to Matthew Schaefer who assisted them in their editorial work.

References

Barrett, D., Kurian, G. & Johnson, T. (eds) 2001. *World Christian encyclopedia: A comparative study of churches and religions in the modern world.* Second Edition. Oxford: Oxford UP.

Bevans, S. 1992. *Models of contextual theology.* Maryknoll, NY: Orbis Books.

Bühlmann, W. 1974. *Wo der Glaube lebt. Einblicke in die Lage der Weltkirche.* Freiburg im Breisgau: Herder Verlag.

Bühlmann, W. 1978. *The coming of the third church.* Maryknoll, NY: Orbis Books.

Camps, A. 1972. Vier sleutelbegrippen voor een meer empirische missiologie. *Vox theologica* 42: p.218–231.

Davie, G. 2002. *Europe: the exceptional case. Parameters of faith in the modern world.* London: Darton, Longman & Todd.

Exeler, A. 1978. Vergleichende Theologie statt Missionswissenschaft. (In Waldenfels, H. (ed). *"Denn ich bin bei euch": Perspektiven im christlichen Missionsbewustsein heute.* Zürich: Benzinger. p.199–211.)

Jongeneel, J. 2001. David Barrett's World Christian encyclopedia. *Exchange.* 30(4): p.372–376.

Jenkins, P. 2002. *The next christendom: the coming of global Christianity.* Oxford: Oxford UP.

Jenkins, P. 2002. After the next christendom. *International Bulletin of Missionary Research.* 28: p.20–22.

Küster, V. 2002. Intercultural theology: a paradigm shift. (In Joneleit-Oesch, S. & Neubert, M. (eds). *Interkulturelle Hermeneutik und lectura popular.* Frankfurt am Main: Verlag Otto Lembeck. p.219–227.)

Krieger, D. 1992. *The new universalism: foundations for a global theology.* Maryknoll, NY: Orbis Books.

Meurkens, P. 2002. Between nostalgia for the past and ethical enthusiasm: half a century of anthropology in Nijmegen. (In Vermeulen, H. & Kommers, J. (eds). *Tales from academia: history of anthropology in the Netherlands.* Part 1. Saarbrücken: Verlag für Entwicklungspolitik. p.493–513.)

Robert, D. 2000. Shifting southward: global Christianity since 1945. *International Bulletin of Missionary Research.* April.

Schreiter, R. 1985. *Constructing Local Theologies,* Maryknoll, NY: Orbis Books.

Schreiter, R. 1998. *The new Catholicity: theology between the global and the local.* Maryknoll, NY: Orbis Books.

Ustorf, W. 2001. Rethinking missiology. (In Houtepen, A. & Ploeger, A. (eds). *World Christianity reconsidered.* Zoetermeer: Uitgeverij Meinema.)

Verstraelen, F. 1995. The genesis of a common missiology. (In Camps, A. Hoedemaker, L. & Spindler, M. (eds). *Missiology: an ecumenical introduction.* Grand Rapids, MI: W. Eeerdmans.

Philip Jenkins

Christianity Moves South

This paper will elaborate on some statements made in the book *The Next Christendom: The Coming of Global Christianity* (2002) such as the following. Over the past half century the centre of gravity of the Christian world has moved decisively to the global South. Within a few decades European and Euro-American Christians will have become a small fragment of world Christianity. By that time the majority of Christians will live in Latin America, Africa and Asia; Christianity in Europe and North America will to a large extent consist of Southern-derived immigrant communities. Southern churches will fulfil neither the Liberation Dream nor the Conservative Dream of the North, but will seek their own solutions to their particular problems.

Ever since the terrorist attacks of September 11, 2001, commentators in Europe and North America have confronted the existence of a great religious tradition rooted in the global South, a religion they perceive as mysterious and fanatical. In trying to comprehend the force of Islam, however, many failed to note the emergence of another great "Southern" religion, namely Christianity. In our time, the heart of Christianity has moved decisively to the global South, to Africa, Asia and Latin America, and that shift represents one of the great movements in the history of the faith. Christianity was born in Africa and Asia, and in our lifetimes, it is going home.

Numbers

Partly, this is a matter of demographic change and the rapid growth of the relative share of the world's population living in Africa, Asia, and Latin America. Since the 1960s, populations have fallen or stagnated in Europe and North America, while global South birth rates have remained far higher—spectacularly so in Africa. Today, there are about two billion Christians, of whom 530 million live in Europe, 510 million in Latin America, 390 million in Africa, and perhaps 300 million in Asia, but those numbers will change substantially in coming decades. By 2025, Africa and Latin America will vie for the title of the most Christian continent. A map of the "statistical center of gravity of global Christianity" shows that center moving steadily southward, from a point in northern Italy in 1800, to central Spain in 1900, to Morocco by 1970, and to a point near Timbuktu today. And the southward trajectory will continue unchecked through the coming century. As Todd Johnson points out, Spanish has since 1980 been the leading language of church membership in the world, and Chinese, Hindi, and Swahili will soon play a much greater role. In our lifetimes, the centuries-long North Atlantic captivity of the church is drawing to an end.[1]

The figures are startling. Between 1900 and 2000, the number of Christians in Africa grew from 10 million to over 360 million, from 10 percent of the population to 46 percent. If that is not, quantitatively, the largest religious change in human history in such a short period, I am at a loss to think of a rival. Today, the most vibrant centers of Christian growth are still in Africa itself, but also around the Pacific Rim, the Christian Arc. Already today, Africans and Asians represent some 30 percent of all Christians, and the proportion will rise steadily. Conceivably, the richest Christian harvest of all might yet be found in China, a nation of inestimable importance to the politics of the coming decades. Some projections suggest that by 2050, China might contain the second-largest population of Christians on the planet, exceeded only by the United States. More confidently, we can predict that by that date, there should be around three billion Christians in the world, of whom only around one-fifth or fewer will be non-Hispanic whites (Barrett et al. 2001; Aikman 2003).

The effects of these changes can be witnessed across denominations. The Roman Catholic Church, the world's largest, was the first to feel the impact. Today, two-thirds of its adherents live in Africa, Asia, and Latin America, and that total does not include people of the global South residing in the North. By 2025, that proportion should rise to 75 percent, a fact that will undoubtedly be reflected in future papal elections. The Anglican Communion—historically, the "English" church—is becoming ever more African dominated, so that the Nigerian branch will soon be its largest representative (Wingate et al. 1998; Presler 2000). The small Seventh Day Adventist Church also epitomizes these trends. In the 1950s, the church had around a million members, mainly concentrated in the United States. Today, the church claims some fourteen million members, of whom only one million are located in the United States; and among even that American million, a sizable share are of immigrant stock (Keller 2005). Of the churches with Euro-American roots, those that are expanding do so by becoming rapidly more Southern in composition. Those that fail to expand retain their Euro-American identity, but they are shrinking perilously in terms of market share. The Orthodox Communion, still firmly rooted in Eastern Europe, offers a worrying

---

1   The religious statistics used here are drawn from Status of Global Mission 2005 at http://www.globalchristianity.org/resources.htm. For future predictions, see Barrett 2001. The map can be found in Johnson & Kim, 2005. The notion of a Euro-American "captivity of the church" dates back to at least Boyd 1974. For the "North Atlantic Captivity," see Stinton 2004.

model of apparently irreversible demographic decline. Christianity worldwide is booming, but at least in relative terms, "Western" Christianity is stagnating, while the old Eastern Christianity may be facing terminal crisis.

Southern Christianities

The concept of a rising global South is fairly recent in historical terms. In the 1950s, emerging African and Asian nations tried to distinguish themselves from what then seemed the rigid separation of the globe between capitalist West and Communist East, proclaiming their membership in a non-aligned Third World. Tragically, that term soon became synonymous not with prosperous neutrality but with grinding poverty and uncontrollable population growth, and that fact led some observers to see the critical global division as one of economics, rather than political ideology. In 1980, at the height of a renewed Cold War, the Brandt Commission portrayed the world enmired in a "Common Crisis" that involved both Global North (Europe, North America, Japan) and Global South, a term that comprised the remaining societies—by no means all of which are located in the Southern hemisphere. In this context, the term "South" is characterized not by geographical location than by relative access to wealth and resources (*North-South* 1980).

Since the 1950s, Christian leaders and religious studies scholars have grown accustomed to the vision of Christianity literally "going South," in the sense of an ever-larger share of Christians being found in the teeming poverty of the Tricontinental world. The theme is well-known in Europe, where African affairs are more attended to than they customarily have been in the US. As long ago as the 1970s, this global change was discussed in well-known works by European scholars such as Andrew Walls (1996, 2001), Edward Norman (1979) and Walbert Bühlmann. Meanwhile, African and Asian thinkers explored the intellectual implications in works such as Kosuke Koyama's *Water-Buffalo Theology* (1974) and John S. Pobee's *Toward an African Theology* (1979). By 1976, African and Latin American scholars joined to form an Ecumenical Association of Third World Theologians. Walbert Bühlmann's term "the Third Church" drew the obvious comparison with the Third World, and further suggested that the South represents a new tradition comparable in importance to the Eastern and Western churches of historical times. Walls likewise sees the faith in Africa as a distinctive new tradition of Christianity comparable to Catholicism, Protestantism, and Orthodoxy; it is "the standard Christianity of the present age, a demonstration model of its character (Fyfe & Walls, 1996, p.3); anyone who wishes to undertake serious study of Christianity these days needs to know something about Africa" (Walls, 2000, p.105). When in 1998 the World Council of Churches commemorated the fiftieth anniversary of its founding, it met in

Zimbabwe, as an explicit recognition of the growing significance of Africa in world Christianity.

Seeing Christianity "going South" in our lifetimes, we think of John Updike's wry comment "I don't think God plays well in Sweden. . . . God sticks pretty close to the Equator." That remark seems true today, and it will be ever more so in years to come.

A Primitive Church?

If these changes meant that the world's Christian population would be very different ethnically and racially from the present reality, that would in itself be a fact of great significance. In practice, though, the new world of Christianity differs even more greatly in its religious assumptions. Of course, we must be careful about generalizations concerning the vast and diverse world of Southern Christianities—and I stress the plural. There is no single Southern Christianity, any more than there is such a thing as European or North American Christianity: each of these terms involves numerous components, some strongly at odds with the others.

Yet we can reasonably say that many global South Christians are far more conservative in terms of both beliefs and moral teaching than are the mainstream churches of the global North, and this is especially true in Africa. The denominations that are triumphing all across the global South are stalwartly traditional or even reactionary by the standards of the economically advanced nations. The churches that have made most dramatic progress in the global South have either been Roman Catholic, of a traditionalist and fideistic kind, or radical Protestant sects, evangelical or Pentecostal. Indeed, this conservatism may go far towards explaining the common neglect of Southern Christianities in North America and Europe. Western experts rarely find the ideological tone of the new churches much to their taste.

Global South Christians retain a very strong supernatural orientation, and are by and large far more interested in personal salvation than in radical politics. As Harvey Cox famously showed in *Fire From Heaven* (2001), Pentecostal expansion across the southern hemisphere has been so astonishing as to justify claims of a new Reformation. In addition, rapid growth is occurring in nontraditional denominations that adapt Christian belief to local tradition, groups that are categorized by titles such as African instituted churches. Their exact numbers are none too clear, since they are too busy baptizing newcomers to be counting them very precisely. By most accounts, membership in Pentecostal and independent churches already runs into the hundreds of millions, and congregations are located in precisely the regions of fastest population growth. Within a few decades, such denominations will represent a far larger segment of global Christianity, and just conceivably a majority. These newer churches preach deep personal faith and communal orthodoxy, mysticism and puritanism, all founded on clear scriptural authority. They preach messages that, to a westerner, appear simplistically charismatic, visionary and apocalyptic. In this thought world, prophecy is an everyday reality, while faith-healing, exorcism and dream-visions are all fundamental parts of religious sensibility. For better or worse, the dominant churches of the near-future could have much in common with those of medieval or early modern European times.

Such a projection carries many implications for the churches of the "old Christendom" of Europe and North America. The greatest temptation, and maybe the worst danger, is to use future projections as a club in present-day arguments. Over the past half-century or so, whenever global South Christianity has gained attention in North America or Europe, it has been through the form of what might be termed two dreams, two competing visions, each trying to deploy that new religious movement for its own purposes. For the left, attracted by visions of liberation, the rise of the South suggests that Northern Christians must commit themselves to social and political activism at home, to ensuring economic justice and combating racism, to promoting cultural diversity. Conservatives, in contrast, emphasize the moral and sexual conservatism of the emerging churches, and seek to enlist them as natural allies. From their point of view, growing churches are those that stand furthest from Western liberal orthodoxies, and we should learn from their success. A Liberation Dream confronts a Conservative Dream. For both sides, though, the new South is useful, politically and rhetorically. Even if activists hold an unusual or unpopular position, it can be justified on the basis that it represents the future: if they wait long enough, they will be vindicated by the churches of Africa (or Asia, or Latin America). Like any true-believing Marxist, one is claiming to be on the side of history, which will absolve its faithful disciples.

I would rather argue that both expectations, liberal and conservative, are wrong, or at least, fail to see the whole picture. Each in its different way expects the Southern churches to reproduce Western obsessions and approaches, rather than evolving their own distinctive solutions to their own particular problems. One difficulty is deciding just what that vast and multifaceted entity described as the Third World, or the Two-Thirds World, actually does want or believe. As I have suggested, the "South" is massively diverse, and conservatism and liberalism are defined quite differently from the customary usages of North American or European churches. Conservative theological or moral stances often accompany quite progressive or radical economic views. And the North-South divergence will probably grow as time goes on. As Southern churches grow and mature, they will increasingly define their own interests in ways that have little to do with the preferences and parties of Americans and Europeans.

The Church of the Poor

In the meantime, though, the newer churches certainly demonstrate many "primitive" characteristics, using that term in its positive, laudatory sense. Partly, this is a matter of the social and economic basis of the new Christian communities, which encourages a strong identification with a Biblically-based world view, and with religious authority.

The average Christian in the world today is a poor person, very poor indeed by the standards of the white worlds of North America and Western Europe. Also different is the social and political status of African and Asian Christians, who are often minorities in countries dominated by other religions or secular ideologies. This historic social change cannot fail to affect attitudes toward the Bible. For many Americans and Europeans, not only are the societies in the Bible—in both Testaments—distant in terms of time and place, but their everyday assumptions are all but incomprehensible. It is easy, then, to argue that the religious and moral ideas that grew up in such an alien setting can have little application for a modern community. Yet exactly the issues that make the Bible a distant historical record for many Americans and Europeans keep it a living text in the churches of the global South.

For many such readers, the Bible is congenial because the world it describes is marked by such currently pressing social problems as famine and plague, poverty and exile, clientelism and corruption. A largely poor readership can readily identify with the New Testament society of peasants and small craftsmen dominated by powerful landlords and imperial forces, by networks of debt and credit. In such a context, the excruciating poverty of a Lazarus eating the crumbs beneath the rich man's table is not just an archaeological curiosity. This sense of recognition is quite clear for modern dwellers in villages or small towns, but it also extends to urban populations, who are often close to their rural roots. And while some resemblances might be superficial, their accumulated weight adds greatly to the credibility of the text, the sense that it is written for a contemporary world. The Bible provides immediate and often material answers to life's problems. It teaches ways to cope and survive in such a hostile environment, and at the same time holds out the hope of ultimate prosperity (Hoppe 2004).

In other ways too, the demographic makeup of Southern Christian churches promotes ideas of religious authority and reliance on inspired texts. Today, half the inhabitants of this planet are under twenty-four, and of those, almost 90 percent live in the global South. What else marks the landscape and soundscape of a Third World society so definitively as the abundance of its children? Young adults predominate in Southern churches—and mosques—and that profile shapes attitudes to faith. We think of the kind of idealism we will find in such a congregation of the young: the fire, the openness to changing the world and overthrowing natural hierarchies, the openness to ecstasy. We think also of the desire for certainty, for absolute standards; the denial of subtleties and compromises, of shades of gray; the rejection of hierarchy and experience, the quest for immediate experience and direct access to the divine; and the need for absolute conviction. In the Euro-American tradition, this demographic profile sounds like the Methodist revival of eighteenth-century England, the American revivals of 1740 or 1798; and that age structure will continue to be the central fact in global religion for at least the next half-century. Such congregations respond avidly to messages grounded in the assured certainty of revealed scripture.

The World and The Devil

For many African and Asian Christians, familiarity with the New Testament world extends to their understanding of evil and sickness. As in the early church, much of global South Christianity today is a healing religion par excellence, with a strong belief in the objective existence of evil, and (commonly) a willingness to accept the reality of demons and the diabolical. Biblical texts and passages that the South makes central are seen by many Northern churches as marginal, symbolic, or purely historical in nature.

The North-South divide is not absolute, and some Euro-American Christians accept theories of the diabolic and demonic, of supernatural warfare and spiritual healing: witness the continued success of a classic such as C. S. Lewis's *The Screwtape Letters*. Yet most Northern-world Christians share the bemusement and the mockery with which the more secular-minded regard such manifestations. For post-Enlightenment Christians in the West, the demonic elements in the New Testament mean so little that they are scarcely even an embarrassment anymore. Many Westerners read over such passages and attribute them to a long-departed stage of scientific development. Most Northern readers today would label believers in demons and witchcraft irredeemably premodern, prescientific, and probably preliterate; and such beliefs would cast doubt on believers' claims to an authentic or intelligent religion.

Yet the supernatural approach certainly harkens back to the ancient roots of Christianity. To read the gospels is to make the intimate acquaintance of demons and demonic forces. Arguing for a social justice approach to Christianity, Jim Wallis rightly points out that excising references to "the poor" leaves very little of the biblical text intact (Wallis 2005). But by the same principle, precious little is left of the New Testament after we purge all mentions of angels, demons, and spirits. Shorn of healing and miraculous cures, the four gospels would be a slim pamphlet indeed (Porterfield 2005).

Under Northern eyes, such demonological readings raise troubling questions about the future of Christianity. Yet a Christian worldview that acknowledges supernatural evil does not disqualify itself from active participation in worldly struggles, including movements for far-reaching social and economic transformation. *Deliverance* in the charismatic sense can easily be linked to political or social *liberation*, and the two words are, of course, close cognates.

Also, we have to situate emerging Christianity in its social and intellectual context. Whatever their spiritual truth—whatever their fidelity to Christian tradition—supernatural approaches can be valuable in moving societies away from pernicious traditional superstitions. For instance, offering distinctively Christian solutions to witchcraft helps disarm the sometimes bloody practices of anti-witchcraft rituals. In a relatively short time, the new Christian emphasis on prayer and Bible reading defuses the fatalism inherent in a traditional system based on notions such as witchcraft, curses, and the power of ancestors. Instead, Christians are taught to rely on faith, and on the role of the individual, who is no longer a slave to destiny or fate. By treating older notions of spiritual evil seriously, Christians are leading an epochal cultural revolution.

The supernatural orientation of contemporary African or Asian Christianity is not surprising given their recent historical inheritance. The ready attribution of evil to powerful spiritual forces reflects the continuing influence of pagan and animist beliefs, and we must remember what a recent presence Christianity is in these regions. In the lands that would become Nigeria, for instance, just between 1900 and 1970, the Christian share of the population grew from roughly 1 percent to around 44 percent, and overwhelmingly, those new converts came from peoples who had earlier been animists or ethnoreligionists. For Africa as a whole, the religious shift during the twentieth century meant that around one-third of the continental population transferred its allegiance away from native religions or animism to different shades of Christianity. Most African Christians are second- or third-generation members of the faith, so that a lively animist presence is always in evidence.

Memories of folk religions also remain strong among Korean and Chinese Christians, most of whom come from families converted over the past half-century. A rich novel such as Han Malsook's *Hymn of the Spirit* (1983) suggests how Korean Christianity established itself in a society deeply imbued with Buddhist and shamanistic elements, in which enormous significance was already attached to dreams, visions, and divination. In Latin America, the surging Pentecostal churches of Brazil commonly draw on believers converted from African-rooted faiths such as Umbanda. Around the world, sorcerers, mediums, spirit healers, and other spiritual professionals are familiar figures in everyday life, much as they were in the milieu of the book of Acts. Then as now, a trip to a marketplace might well mean an encounter with a magician claiming to invoke pagan forces.[2]

---

2   For conversion statistics, see Barrett 2001; Meyer 1999; Metuh et al 2002.

Pagan and primal religions teach the existence of spiritual menaces facing society, but they also provide means to combat those dangers. A crucial flaw of early white missionary activity in Africa and Asia was that it forbade these solutions, whether amulets, fetishes, spells, charms, or ceremonies, since all were conspicuous symbols of pagan practice. At the same time, though, missionaries rarely offered plausible spiritual resources to combat what were still universally seen as pressing menaces. For most missionaries, New Testament stories of healing were interpreted "either as spiritual lessons having little to do with prayer for sick bodies, or as a call to found clinics and hospitals." As Grant LeMarquand comments, "The latter they ought to have done, not neglecting the former" (2000, p.87). Newer indigenous churches succeeded by taking seriously the danger posed by the demonic and supernatural—indeed, in interpreting these forces firmly in the ancient Christian tradition. They allowed believers the right to bear arms for spiritual self-defense, though protection was now characterized in strictly Christian terms.

The sense of confronting a vast empire of evil does not cause believers to despair, since the Christian message teaches that the powers of good have already triumphed over these forces, through the Incarnation and Resurrection. Christ's victory is epitomized in the cross and crucifixion, themes that are absolutely central to hymns and forms of popular devotion. Jesus defeated death and sin not just in this world, but in any conceivable realm of spirits or ancestors. Indeed, early Christian apologists repeatedly used the evidence of spiritual triumph as a key selling point for the faith. For Justin Martyr or Origen, the truth of Christianity was proved every time an ordinary Christian cast out demons, not through great occult learning, but through prayer and simply invoking the name of Jesus. As Tertullian boasted, "All the authority and power we have over them is from our naming of the name of Christ."[3] In much of today's Christian world, such arguments still ring true. Reading Hebrews, African Catholics learn that Jesus "is superior to the angels and spirits and to any ancestor one might think of; he surpasses in dignity and efficacy all soothsayers and sacrificers."[4] In Korea too, where "the power of the dead is stronger than that of the living . . . the traditional faith of Koreans in the power of ancestors and the influence of the killed for justice is in accord with the Christian faith in the death and resurrection of Jesus" (Park 1995; Lung-Kwong 2003).

Biblical descriptions of Jesus' triumph over evil imagine a king dragging his defeated enemies behind him, while rewarding his followers: "Having spoiled principalities and powers, [Christ] made a shew of them openly, triumphing

---

3   Justin Martyr, *Second Apology,* ch. 85; Origen, *Contra Celsum,* 7:4; Tertullian, *Apology,* ch.22–23.

4   *The African Bible.* Nairobi: Paulines Publications, 1999.

over them in it" (Colossians 2:15) and "When he ascended, he led captivity captive, and gave gifts unto men" (Ephesians 4:8). These heroic images still make wonderful sense for anyone accustomed to traditional African or Asian cultures. One hymn from the Transvaal declares,

> Jesus Christ is Conqueror
> By his resurrection he overcame death itself
> By his resurrection he overcame all things
> He overcame magic
> He overcame amulets and charms
> He overcame the darkness of demon possession
> He overcame dread
> When we are with him
> We also conquer (Chandler, 2000, p.102).

Such a hymn could easily have been sung by Mediterranean Christians of the first three centuries after Jesus' time. Still more startlingly martial is a hymn of the Ghanaian Afua Kuma:

> If Satan troubles us
> Jesus Christ
> You who are the lion of the grasslands
> You whose claws are sharp
> Will tear out his entrails
> And leave them on the ground
> For the flies to eat (Bediako, 2004, p.11).

Victorian hymn writers had little to teach their modern counterparts about utilizing bloody or militaristic imagery.

Ideas of spiritual warfare and deliverance span the globe, in the sense that they are found wherever charismatic churches exist. The doctrine is grounded in a passage from the letter to the Ephesians, "we wrestle not against flesh and blood, but against principalities, against powers, against the rulers of the darkness of this world, against spiritual wickedness in high places." Across Africa and Asia, spiritual warfare is a familiar component of most Christian practice, even among denominations that in the global North would scorn such approaches. The boundaries separating evangelical and charismatic churches are very porous in the global South, so that African and Asian evangelicals demonstrate little of the coolness to "Pentecostal excesses" that marks their North American brethren. Moreover, mainstream liturgical churches (Catholic, Anglican, Lutheran) have adopted at least elements of the spiritual warfare worldview, largely through sincere conviction, but also from the urgent need to compete with Pentecostal, charismatic, and independent congregations.

Demonology is thus credible for African and Asian churches, in a way it can scarcely be for most educated Westerners, and so is the idea of exorcism. I once heard a white American Adventist clergyman recount a hair-raising tale

of his visit to a packed church service in southern Africa. Though initially star-
tled to see a white face in its midst, the hospitable congregation was delighted
to find that the visitor was an ordained pastor. Happy to welcome the new
arrival, the church's minister announced that Pastor Smith had come all the
way from America to visit them, and that he would be conducting tonight's
exorcism. Pastor Smith, needless to say, had no experience whatever of such a
practice, and he had to improvise speedily.[5]

Not all African churches offer exorcism and spiritual healing on a routine
basis. For many clergy, counseling is the correct response for a person who comes
forward reporting being possessed or bewitched. Even in such cases, though,
the powerful example of the Bible means that the sufferer's belief system must
be treated with total respect, and spiritual intervention must be offered as a last
resort. Having said this, the normality of spiritual healing is in some form
accepted across most denominations, including those that in Europe or North
America would be regarded as strictly mainstream. At a healing revival in
Uganda, a woman reported being cured of a spinal complaint. After this event,
"a whole stream of people . . . stood up one by one to declare joyfully what Jesus
had done for them. They had been dumb, mad or psychologically disturbed; crip-
pled, epileptic, hemorrhaging; they had had cancer, epilepsy and asthma. By turns
they declared that they had been healed by prayer and the power of the Lord
Jesus. So many people wanted to testify that in the end the parish catechist
simply resorted to calling out the afflictions and doing a headcount of those
who had been healed" (Cooper 2002). This may sound like the typical currency
of charismatic movements the world over, except that this particular example
occurred in a Roman Catholic church, through the ministry of an Indian priest,
and the initial miracle described took place during the exposition of the Blessed
Sacrament.

Incidentally, the power of the spiritual warfare perspective helps explain the
vigor of contemporary North-South controversies over recent sexual controversies, for instance within the Anglican Communion. When conservative African
and Asian clergy invoked the language of the diabolical in these conflicts, they
were not just indulging in overheated rhetoric. Reacting to the proposed ordination of a gay bishop in the Church of England, Nigerian primate Peter Akinola
proclaimed, "This is an attack on the Church of God—a Satanic attack on God's
Church." Speaking of the U.S. Episcopal bishops who refused to approve the ordination of Bishop Gene Robinson, Akinola applauded "the admirable integrity and
loyalty of those gallant 45 Bishops of ECUSA who have refused to succumb to
the pressure for compromise. In the language of the Bible, they have refused to

---

5   For the relationship between mainstream and independent churches, see Adogame & Omyajowo
     1998; Bergunder 2001.

bow their knees to Baal" (Akinola 2003). Another conservative, southeast Asian primate Datak Yong Ping Chung, similarly portrayed Episcopal liberals as compromising with evil forces. He protested, "The enemy, the devils, try to discount and destroy the church by promoting the so-called critical approach to the Bible" (Stammer 2001). Bowing to idols and serving demons might be familiar enough metaphors in Western society. The imagery has quite different connotations when used in societies in which fertility rituals, animism, and image worship still exist; and in which, moreover, these customs are not seen as quaint parts of the tourist heritage, but as living manifestations of devil worship.

Martyrs

I would also highlight another critical North-South difference, namely in attitudes towards the secular state. The New Testament portrays persecution as a likely if not inevitable consequence of Christian belief. In Mark's Gospel, Jesus warns his followers of bleak times yet to come, warns about *when* they lead you before a court, not *if*. Most Western readers see in such passages only historical references to long-gone times of persecution. These prophecies, after all, belong to a time when expulsion from the synagogues was a nightmare to be dreaded. In contrast, persecution is a quite real prospect for much of the new Christianity, and martyrdom is both a recent and a continuing reality for many African and Asian churches.

When Euro-American Christians hear the word "martyr," the images that come to mind have an ancient air, perhaps white-clad men or women facing lions in an arena reminiscent of the film *Gladiator*. The connotations for modern African and Asian Christians are quite different and, of course, contemporary. Not long ago, the Kenya-based Pauline Publications produced its sumptuous *African Bible*, which applies the scriptural text to contemporary African conditions. The cover portrays what at first sight looks like a Maltese cross design, but the underlying story is rather more complex. The design "is based on metal crosses made by Philip Makuei, of the village of Jalé in Bor area, southern Sudan. . . . One day, searching for metal to use in his craft of mending canoes, he discovered that the gas tank of the MiG fighter which had crashed nearby provided metal that could be easily worked." He took special delight in transforming the scrap metal into crosses. "The area had experienced bombing from such MiGs as the one Philip used for his crosses. Some people have seen in the cross the representation of four MiG fighters colliding—the emblems of death being transformed into the emblem of life."[6] For a global North Christian, the

---

6   *The African Bible*. 1999. Nairobi: Paulines Publications. p.2176.

word "martyrdom" implies a cinematic lion; for an African, it suggests a jet fighter in the service of a strictly contemporary regime.

The difference of expectation about the secular state has many implications. All too often, secular ideologies appear false and destructive; their claims to provide growth and improvement are farcically inaccurate; and they sometimes involve bloody repression. Even when states are not actively homicidal, the common assumption—in the twenty-first century, as in the first—is that the state is a hostile institution, and that secular society must be seen as enemy territory, in which believers tread at their peril. Christians are rarely wise to put their faith in princes or presidents. Because of their modern historical experience, many Southern Christians easily identify with the profoundly antistate and separatist texts in the New Testament produced by early believers living within the Roman Empire, who themselves faced the danger of imminent persecution. Such diffidence—to say the least—about the secular world contrasts sharply with attitudes in the global North. If global South believers are accused of "supernaturalism," we might well ask what grounds they have for putting their trust in developments in this unjust world.

Missionaries

I could point to many other critical differences between what passes for mainstream belief and practice in North and South, but these examples will serve as illustrations. Apart from its intrinsic interest, Southern and especially African Christianity is likely to become an ever-better known phenomenon in the global North as a result of immigration, but also through deliberate evangelistic activity undertaken throughout Europe and North America.

Perhaps the most successful example of such evangelism today is the Kiev-based church founded by Nigerian Sunday Adelaja, the Embassy of the Blessed Kingdom of God for all Nations. Sunday Adelaja was one of many bright African and Asian students brought to the Soviet Union to receive an education, and ideally to become a future advocate of pro-Soviet views. Within a couple of years, the Soviet Union itself dissolved, and in 1994 Adelaja founded a Pentecostal congregation in the new Ukrainian republic.

From seven founding members, the church soon claimed thirty thousand adherents, overwhelmingly white, and the church spread widely. As the church reports, "Over twenty services are held every Sunday in various auditoriums of Kiev, Ukraine. There are over fifty daughter churches functioning in the Kiev region. More than a hundred daughter and satellite churches exist in the cities and villages of Ukraine. Over two hundred churches in the countries of the former Soviet Union, the USA, Germany, UAE, Israel, and Holland have been founded. . . . The church's Christian television and radio programs reach approximately eight million people."[7] Within the Ukraine, the church's main dilemma, in fact, was in finding facilities large enough to accommodate its numbers, but fortunately the old Soviet Union had built many grand auditoriums for union functions and sports gatherings. Wry observers suggest that perhaps at last, Christians can understand the historic role of Communism, in building facilities large enough to cope with Pentecostal churches. Sunday Adelaja's Embassy bases its success largely on its promise of healing, and its website offers testimonies from Russians and Ukrainians who report being healed from all manner of complaints, including AIDS and cancer. Boris, a police lieutenant, reports being raised from the dead.

Calling a New World into Being

In some cases, the churches of the global North have deliberately sought to draw on the new religious manifestations emerging in Africa, especially. The moral and sexual conservatism of Southern believers is music to the ears of North Americans or Europeans who find themselves at odds with the progressive leaderships of their own churches. When they suffer an ideological defeat at home—when for instance a new denomination approves same-sex marriages—conservatives are tempted to look South and to say, in effect, "Just you wait." History is on the side of the Southern churches, which will not tolerate this nonsense. These observers echo the hopes of George Canning, the British statesman who looked at the newly independent Latin America of the 1820s and declared that "I called the New World into existence to redress the balance of the old." Finding Southern allies is doubly valuable for traditionalists, since conservative positions stand a much better chance of gaining a hearing in the mainstream media when they are presented by African or Asian religious leaders rather than the familiar roster of white conservatives. Also, Northern traditionalists are tempted to believe that the tides of history are clearly running their way. As the old liberal mainline churches lose their influence in the face of changing world demographics, so their progressive ideas are expected to fade along with them.

But Northern world conservatives have not been content to wait for the currents of history, and especially in North America, some have sought to use like-minded Southern churches for their own purposes. In 2000, some conservative U.S. Episcopalians took a step that was remarkable enough at the time, and would have been shocking only a few years earlier. Two (white) American

---

7   http://www.it-is-easy.org/contact/friends/sunday.php. Dawn Herzog Jewell, "From Africa to Ukraine," (2005), at http://www.christianitytoday.com/tc/2005/006/4.42.html.

clergy traveled to Singapore where they were ordained as bishops by conservative Archbishops Tay and Kolini, as well as several other African and American clerics. By ancient tradition, an archbishop is free to ordain whoever he pleases within his province, so that one of the US dissidents legally became a bishop within the province of Rwanda. In addition, though, these Americans assumed a radical and controversial new role within North America. They effectively became missionary bishops charged to minister to conservative congregations, where they would support a dissident "virtual province" within the church. They, and their conservative colleagues, were now part of the Anglican Mission in America. This grouping aspired to help "lead the Episcopal Church back to its biblical foundations," to restore traditional teachings on issues such as the ordination of gay clergy, and blessing same-sex marriages: in short, to combat the "manifest heresy" of the U.S. church leadership. Since 2001, several more American bishops have been consecrated to serve what looked increasingly like a new denomination (Bates 2004).

Within both the US and Canada, though, many rank and file Episcopalians expressed sympathy for the new bishops and their international sponsors—all the more so after the 2003 decision to ordain Bishop Gene Robinson, a noncelibate homosexual. North American conservatives found themselves much closer politically to the upstart churches of Africa and Asia than to their own church elites, as they looked to Singapore and Rwanda to defend themselves against New York and Ottawa. Thirty or so conservative Episcopalian congregations physically located in North America are now technically part of the jurisdiction of the Archdiocese of Rwanda, white soldiers following black and brown generals (Rodgers 2005).

Since 2003, the conservative wing of the Episcopal church has been in ferment, with an upsurge of new networks and pressure groups such as the American Anglican Council and the Anglican Communion Network, the latter operating under a Pittsburgh bishop. AMIA also still flourishes. As the use of the "Anglican" term suggests, conservatives were seeking to place their own views in the global context, rather than merely using the local US term "Episcopal". More conservative Anglicans have placed themselves under global South prelates, as perhaps a hundred parishes tried to secede from their own dioceses. Some look to the Province of the Latin American Southern Cone, as priests resident in Baltimore or Philadelphia notionally serve the Anglican Church of Chile or Bolivia. African and Asian prelates are now a familiar sight at US Anglican gatherings, as conservatives seek alliances with orthodox and traditional believers across the ecclesiastical spectrum.[8]

---

8   For more information see http://www.americananglican.org/; http://acn-us.org/; http://www.mereanglicanism.com/. For Canadian developments, see http://www.anglicanessentials.ca/.

The existence of AMIA and other conservative breakaways is in itself a remarkable statement of changing perceptions of Christian orthodoxy, and the geographical bases of authority within the church. For many conservative American believers, orthodoxy travels from the South to the North. After a visit to his distant archdiocesan home in Africa, one AMIA cleric asked wonderingly, "Who should be missionaries to whom?" (Niebuhr 2001). For many, that question is now thoroughly settled.

Nor, as noted earlier, are the Anglicans unique in seeking to turn the ecclesiastical world upside down. The closest present-day analogy to Anglican circumstances occurs among the world's Lutherans, another church that originated in Northern Europe, but which now finds its chief centers of growth in Africa and Asia. Though Lutherans claim 66 million members worldwide, a large proportion of these are at best nominal adherents of the historic state churches of Scandinavia, Germany and the Baltic states, and these bodies are stagnant or declining. In contrast, membership is soaring in the upstart African churches, which together account for some fourteen million Lutherans. Just between 2001 and 2003, membership of African Lutheran churches grew by an enviable nine percent. The most amazing example of such growth must be the Ethiopian Evangelical Church Mekane Yesus, formed in 1959 with twenty thousand members. The church grew to over a million members by 1991, topped four million by 2003, and continues to boom. As a Lutheran church report notes, in a surprisingly matter of fact tone, the EECMY "has experienced a 15 percent per year growth rate for many years."[9]

As in the Anglican case, the Northern branches of the Lutheran denomination are highly liberal, and seek to enforce progressive views on conservative clergy. Those clergy in turn sought the help and protection of traditional minded African prelates, such as Kenyan bishop Walter Obare Omwanza, who denounced the official church for practicing "a secular, intolerant, bureaucratic fundamentalism inimical to the word of God and familiar from various church struggles against totalitarian ideologies during the 20th century." He attacked the Swedish ordination of women as "a Gnostic novelty," which "cannot tolerate even minimal co-existence with classical Christianity."[10]

Schism?

Quite probably, the story of Christianity over the coming decades will be marked by new schisms that broadly follow the North-South division, conflicts for which

---

9   For information see: http://www.lutheranworld.org/News/LWI/EN/1404.EN.html; http://www.elca.org/countrypackets/ethiopia/church.html.

10   See http://www.missionsprovinsen.se/the_letter_from_bishop_w_obare_to_the_archbishop_kg_hammar_(eng).htm.

the present Anglican/Episcopalian rift provides a sour foretaste. Unless both North and South, liberals and conservatives, make a heroic effort to understand the language of their opponents, and the historical and cultural values in which it is based, schisms are all but certain. We can also predict with fair confidence the rhetorical approaches of both sides, as Northern liberals denounce intolerant fundamentalism, while Southern churches assert fealty to biblical foundations. The word "primitive" will be freely thrown around, though with radically different meanings, positive and negative. In themselves, such splits are not necessarily to be dreaded: cultural differences often have fragmented Christian congregations in the past, and they will do so again. But it would be a tragedy if each tradition, each region, sundered itself from the cultural and spiritual resources offered by its rival.

To illustrate the nature of these conflicts, I will describe an actual conversation between a representative of a solid mainstream denomination, and an upstart church from the newly evangelized world, though I admit that I am doctoring the quote, altering one key word. The mainstream cleric complains that, "your beliefs are too young," suggesting that the new churches simply did not have the intellectual capacity to understand the sophisticated theological debates then roiling the advanced world. But the man from the emerging church stands his ground. He retorts that "All heresies have emanated from you, have flourished among you; by us, that is by the Southern nations they have been here strangled, here put an end to": the new churches are the defenders of orthodoxy. The upstart cleric concedes the charge of youth and inexperience, which he holds out as a virtue. An ancient church, he replies, is a weary and decadent one, and has compromised with worldly wisdom. "Since you declare the faith of the Africans to be young, I quite agree with you; for always the faith of Christ is young. . . . Where faith is not accompanied by works, then faith is not young but old, and people make fun of it for its age, like an old worn out garment."[11]

This dialogue occurred in Constantinople around 970 between a leading cleric of the Orthodox Church, and the Western visitor, Liutprand of Cremona, who was defending the Western nations, not the Southern. But the accusations between the two sides seem familiar today. The over-sophisticated Byzantines produced heresies, Western Popes suppressed them: new churches are the defenders of orthodoxy. "The race of the Saxons, from the time when it received the holy baptism and the knowledge of God, has been spotted by no heresy which would have rendered a synod necessary of an error which did not exist." Do I draw too improbable an analogy by applying this passage today, substituting

---

11   Liutprand of Cremona, "Report of his Mission to Constantinople," at http://medieval. ucdavis.edu/ 20A/Luitprand.html.

for the defiant Liutprand an African or Chinese bishop; for the arrogant Byzantines an American or European?

As a coda to that story, we recall the final decisive break between the churches, the still unhealed schism of 1054. Remarkably for such a vast event, its causes lay less in great issues of theology than in matters that seem culturally driven, more symbolic than substantial: the use of unleavened bread in the Eucharist, and whether priests should be clean shaven. In retrospect, most appear on a par with Gulliver's discovery of two nations divided over the proper end to open an egg. But while priest's beards scarcely seem sufficient reason to divide Christ's church, the incident reminds us of a powerful fact. Divisions that are "just cultural" are often the most deeply felt, especially when one party feels such a sense of grievance and historic exploitation (Chadwick 2003; Chadwick 2005).

As we examine the growing churches of the global South, we can reasonably ask whether the emerging Christian traditions of the Two-Thirds World have recaptured themes and trends in Christianity that the older churches have forgotten, and if so, what we can learn from their insights. What can, or should, be done about that cultural gap? For anyone accustomed to living in the environment of "Western Christianity," the critical question must be to determine what is the authentic religious content, and what is cultural baggage. What, in short, is Christianity, and what is merely Western?

References

Adogame, A. & Omyajowo, A. 1998. Anglicanism and the Aladura churches in Nigeria. (In Wingate et al. 1998. p. 90–97.)

Aikman, D. 2003. *Jesus in Beijing*. Chicago: Regnery.

Akinola, P. 2003. Statement from the bishops of the Anglican Church of Nigeria, 21 November 2003. http://www.anglican-mainstream.org.za/nigeria.html

Barrett, D., Kurian, D., & Johnson, T. 2001. *World Christian encyclopedia*. 2nd ed. New York: Oxford UP: p. 12–15.

Bates, S. 2004. *A Church at war*. New York: I.B. Tauris.

Bediako, K. 2004. *Jesus and the gospel in Africa*. Maryknoll, NY: Orbis.

Bergunder, M. 2001. Miracle healing and exorcism. *IRM* 90: p.103–112.

Boyd, R.H.S. 1974. *India and the latin captivity of the church*. New York: Cambridge UP.

Bühlmann, W. 1976. *The coming of the third church*. Slough, UK: St Paul.

Chadwick, H. 2003. *East and West — the making of a rift in the church*. Oxford: Oxford UP.

Chadwick, H. 2005. *The early church*. London: Penguin.

Chandler, P. 2000. *God's global mosaic*. Downers Grove, IL: InterVarsity Press.

Cooper, K. 2002. Spiritual warfare in Africa. *Tablet*. 28 September.

Cox, H. 2001. *Fire from heaven*. Cambridge, MA: Da Capo Press.

Fyfe, C. & Walls, A. (eds) 1996. *Christianity in Africa in the 1990s*. Edinburgh: Centre of African Studies.

Hoppe, L. 2004. *There shall be no poor among you*. Nashville: Abingdon Press.

Johnson, T. & Kim, S. 2005. Describing the worldwide Christian phenomenon. *International bulletin of missionary research.* 29(2): p. 80–84.

Keller, E. 2005. *The road to clarity.* New York: Palgrave Macmillan.

Koyama, K. 1974. *Water buffalo theology.* Maryknoll, NY: Orbis.

LeMarquand, G. 2000. New testament exegesis in (modern) Africa. (In West, G. & Dube, M. (eds). *The Bible in Africa.* Leiden: Brill. p.72–102.)

Lung-Kwong, Lo. 2003. The nature of the issue of ancestral worship among Chinese Christians. *SWC* 9 (1): p.30–42.

Malsook, H. 1983. *Hymn of the spirit.* New York: Fremont Publications.

Metuh, E.I. (ed) 2002. *The gods in retreat.* Enugu, Nigeria: Fourth Dimension Publishers.

Meyer, B. 1999. *Translating the devil.* Trenton, NJ: Africa World Press.

Niebuhr, G. 2001. Episcopal dissidents find African inspiration. *New York Times* 6 March.

Norman, E. 1979. *Christianity and the world order.* Oxford: Oxford UP.

Norman, E. 1981. *Christianity in the southern hemisphere.* Oxford: Oxford UP.

North-South: a programme for survival. 1980. Cambridge, MA: MIT Press.

Park Jae Soon. 1995. Cross: from killing to interliving. *CTC Bulletin* 13 (3).

Pobee, J. 1979. *Toward an African theology.* Nashville: Abingdon.

Porterfield, A. 2005. *Healing in the history of Christianity.* New York: Oxford UP.

Presler, T. 2000. Old and new in worship and community. *Anglican theological review* (Fall, 2000).

Rodgers, A. 2005. Priest, deacons ordained to serve Episcopal splitoffs. *Pittsburgh Post-Gazette* 13 November.

Stammer, L. 2001. Their truths shall set them apart. *Los Angeles Times.* 30 June.

Stinton, D. 2004. *Jesus of Africa.* Maryknoll, N.Y.: Orbis.

Torres, S. & Fabella, V. (eds) 1978. *The emergent gospel.* Maryknoll, NY: Orbis.

Wallis, J. 2005. *God's politics.* San Francisco: Harper San Francisco.

Walls, A. 1996. *The missionary movement in Christian history.* Maryknoll, NY: Orbis.

Walls, A. 2000. Eusebius tries again. *International bulletin of missionary research* 24(3): p.105–111.

Walls, A. 2001. *The cross-cultural process in Christian history.* Maryknoll, NY: Orbis.

Wingate, A., Ward, K., Pemberton, C., Sitshebo, W. (eds) 1998. *Anglicanism.* New York: Church Publishing.

Werner Ustorf

Global Christianity, New Empire, and Old Europe

This paper offers a debate of some of the theses put forward by Philip Jenkins. Some theses only, because others have been known to missiologists for quite a while; whereas some of the assumptions underlying his work can be traced back to the beginning of the modern missionary movement itself. Rather more interesting is Jenkins' forecasting of the continued rise of the public importance of religion, and the inevitability of "Christendom" or of the global retreat of modern nation state structures and the advance of powerful political religions. Fanatic political faith, however, is, theologically, non-Christian faith. It needs to be opposed even if it comes along in Christian garments: this is a lesson we learnt, e.g. in the struggles of the 1930s. All these phenomena of faith regression into idolatry are related not so much with (medieval) Christendom (or, as in Jenkins' argument: the South), but rather the totalitarianism or the new nationalism of the North and, therefore, the religious production of a highly modern conception.

Christianity does not just represent the religious past of the West. There is a phenomenal rise of Christian activity in the South and, more specifically, of Pentecostal and charismatic enthusiasm, making this religion, despite the history of Fascism and Socialism, the most successful social movement of the 20th century and, very likely, a global political force in the next.

This was the message Philip Jenkins was driving home in his pre-9/11 book on *The Next Christendom*. It did indeed need to be driven home because the media and the academy in the West, in Europe in particular, for a century or so were blasé about Christianity and mesmerised and blinkered by their belief in secularism and the end of religion. But it was a message that had been shared among missiologists and experts, who, since the 1960s, were carefully taking account of the surge of Christian dynamism in Africa, Asia, Latin America and the Pacific and, in the 70s already, predicted the coming of the *Third Church* or the *Thirdworldliness* of Christianity's future (Jenkins 2002). The difference to such experts, for example Walbert Bühlmann (1976), David Barrett (1982) or Hans Jochen Margull (1974), my own teacher, seems to be the way Jenkins put forward his evidence. *The Next Christendom* addressed the question on a very wide canvass and on the basis of an excellent collection of secondary sources and a critical discussion of global statistical and demographical data. He showed himself in command of these diverse materials that were presented in such a spectacular way that people would listen; but it is also true that since 9/11 religion has re-entered the arena and made the public more receptive towards the kind of questions discussed in the book. However, even for missiologists and mission agencies, though more or less familiar with the main argument, Jenkins offers new and spectacular insights as to the ecclesiological and political implications the concentration and radicalization of Christianity in the South may have for the world. There is no question that his book on the Coming of Global Christianity is one of the most challenging publications in the field of world Christianity at the beginning of the 21st century. The *narrative* Jenkins has offered is convincing in many ways and, within this narrative, what he says makes sense. However, it is possible to tell the story in a different way and give it another ending. This is what I am trying to do here. I am not sure that I have found a happy end though, but at least one that is different and provides us with an alternative. I will organise my thoughts in two steps: in the *first* section I want to indicate at which point I am uneasy with Jenkins' narrative, and I will ask what questions are underlying this uneasiness. A selection of these questions will then be discussed in the *second* section, before I present my alternative ending by way of conclusion.

Uneasiness

My uneasiness is, of course, not simply self-generated. I have discussed the book with an international group, colleagues and research students.[1] Most of us are fascinated by the scenario; we agree that it is easier to identify Christian action in the South than in the North and that most of the action is indeed taking place in the South. There is an awareness that Rome, Wittenberg, Geneva or Canterbury must rethink their policies with a view of accommodating the new majorities. We also think that the global trends of world Christianity ought to be taken better account of in the places of theological education in the West. However, the interesting thing is that, when asking ourselves whether we think our own position or that of our respective contexts are truthfully portrayed in Philip Jenkins' book, most of us cannot persuade ourselves to say we do. There are reasons why one can be fascinated by his grand scenario and, at the same time, feel that it does not properly fit when applied to one's own context. I wish to explore this uneasiness.

1. It is clear to me that Jenkins—in the interest of his *big picture*—has used a typological approach; that is, he reduced the complexity on the ground and

---

1   Special thanks go to my research students and to prof. Heinrich Balz, Berlin and Makumira, Frieder Ludwig, St. Paul/Minnesota, and R.S. Sugirtharajah, Birmingham, whose thoughts I have profited from.

introduced broad categories, such as the distinction between a "Northern" and a "Southern" form of Christian experience. Types of Christian experience are meant to be a simplified model of reality without being simplistic. But I think he went too far when characterizing the acceptance of the whole package of orthodox belief and the expectation of God's direct intervention in a life that is troubled by alienation and demonic forces as a specifically southern phenomenon. Equally overstated, on the other side, is the characterization of northern experience as a process of pick and mix, with the modern liberal mythology acting as the decisive element and therefore inevitably leading to the abandonment of Christian belief. Processes of religious pick-and-mix are not unknown in the South. In fact, a sociological or cultural definition of *northern* and *southern* would be more adequate and helpful than its geographical fixation. This means that the types are useful, but their geographical fixation is problematic. It does not really help either that the typology is charged by some kind of agenda, visible when he preaches against "Northern liberals" and their "dilettantish kind of cafeteria religion" (p.197) and when he juxtaposes this with his cautious fascination with the "exotic beast" of Southern "jungle religion" (p.162, p.220). The anti-liberal agenda certainly has a high priority among US evangelicals and their friends, also to some extent for the Vatican, but it is also an issue that is discussed controversially in the Church universal. There are numerous Christian groups in the North that are evangelical and whose faith we must regard as orthodox. Orthodoxy, however, is not equivalent to obedience to Christ. This is a different question, I know, but I want to flag it here. The orthodoxy of their beliefs, for example, did not prevent many theologians, mission leaders included, from supporting Hitler and his political religion of Nazism (Ustorf 2000). In other words, geography and orthodoxy do not seem to be sufficient criteria for a qualitative distinction between Christians in the North and the South.

2. Jenkins is probably right with his prediction, already implicit in the first point, that the future of global Christianity will be more conservative and traditional, perhaps even "fundamentalist", when compared to that type of Christianity that has grown in the West and takes its cue from liberal theology and Vatican II. However, it does not follow from this that the Christian traditionalism of the South will be of one kind only. The likelihood is that there will be a plurality of conservatisms and even mutual ecclesiological and theological disagreement. The diversification of the Christian tradition has been keenly observed since the 1950s. I am quoting the example of 1954 when the *International Missionary Council* commissioned a series of depth studies of churches in the non-western world, in the sixties then published by the Division of World Mission and Evangelism of the *World Council of Churches* under the title *World Studies of Churches in*

Mission.[2] Its approach was new and reflected, on the one hand, the process of decolonization, on the other, a shift in missiological methods: instead of coming with pre-established biblical criteria against which to measure these churches, the process was reversed, with the hope being that the life of these churches would in turn generate a new interpretation of scripture. When in the sixties, following the slogan of the world mission conference of Mexico City of 1963, "mission in six continents", a couple of Western church contexts were hastily added to the study series, it was made sure that non-Western scholars authored or at least co-authored these volumes.[3] The purpose of the study was to take account of the variety of church contexts and of the diversity of Christian responses to different cultural and social situations. The great surprise, however, was that the emerging variety and diversity were far greater than had been anticipated. In fact, the study was, as the evaluation volume put it, "gloriously disappointing" (Mackie, 1970, p.79). It is quite ironic to note that one of the proposals of the WCC conference of Uppsala in 1968 had been to examine the worldwide church through field studies and decide "whether any general principles emerge from them" (Goodall, 1968, p.202), and here was such a field study which found *no such principles*, unless 'diversity' as such is seen as a general principle. A simple and general pattern in church development could not be established, and none of the many possible definitions of "the Church" seemed to describe a single one of the churches analysed in the study. The differences ran much deeper than surface level, and every church situation was different, its history, the cultural patterns, the self-definition, and the ways in which the boundaries to the environment were drawn; even biblical interpretation differed from context to context. The tighter the description was the more contradictions surfaced, and the more elusive became the notion of the church. There was no discernable unifying principle. The comparison of churches did not lead to a safe knowledge about the church, and the whole evaluation ended in "a very humble agnosticism" (Mackie, 1970, p.101).

I do not see that these findings of the early seventies have been invalidated by the ecumenical developments in the last three decades. The opposite is more likely. This means that the process of going south and going traditional is not equivalent to a reduction of diversity. The re-appropriation of the Bible in the Base Christian Communities and in the Pentecostal movement,

---

2   In 1970 thirteen volumes had been published. An overall assessment of the study process is
      contained in Mackie 1970.

3   The church study on Birmingham, U.K., e.g. was done by a theologian and sociologist from
      Ghana, cf. Busia 1966.

the rather diverse contextual theologies,[4] and, for that matter, the Synod of Bishops in Asia in 1998,[5] are all very distinct phenomena. Their theological stance, when compared to the standard of "cafeteria religion" may be called *traditional*, but this does not imply that we have a Southern agreement, for example, with the theological conservatism of the Vatican or the New Christian Right in North America.

3. I am terrified by the prediction that a dominant, but also fundamentalist and even "reactionary" and "fanatic" Southern Christianity[6] will somehow gang up and merge into an "axis" of global *Christendom*, and I hope that this will indeed not happen. The prediction implies that passionate religious identification takes precedence over any allegiance to the secular political order, such as that of a nation-state. We have heard this before, of course, from Huntington and a number of other scholars.[7] The focus of loyalty, it is said, is not the individual state, but the overarching unity of an imagined sacred empire. Jenkins speculates, using Max Weber's and Ernst Troeltsch's typology of church and sect, as to whether, in the distant future, this seething cauldron of turmoil will simply boil to nothing, leaving, as it were, a residue in which Southern Christendom again becomes a plurality of churches. But, for the foreseeable future, the religious imagination of the South would have serious and direct political consequences: in practice, some form of crusading theocracy engaged in a series of violent conflicts with Islam, but carried out with modern weapons. The structures of this "Christendom", Jenkins thinks, would have much in common with those Europe had exhibited in the past, particularly during the Middle Ages. Why Southern Christianity, with its varieties of distinctly different cultural, religious, and contextual backgrounds, should follow a medieval European trajectory is not clear.[8] However, I do not think that Jenkins is using the idea of *Christendom* as a tool of historical analysis. He has tried instead to find a historical analogy that is able to express this *nightmare* scenario.[9] Few of the examples quoted by Jenkins could be classified as a politicization of the sacred. He has thrown rather heterogeneous political phenomena into a single conceptual basket: politicians manipulating religious bodies, self-styled

---

4   For an overview see Fabella and Sugirtharajah 2003.
5   Cf. Fox 2002.
6   Jenkins used these terms in *The New Christendom*.
7   Cf. for example Rudolph 1997.
8   It is also not clear whether the South alone would be responsible for the decline of the nation-state. Jenkins himself argues that factors generated in the West, such as information technology, markets, globalization or the emergence of the European Union, are anyway busy in eroding the sense of belonging to a particular state.
9   *Nightmare* is a term used by Jenkins himself.

messiahs meting out apocalyptic violence, Church leaders challenging the political authorities in the area of human rights, or churches offering a kind of parallel administration in states where the infrastructure has collapsed. Such examples, valuable as they are individually, are not or, to be more cautious, not yet supportive of his thesis of a global southern trend towards a "political ideology" of Christendom or the emergence of a violent "theocratic Christian state" (Jenkins, 2002, p.141–159). These are, so far, nightmares, projections perhaps. But where did they come from in the first place? The great liberal church historian Adolf Harnack described the transition from St. Augustine to Pope Gregory I in the following, rather dark words:

At the end of our period, when night covered the occident completely, the great monk-pope and father of superstition had prepared the Church for the Middle Ages in exactly the way the primitive nations required it. He did not need to force himself because culture declined anyway and turned to barbarism.[10]

Has Jenkins sought to exorcise the demon of barbarism by projecting it on to the South? This is not a rhetorical question for there are and were fanatical forms of Christianity. It is undeniable that violence is a major problem throughout Christian history. Christianity is not immune from regressing into barbarism, not in Europe and not in Africa. It would be insufficient to celebrate the creative sides of African Christianity for example without acknowledging its shadow side. Jenkins is right to put his finger here. But if and when Christian barbarism comes, what do we do? Can we restrict our reactions to the political domain and to strategic considerations, as Jenkins seems to suggest, or do we react as theologians? Does the Church have to fight the barbarism in its own midst? I will return later to this question.

4. Jenkins is entitled to apply a market model to religion and to ask how Christianity can "dominate the religious economy" (2002, p.212). He is free to criticize the churches of the West for paying too little attention to the possibility that Christianity's battle for supremacy in the world market of religion might be won or lost in the mega-cities—not those of the North, but of the South. He predicts that a religion that "builds there today is very likely to be profiting richly in a decade or two". But he seems to use a geo-religious map that has the West and the United States as its point of reference. The origin and the threat of religious violence are firmly located in the outside, mostly in the South. This comes as a surprise to everyone who has experienced the political history of the last half-century with open eyes. If

---

10   Von Harnack, 1890 vol. 3, p.239 (my translation).

something like a "theocratic absolutism" is underway in Christianity, to quote the writer Philip Pullman, it is more likely to come out of Tony Blair's Britain, where there is a trend to let "obnoxiously superstitious and self-righteous" people have their way (2005, p.18–19). Or it may come out of the United States, where the linkage between state policy and religious fundamentalism can hardly be ignored. Concerning violence, from Vietnam to Iraq, just to name the two, there is a history of conflicts, military interventions and even wars originating from the US (sometimes Britain) and fought in such names as freedom and war on terror. I would not dispute that the pursuit of freedom and the combat of terror were among the motives triggering these conflicts, but I would think that the political self-interest of the world's superpower and its ambition for global hegemony played an equally strong role. The ambitions of the leading western powers are themselves a cause of war and, very likely, will continue to be so. Adrian Hastings, in one of his last publications, said:

What none of us anticipated at the time [the 1950s] was that the gravest nationalist threat to Christianity by the late twentieth century might come from the United States, essentially a rehash of the traditional Christian imperialism of western European countries. It is just the latest example of a self-appointed 'chosen people' carrying forth a gospel message reshaped by its own values and bonded to its own political expansion.[11]

We have reason, therefore, to look more closely at how Jenkins' scenario fits into the western discourse of power. He addresses his ideas explicitly to "our political leaders and diplomats" (2002, p.13). In other words, this influential study is not simply the academic exercise of a disinterested historian, it is meant to have an impact on the discourse on policy and strategy of, in the first place, the leading world power. If I were a sort of youngish Henry Kissinger, I would hear Jenkins say something like the following: The continuation of the role of the US as a leading world power is dependent on more than oil and military force. As an empire that is shaped and continues to be shaped by Christianity (thanks to Mexican-Catholic immigration) it requires an uncompromising religious vision and must bring this to bear in the global religious conflicts of the future. The main conflict will be between Christianity and Islam. This conflict may result in global wars that will originate in the Third World. The super power, because it can no longer rely on Europe's shrinking Christianity (Europe, despite Christian immigration from the South, will be either Muslim, secular or itself a zone of conflict), must look for the big battalions of the Christian South. In order to do so it must be ideologically in agreement with southern Christianity, marginalize liberal forms of Christianity at home, and support

---

11   Hastings, 2003, p.32. See also his publication of 1997.

southern Christianity in the urban centres of the Third World.[12] I repeat, this is not what Jenkins says, it is what I am hearing.[13]

These are four areas of uneasiness. The *first* one implies that *northern* and *southern* types of Christianity cannot simply be geographically defined and that the presence of orthodox belief is not a sufficient criterion for the measure of Christian faith. The *second* area of uneasiness highlights the ecumenical experience that Christianity's current migration to the South and to "tradition" is not equivalent to a reduction of diversity or, for that matter, to a southern agreement with the theological conservatism of the North Atlantic. The *third* area concerns Christian ethics: does the Church have to fight the barbarism in its own midst? And the *last* area relates to the task of distinguishing between the future of Christianity and the future of the United States. These are big questions and it is impossible to deal with them adequately in the remaining space. The underlying issues have to do with two even more fundamental and inter-related questions, namely how to measure what it means to be Christian and whether we can and must learn from the numerous advances and recessions of Christianity in its history of two millennia.[14] I am far from having resolved these issues, but I will try to make them at least more explicit in two brief sketches. These sketches attempt to pinpoint two rather diverse sets of mind or two tales (narratives) of Christianity, both in combat with each other. I have given them topical political labels and called the one *New Empire* and the other *Old Europe*. It looks like a transatlantic problem then; however, I am offering not geography, but a typology of two ways to tell the Christian story. *New Empire* stands for a symbolic experience that wants to become historical experience, *Old Europe* for a historical experience that wishes to be part of the symbolic universe.

Old Europe

Common to all Christian theology, from the days of St. Paul on, is the awareness that our search for God is only a pointer to what this search itself is not. In the West, this search has inevitably acquired particular forms, two of which I wish to highlight: when responding to its own cultural context of early modernity,

---

12   Interestingly, Tony Blair—after the no-vote in France and the Netherlands on the European Constitution and addressing his imminent talks with George Bush—is said to have made the remark "Africa is worth fighting for. Europe, in its present form, is not." Quoted in *The Sunday Telegraph*, 5th of June, 2005, page 1.

13   At the conference in Nijmegen Philip Jenkins did unfortunately not find the time to respond to this.

14   The oscillation between recession and advance is the structural theme in Latourette 1937–1945.

the Reformation stopped reading a book that up to the time of Nicolas of Cusa was generally regarded as the *other book* "written by the finger of God", namely nature or the created world, inclusive of its history. The Reformation restricted itself and the faithful to reading only one book, the Bible, leading to a substantial injection of individualism into faith. When this book came under attack during the Enlightenment period, figuratively speaking, none of the books written by the finger of God were left to read, at least not for Europe's developing mainline that is secular, culture. The academy had taken over both books, excluding the Church, perhaps because the academy itself implicitly wanted to be the one and only church. In this context a split developed in western Christianity between what I call *New Empire* and *Old Europe*.

The modern revivalist, evangelical and missionary movements forged a new synthesis between the bible-orientation of the Reformation and the universalism of the Enlightenment. The result was a competitive and often highly subjective faith that rivaled the assumptions of the secular mainline culture, declared their own religious convictions as biblical and, moreover, as "biblical facts", thus as an alternative to the world of the sciences, and aimed at universal dominance.[15] This type, the *New Empire*, is a thoroughly modern, Western dream and very much informed by Enlightenment thought. The other type is represented by liberal theology from Friedrich Schleiermacher to Paul Tillich (both, by the way, had explicit ideas in favour of Christian mission); this is *Old Europe*, because it returns to the tradition of the unity of theology and the sciences and thus tries to reclaim the two books "written by the finger of God". It assumes that the different disciplines have created new materials and tools by which to explicate the faith. This is how theology functioned before the Reformation as well. Let me give an illustration: one of the largest libraries in Europe was the *Bibliotheca Palatina*. Before it was taken away to Rome in the 30 Years War by General Tilly, its home was the Holy Spirit Church in Heidelberg. The knowledge of the world, as it existed then in Europe, was accessible in the Church. Britain's Cathedral libraries and the foundation of the medieval universities tell a similar story. Liberal theology, then, is using an old approach when it reinterprets the faith in the light of the knowledge and the questions of the time.

What were these questions? *Old Europe* would perhaps have said the following: we read the gospel narratives on the basis of our cultural paradigms that include such issues as freedom and equality and in discussion with the ever-growing body of knowledge that is constituted by the humanities and the sciences. Thus, we may have to revise our assumptions in due time. Yes, we address issues of faith from within our culture; we apply the hermeneutics of suspicion, which is to say, the organized application of doubt; we discover the

---

15   Cf. Stanley 2001; also Ustorf 2004.

love of God in social action; we think that we need control mechanisms against those in power, including the separation of the religious from the political; and we are convinced that the conscience of the individual must not be suppressed in the name of the many. And, when asked, why these cultural paradigms should be of any importance for the faith, *Old Europe* would perhaps have answered that God has revealed Godself not only in a text, but is believed to continue to do so in life and history, in the *world* in brief, though in a broken way only. Why broken? Because the last two hundred years of history in general have taught us two very basic lessons: there are doubts as to the reliability of religion as a force for good and a power directed towards the healing and saving of humanity. There are also doubts regarding the reliability of reason as the panacea for the world's problems. Reason turned out to be as prone to misuse and temptation as religion proved to be. On both counts our experience is a broken experience.

Liberal theology is a particular answer to a particular context, no doubt. This answer can and has to be questioned. But I cannot see, as Jenkins seems to suggest, that liberal Christianity can be disregarded as a pure matter of statistical euthanasia. It has survived major challenges as well as many attempts at converting it to orthodoxy or neo-orthodoxy. The death of liberal Christianity has often been proclaimed, but the tradition has turned out to be extremely resilient. The reason for this is the very distinctive way it managed to assimilate the biblical message within a post-Christendom context. I would agree that it has been caught unguarded by the return of "religion". I agree that its parameters are too narrow to contain the new quest for spiritual discovery that is indicative of the transformation of the religious landscape in the West. But the core questions liberal Christianity is struggling with are still very much alive. The new kind of European spirituality, as described (or, rather, postulated) for example by Linda Woodhead and others,[16] is more or less continuing these questions though giving them, very much in line with the charismatic movement, a more experiential drive. If there really is, as it is claimed, a cultural move away from a religiously transcendental mode and towards a new type of immanent religion (or spirituality), a religion rejecting an image of God as the judge forcing the believer into obedience and submission, then this must be a critique of both *New Empire* and *Old Europe*. If this assumption is right, the chances for a new Christian traditionalism in the West are limited.

New Empire

Now, let me unfold my ideas about *New Empire*. This theological set of mind attempts to interpret culture in the light of the gospel. We can expect *New*

---

16   Cf. MacLaren 2004; Heelas et al 2005.

Empire theology to be reluctant to give experience and history, including the history of mission, the decisive word because, in principle at least, its argument claims a divine and eternal, not a temporal ground. David Bosch says, in his much acclaimed volume *Transforming Mission*, that mission has to be defined in terms of its nature, not in terms of its success, non-success, statistics and demography or even the addressees of mission, that is in terms of context or inculturation. In an almost Barthian fashion he states that mission comes as a dictator. Mission is "that dimension of our faith which refuses to accept reality as it is and aims at changing it" (Bosch, 1991, xv).

But, as was shown, the idea that mission comes as a dictator, is itself an idea with a rather recent history. Its context is the cultural civil war of the West about its dominating symbol system. In practical terms, not even Bosch is able to disregard this reality when describing the series of the diverse paradigms of mission theology in history. It is not only the World Mission Conference of Edinburgh in 1910 that can be accused, according to Bosch, of substituting the theology of mission by statistics, demography and cultural optimism; the very slogan "evangelization of this world in this generation" has a very unappetizing prehistory. A considerable role in this plays Josiah Strong's very popular missionary manifesto of 1885 *Our Country*, depicting the United States not only as the apex of Christian civilization, but a nation of racial (Anglo-Saxon) and spiritual purity with a "God-given" mandate to spread the gospel to a less fortunate world (Deichmann Edwards 2004). The problem with *New Empire* theology is that despite its claims it is not exempt from the temptation of siding with the principalities and powers of the time. That is why history matters even for a theological approach that has difficulties with acknowledging its own historicity.

In times like ours, when diversity has become an established fact of life, it is increasingly difficult to maintain rigid religious and cultural boundaries, yet the geopolitical and economic demands of the superpower require a strong imagination or vision. Jenkins offers New Empire as just such a geopolitical vision, comprising a sophisticated imagination, but involving as well a tightening up of religious core values in the West. He borrows extensively from Samuel Huntington's approach of a "clash of civilizations"[17] and it is important to find out where the two differ. Significantly, both presuppose that different cultures are incapable of talking to and learning from one another. It is this very fact, however, this unwillingness to talk and to learn, that is the logical precondition

---

17   Huntington 1998. Huntington in turn has consulted Oswald Spengler's *The Decline of the West*, and distanced himself sharply from F. Fukuyama's scenario of universal history and rationality, the "illusion of harmony", with its unfettered westerness and its disregard for the world's cultures and religions (Huntington had been Fukuyama's tutor at Harvard.). However, I cannot address these issues here.

for the conflict and war that are so central to their narratives. The idea at the
heart of this scenario is that there are solid and insurmountable boundaries
between religions and cultures.

This idea is another idea with a history. Its recent history is the need of the
colonial empire to have clearly defined boundaries between "us" and "them".
And it is at this point that the clash of civilizations scenario is in direct conflict
with the universalist tradition (both in its religious and secular version).
Huntington's well-known advice to the US foreign policy makers was always
to keep in mind that violent conflicts between the world's leading civilizations
are inevitable, whether these be local "fault-line wars" or major global confronta-
tions. This resonates, of course, with Jenkins' prediction of crusade and violence
in the Christendom of the South. For Huntington the world is divided in a
familiar "West and the rest" manner. The West is seen as fundamentally different from the rest. Unlike Jenkins, however, Huntington does not speak as such
of the global South, but instead highlights the existence of eight very diverse
civilizations outside the West: Latin American, African, Islamic, Sinic, Hindu,
Slavonic-Orthodox (interestingly), Buddhist and Japanese. This is not the place
to discuss this. Huntington predicts not only a comprehensive decline in the
importance of the West, but also forecasts dangerous conflicts taking place not
so much between social classes or the rich and the poor, and not even between
nation-states, but between peoples espousing different cultural and religious
identities. What distinguishes the West from other civilizations is not modernization but a particular mix or cultural inheritance, which includes the phenomena of the separation of religion and politics or, if you will, of spiritual and
temporal authority—"an idiosyncratic product of Western civilization", as
Huntington would have it (1998, p.54). With the decline of the West, this separation would also decline and result in the intrusion of religion into international politics. Jenkins' work complements this line of thought, but there is
also a major point of departure here in that he focuses on, and in fact adds, a
civilization that Huntington has refused to acknowledge in his overview,
global Christianity. By focusing on the Catholic, Protestant and Pentecostal
sections of this religion Jenkins shows that a massive fault-line runs through
it.[18] In other words, Jenkins is saying what many critics have also said, that most
conflicts are not between civilizations but *within* them. But he also goes beyond
Huntington, by stating that the Christianity of the *global South* no longer shares
the core values of western mainstream Christianity. But all the other elements
of Jenkins' approach, the focus on the shifts in global demography, the prediction

---

18   Jenkins has almost completely omitted the various strands of the family of Orthodox
      churches—in Europe, but also elsewhere. This omission is quite surprising given the fact
      that Huntington explicitly acknowledges a "Slavonic-Orthodox" civilization.

that Islam and Christianity will battle it out in the new growth areas, are established themes in Huntington's work. Like Jenkins, Huntington, in his last chapter, deplores the moral decline in the West. The internal self-destruction leads to a stage where Western civilization is no longer willing to defend itself and is wide open to "barbarian invaders".[19] This kind of development, if unchecked, could destroy Western civilization. Jenkins follows this decline of the West narrative, but he seems to think that American civilization at least can survive, namely with the help of the New Empire Christians of the South.

Conclusion

Jenkins has written one of the most impressive pieces of contemporary missionary apologetics. His expectations in Southern Christianity are high, perhaps too high. What he has not done is to engage theologically with the Christian experience of the "South". Theologically, the image of the *Next Christendom* is not a particularly attractive one. Is the nightmare that Jenkins describes under the banner of Christendom, not a form of religious nationalism or, perhaps, the politicization of the sacred?[20] And is this type of Christianity, whether in the shape of southern theocracies or in the milder form of making leaders of evangelical agencies principal advisors to the US president,[21] not in danger of being victorious precisely because it is in bed with powers that are not genuinely Christian—like other expressions of Christendom before it, as I hasten to say? Must missiologists, instead of tactical and strategic considerations, not reflect in the first place on what these powers are? And can missiologists afford the luxury of not consulting the liberal experience of their own tradition? Violent religion would not be any less disastrous if it came along in Christian garments, whether these originated in the South or the North. Must we not look up the pages of Christian history and find out what antidotes are available when Christians become fanatic, fundamentalist and a danger to peace? My students dubbed Philip Jenkins' book a "wake up call". When Christians, where ever they are, claim Paradise, the Kingdom of God, and the Resurrection for their imagined political-religious empire and their religious vision demand the merger of God and man and of eternity and history, then we must wake up to this.

---

19   But these invaders have already arrived in the shape of "a small but influential number of
      intellectuals and publicists. In the name of multiculturalism they have . . . denied the existence of a common American culture, and promoted racial, ethnic, and other subnational cultural identities and groupings" (Huntington, 1998, p.305).
20   For terminology, cf. Gentile 1996 and Gentile 2000.
21   Hastings, 2003, p.33, quotes the case of Robert Seiple, the President of World Vision, the
      largest evangelical mission body in the US.

Must we not insist that violence is the inevitable outcome of this removal of the distance between God and man? Fanatic Christians would be in danger of switching their mode of believing from *faith* to *obsession* or, to use a strong formula, from the *terror of uncertainty* to the *certainty of terror.*[22]

References

Barrett, D. (ed) 1982. *World Christian encyclopedia* 1900–2000. Oxford: Oxford UP.

Bosch, D. 1991. *Transforming mission*, New York: Orbis.

Bühlmann, W. 1976. *The coming of the third church: an analysis of the present and the future of the Church*, Slough, UK: St. Paul.

Busia, K.A. 1966. *Urban churches in Britain: a question of relevance*. London: Lutterworth Press.

Deichmann Edwards, W.J. 2004. Forging an ideology for American missions: Josiah Strong and manifest destiny. (In Shenk, W. (ed), *North American foreign missions, 1810–1914*. Grand Rapids, MI: Eerdmans. p.163–191.)

Fabella, V. & Sugirtharajah, R.S. (eds) 2003. *SCM dictionary of third world theologies*. London: SCM Press.

Fox, T.C. 2002. *Pentecost in Asia: a new way of being church*. New York: Orbis.

Gentile, E. 2000. The sacralisation of politics: definitions, interpretations and reflections on the question of secular religion. *Totalitarian movements and political religions*. 1 (1): p.18–55.

Gentile, E. 1996. *The sacralization of politics in fascist Italy*. Cambridge: Harvard UP.

Goodall, N. (ed) 1968. *The Uppsala report*. Geneva: World Council of Churches.

Harnack, A. von. 1886–1890. *Lehrbuch der Dogmengeschichte*, three vols, Freiburg: J.C.B. Mohr.

Hastings, A. 2003. The clash of nationalism and universalism within twentieth-century missionary Christianity. (In Stanley, B. & Low, A., (eds). *Missions, nationalism, and the end of empire*. Grand Rapids, MI: Eerdmans. p.15–33.)

Hastings, A. 1997. *The construction of nationhood: ethnicity, religion and nationalism*. Cambridge: Cambridge UP.

Heelas, P., Woodhead, L., Seel, B., Szerszynski, B. & Tusting, K. 2005. *The spiritual revolution: why religion is giving way to spirituality*. Oxford: Blackwell.

Huntington, S.P. 1998. *The clash of civilizations and the remaking of world order*. London and New York: Touchstone Books.

Jenkins, P. 2002. *The next christendom: the coming of global Christianity*. Oxford: Oxford UP.

Latourette, K.S. 1937–1945. *History of the expansion of christianity*, seven vols. New York and London: Harper.

Mackie, S.G. (ed) 1970. *Can churches be compared? reflections on fifteen study projects*. Geneva: World Council of Churches. (Research Pamphlet No. 17)

MacLaren, D. 2004. *Mission impossible: restoring credibility to the church*. London: Paternoster Press.

Margull, H.J. 1974. Überseeische Christenheit II: Vermutungen zu einer Tertiaterranität des Christentums. *Verkündigung und Forschung*, 19 (1): p.56–103.

Pullman, P. 2005. *The Times higher education*. 22 April: p.18–19

Rudolph, S. 1997. *Transnational religion and fading states*. Boulder, CO: Westview.

---

22   I am using here ideas introduced by Egon Voegelin and Paul Schütz during the rise of National Socialism. Cp. Ustorf, 2005, p.5–14.

Stanley, B. (ed) 2001. *Christian missions and the enlightenment.* Grand Rapids, MI: Eerdmans.

Ustorf, W. 2000. *Sailing on the next tide: missions, missiology, and the third reich.* Frankfurt: Lang.

Ustorf, W. 2004. Wissenschaft, Africa and the cultural process according to Johann Gottfried Herder (1744–1803). (In Ludwig, F. & Adogame, A. (eds), *European traditions in the study of religion in Africa.* Wiesbaden: Harrassowitz. p.117–127.)

Ustorf, W. 2005. Political religions—a theological perspective. (In Heuser, A. & Weisse, W. (eds), *Neuere Religiöse Bewegungen in internationaler Perspektive.* Aachen: Verlagshaus Mainz. p.5–14.)

Ben Knighton

Christian Enculturation in the Two-Thirds World

Where does agency lie in mission? Is it in the sending north or the receiving south? This paper will take a lead from recent African Studies that the power of the north, reinforced by globalization, does not determine the cultures of the Two-Thirds World. These are most effectively redeemed from within. The historically mediated message of Jesus of Nazareth needs to be connected with the cosmic Christ present in each culture, if its various aspects: military, legal, political, social, economic, religious and so on are to be redeemed through the Holy Spirit working in actors and structures. Without the process of such a holistic transform-ation, individual converts and churches will be left with the norms of churches in the North, imposed as a universal theology. Christian enculturation values the local, not the global when it is merely a metonym for the USA, whose interests are the concern of Philip Jenkins.

The renowned historian Hugh Trevor-Roper continued to declare during the 1960s in the University of Oxford that Africa has no history.[1] In the history of this idea it followed that only contact with Europe could redeem it (Bernasconi, 1998, p.59). Thus in mission studies it was expatriate missionaries and their missiologies who were the focus of attention. Only after their advent came the redeemed life. However, closer studies of African conversion, such as Louise Pirouet's *Black Evangelists* (1978), revealed that it was African catechists who were immediately responsible for spreading the faith as missionaries to Africa frequently found it most difficult to convert Africans soundly themselves. The legacy of their mission depended to a very large degree on one or two who had caught a Christian vision and were able to spread it themselves. In some cases, as with Samuel Mukuba,[2] a Mukamba who brought a Christian message 400 miles from the Indian Ocean coast to the slopes of Mount Kenya, unpaid, self-appointed evangelists found a new faith on the fringe of churches far away from home and then spread it to their people before any expatriate had reached them.

Thus African agency, initiative, and activity have come to be much more, if not universally, emphasized (Barrett 1971; Stanley 1978; Ranger 1999;

---

1   Prof. Terence Ranger, personal communication.
2   The author knew his widow, Jessie Mukuba before she died in Ngiriambu, near Mount Kenya.

Maxwell 1999, 2000; Maxwell & Lawrie 2002; Lonsdale 2002; Peel 2003).[3] Now Africans are seen not to have passively received a preformulated gospel rhetoric for replication, but to have worked on it in many subtle and found ways, translating the message, appropriating Christian traditions, resisting the formation of social institutions and buildings so that they are not totally alien as the mind of the missionary might have them, but local enough to be owned, valued, and maintained.[4] On the underside of history they may not appear authentically African either to the traditionalist there nor to the Western observer, but where power is lacking to overturn the Western ecclesiastical insertion, small adjustments to the incoming tradition were significant ones. There were considerable benefits on offer to adopt a Western religious tradition in order to progress under colonial government.

However fast assimilation to external trends may not always be sustainable despite neo-colonialism and glocalization, not only because of the resistance that turns it into globalization (Robertson 1992, 1994; Knighton 2001b), but also because being integrated into the global economy by producing commodities whose price is determined by Western markets, or depending solely on one's labour value, leads to a yet further loss of autonomy and freedom (Knighton 2005a; Meyer & Geschiere 1999). Expatriate missionaries have deliberately attempted not only to bring rural Africa into their orbit across the North Atlantic, but also to recreate bucolic idylls of Northern Europe (Casson 1998).

Yet the major thrust of this paper is that in the long run Christian faith is propagated not so much by the "senders" in mission, but by the "receivers", or rather the appropriators, and that mission would be much more effective is they were enabled to do this more by constructing a local theology (Schreiter 1985). From beginning to end the Christian mission frequently tends to turn out looking very different from what its foreign founders intended. Both message and institutions quickly take on a life of their own, which become intractable from any the control of an individual. Once the Word is out it quickly becomes enfleshed in the lives, not so much of those who passively receive it, but of those who actively accept and, in doing so, remould it. The founders may become deeply frustrated and try to increase their control, leading to schism or their

---

3   The trend of the last thirty years is opposed by the kind of anthropology produced by the Comaroff (1991) on the Tswana, which highlights how their missionized lives were written into Victorian discourses and designs, and by the merely political description of African churches that sees right-wing politics as ideas imported from North America (Gifford 1991, 1998).

4   For the concept of appropriation see Fabian (1986). As the one-time Chief Education Adviser to the British Secretary of State for the colonies put it in regard to education: 'in the long run Africa would take what it wanted, digest it slowly, and assimilate what it did not spit out again' (Whitehead, 1988, p.225).

exeunt, or they may learn from the process and make their mission more sustainable. Even if there is no dialogue worthy of the name there is a cosmological dialectic, however much embedded in the difference of lives and traditions.

Local and Global Histories

Philip Jenkins' roots as an historian lie in the study of early modern Britain. He has latterly blossomed as a commentator on the contemporary USA, where he now lives and works. Thus his book, *The Next Christendom* (2002), is based on Anglo-American perspectives in history and international relations. He has done well to note that the Christian faith in Africa has significantly different expressions from that in North America and Europe and will continue to do so. If Africa is to be well understood, then, it is vital that its religions should be paid very careful attention. He is quite right to point out the lack of serious analysis of Africa in some circles, to which he belongs and in which he shared until researching this book: "Northerners rarely give the South anything like the attention it deserves, but when they do notice it, they tend to project on to it their own familiar realities and desires" (Jenkins, 2002, p.13). Christian mission has long taken Africa more seriously, combining with anthropologists, indeed being amateur anthropologists, to found scholarly journals like *Africa, African Affairs*, and *Journal of Religion in Africa*, which hardly figure in Jenkins' research. The growth in the academic field of African Studies, especially history, is not reflected in Jenkins' account, for "so much of this book concerns numbers" (Jenkins, 2002, p.86). Yet to give it coherence, Jenkins falls back on his understandings of European history and the American experience of the rest of the world.

Fitting Africa into a cosy simplification of European history may be an attempt to make Africa intelligible to a wider readership, but it is also the default method by which Jenkins makes Africa intelligible to himself, when he writes:

> In twenty-first Africa, as in second-century Rome, baptism is an awe-inspiring symbol . . . in many ways, Southern Christianity today stands in much the same relationship to the wider society as it did in the Roman Empire, before and during the great age of conversions. (Jenkins, 2002, p.134)

Bringing together the histories of Rome and modern Christian mission in Africa was the idea of Andrew Walls (1998) and Kwame Bediako (1992)[5] in order to combine their different realms of knowledge in patristics and the contemporary African church. Jenkins prefers another perpetual parallel for the

---

5   The idea of Africa being the current locus for the renewal of Christianity as an originally non-Western religion anyway is also from Bediako (1995).

purpose of his book, which is not as convincing as Bediako's careful discussion of similar ranges of theological response to culture.

"Many societies of the global South," Jenkins (2002, p.141) writes, "live in an intellectual world far closer to the medieval world than Western modernity". The "dominant churches of the future could have much in common with those of medieval or early modern European times" (Jenkins, 2002, p.8). He makes President Moi of Kenya behave like a "medieval king", becoming saintly through paying "penance" to the church for misdeeds. In fact Moi came to politics with a born-again reputation forged in the Africa Inland Mission. He confessed no fault when he was attacked by the mainstream churches, but rather favoured his own Africa Inland Church and right-wing Evangelical mission-church in order to ruin a comprehensive united stance on constitutional review by the National Council of Churches in Kenya. He paid no penance, but made his usual cynical political machinations to a political problem, instead of the political error of persecuting the church. This issue of republican constitutions was far beyond parallels with the rule of medieval monarchs.

Similarly Jenkins (2002, p.155) situates recent African conflicts, which he claims have "a linkage between tribalism and religious zealotry", in the wars of religion following the Reformation on the European scale of history. Despite the highly secular research in economics being carried out on behalf of the World Bank by Paul Collier (2003) and Anke Höffler (2001), religion has not been at the centre of African conflict which has usually been over who can hold or use state power. This is certainly true of Rwanda, Darfur, Congo, Ethiopia, and Eritrea where antagonistic combatants have shared the same religion. There has been religious conflict in the Sahel region between Muslims and Christians, but there antagonistic combatants have often come from the same tribe. To align himself with the positivist economist approaches of Washington to Africa is to fall into the same secular hole that he claims to be filling: inadequate attention to the religious reality of Africa. Instead the reader is bidden see the deaths in Rwanda and Congo as "Africa's equivalent of the First World War" and to "imagine the world of the thirteenth century armed with nuclear warheads and anthrax" (Jenkins, 2002, p.189).

Jenkins finds religious conflict in Mexico parallel to the European reformation, so "it would be wonderful if Latin American struggles could have such a bloodless and well-organized outcome" as in the British solution of forming Conservative, Liberal, and Labour parties in the nineteenth century. This rehistoricization condemns the Two-Thirds World to centuries of conflict, for "in Europe modernization and state-building could only advance once the wars of religion had been fought to a standstill" (Jenkins, 2002, p.156). As it was "a piecemeal process taking centuries, and it is unlikely that a parallel change in Africa or Asia would be much more rapid", clearly Jenkins assumes that Africa will not advance in modernization for hundreds of years yet. The Congo has become "a perpetual war zone reminiscent of Germany during the Thirty Years War" (Jenkins, 2002, p.189), though not many Congolese will be reminded of Northern Europe 1618–48. His history provides no options, so the end of religious wars is not in his sight of Africa.

Moreover "Southern Christianity" is to be defined in terms of the Shi'ite Muslims of the 1980s: "fanatical, superstitious, demagogic; politically reactionary and sexually repressive". Iran has never been allowed to shake off its medievalist tag ever since Jimmy Carter's Democratic administration foundered on the theocratic revolution there, but the similarities with the increasingly secular state constitutions of the Two-Thirds World is not clear, except that Jenkins is positing both as a threat to the USA, and therefore an obstacle to advancement, "progress", for which "medieval" is a suitably pejorative adjective in the age of globalization. Further, the medieval parallels are necessary to make the title of the book fit, when Christendom was a notion of the Middle Ages in Europe. For Islam the "the age of the Crusades" is not long past and "The Last Crusade" is still to come, when the world will be brought back "full circle to the worst features of the thirteenth century" (Jenkins, 2002, p.186, 190).

To his credit Jenkins is opening minds as to what is out there in the Two-Thirds World,[6] but at the same time, despite the breadth of material he has gathered, he has not deeply revised his own pre-existing understanding of history, but accommodated Africa to it, thereby falling foul of his criticism of projecting on to it "familiar realities". He calls it an "emerging world", but when human life and civilization began in Africa and Asia, the term only makes sense in the consciousness of North America. Both Africa and Europe have long shared a sense that the former continent was more religious, and was becoming more Christian, than the former. After independence this was one of the few aspects of life where Africans could detect a superiority over the colonizers.

Jenkins (2002, p.6) spices his script with some heart-warming insights: "European Christians interpreted the faith through their own concepts of society and gender relations, and then imagined that their culturally specific synthesis was the only correct version of Christian truth". Yet he does not impart a

---

6   It is important not passively to accept Jenkins' terminology, since that collaborates in the same suspect definition of the world and its 'hemispheric division' due to the Brandt Report (Jenkins, 2002, p.223). All the non-polar continents have territory in the northern hemisphere, apart from Australasia, which is dominated by occidental culture and so excluded by Jenkins. The USA shares latitudes with North Africa, the '10-40 window', of which he speaks (Jenkins, 2002, p.172), and East Asia. It is easy for South to become adjectival to North, especially in political, economic, and military terms. On the other hand 'Two-Thirds World' makes the very point that is the foundation for his book: that is, the section of the globe, which does not own occidental culture, does contain the majority of the world's population and land.

clear awareness or theory of the history of religion in Africa. Inevitably, not addressing the problematic explicitly means that any writer is likely to fall back on assumed and implicit theories without having subjected them to critique. Thus Jenkins (2002, p.133) appears wedded to an evolutionary theory applied even to Christian religion that moves through preset stages of development. Thus on the 2000-year scale of church history the Two-Thirds World is planted firmly if sporadically in the first two centuries, the thirteenth century, or the sixteenth. This give it a certain affinity with the ancient cultures of the bible, vigour, and freshness, but it is not yet enlightened or unrepressed and has a long way to go to meet the ideals of vital Christian faith in the West.

Presumably the church at its best is in the USA, which according to the CIA, is still going to be the largest Christian county by a distance in 2025 and 2050 (Jenkins, 2002, p.135), where religion has nothing to do with politics and conflict: "I personally believe that religion flourishes best when it is kept farthest away from any form of government intervention" (Jenkins, 2002, p.103). This is not the Hegelian apotheosis in the minds and culture of human beings, but it is the neo-Conservative dream of the USA. Threatening the land of the free with the big state that turns its unwelcome attention outwards, instead of in on its own citizens, is the uncongenial, "emerging Christian world" (Jenkins, 2002, p.14) whose authoritarian and illiberal impulses betoken war without and confusion within. This is not Jenkins' way to Progress through modernization.

Culture

In his search for the global, Jenkins does not take culture very seriously; it does not appear in his index and terms like Christendom and Southern Christianity reflect fascination with large-scale uniformity. However Christians from Latin America, Africa, and Asia, as can be heard weekly by research students in the Oxford Centre for Mission Studies, say that their culture is important to them and is distinct from others. There is no organization like the Holy Roman Empire of the Middle Ages to ensure the unity of rule on which Christendom was founded. The World Council of Churches embraces cultural difference while not pretending to transcend it, while Rome finds herself having to negotiate with it, balancing conservative cultures with liberal postmodern ones. The Anglican Communion does not even have the central authority necessary to sustain this, while the Archbishop of Canterbury warns "that the worldwide Anglican Church faces a fundamental 'rupture' on the issue of homosexuality" (BBC News 2006). This is a postmodern world where the challenge to the sustainability of a concept of culture comes not from an imposed medieval universalism, but from individual demands for the right of each to construct their own personal identity.

Culture is a term that, even if abused, is certainly widely used in many disciplines and at many social levels around the world today. An African's rationale in English for many beliefs and practices is simply, "It is our culture", as though it were a self-evident charter of freedom. The downside of much use is that it means contradictory things to different people. The main trap is that culture's meaning is confined to aesthetics represented in the West by fine art, Classical music, and ballet to a normative high culture. On the other hand cultural studies have tried to chaperone the term into the representations of mass media and popular culture.[7] However both usages are prisoner to professionalism and captive to celebrity cults, when such elite groups set the norms and fashions of a culture. Yet aesthetics is but one aspect of any culture, not "that complex whole which includes knowledge, belief, art, morals, law, custom and another capabilities and habits acquired by man as a member of society" recognized by nascent anthropology (Tylor, 1871, p.1).

Not all thinkers admit to a concept of culture but the alternative is to see cultures as "superficially different representations of one abstract culture, human culture" (Sebeok, 1987, p.165). To Roland Barthes (1975, p.20) "the cultural code is virtually an epistemological category. It represents a system of knowledge and values which are 'accepted', stereotyped, or perceived in the story as 'common knowledge'". For Umberto Eco "To communicate is to use the entire world as a semiotic apparatus. I believe that culture is that and nothing else" (Thiselton, 1992, p.98). Even grand social theorists such as Habermas (2005) have recently taken the cultural turn.

Culture is here taken to be a community's accumulated and patterned response to its environment, where "environment" is given its widest possible sense as the aggregate of all the external conditions and influences affecting life. It combines both "habitat", the natural setting of human existence with its physical features and primary resources, and "culture", which varies in form according to the different societies that share the same habitat and whose very plurality goes to show that culture is the immediate conditioning factor behind human belief and behaviour.

Humans, through the expression of their culture, work on their habitat and so, to a certain extent, mould their own environment (Leach & Mearns 1996). Culture is inside and outside humanity. The concern for super-organic elements should not repeat the theological error of retreat into a purely metaphysical, spiritual world. Culture is that part of the environment which gives direction and intensity to human life as a response to it. It maps a matrix of military, economic, and social forces that are the material and efficient causes in a system,

---

7   It is interesting to see that the academic movement of cultural studies has already run into self-doubt as the 'geo-political conjuncture' changes as being too centrist (Grossberg 2006).

while culture as a field or pattern is a formal cause. Culture, then, is neither physical, nor is it just the force of individual human minds, yet it is their context which is omnipresent to shape human belief and behaviour and so, the whole environment. Thus "all cultural behaviour is patterned", so that the beliefs and behaviour of members of a society are directed towards broad channels, whose courses are implicitly known to all (Herskovits, 1950, p.212).

Jenkins takes religions and categorizes them as Southern and Northern or at most continental. He acknowledges the problem of "regional differences within vast states". "In Africa, the new Christianity defines itself against a pagan society, while Latin America Pentecostalism emerges from a matrix that is thoroughly Christian", but in practice African Instituted Churches (AICs) avoid the concept "pagan" as being colonial, while the depth of conversion in Latin America is "questionable" (Jenkins, 2002, p.29). Yet Jenkins still insists on generalizing across the Two-Thirds World before he has acknowledged any ethnic differential that:

> the new churches do have certain features in common, which set them apart from the traditional Christianity of Europe and North America. In this regard we can understand the African independent congregations in very much the same context as the Pentecostal movement of Asia and Latin America (Jenkins, 2002, p.72).

To select just one contextual factor for scrutiny, the AICs are largely rural in a continent that is largely rural, while the Pentecostalism of Asia and Latin America grows best in the megacities.

Religion, even with the contradictions of rival religious traditions, forms only one aspect of culture alongside other aspects as political, social and economic. The lack of cultural specificity means that the African religious scene is rather misrepresented. Jenkins (2002, p.133) uses generalities as if there were one African Christianity, and this is typified by AICs that, while orientated to African culture, conveniently subscribe to three "fundamental beliefs": strict monotheism, recognition of Christ's unique role, and the division between the divine and the human realms. Yet the use of intermediaries and the messianic movements that he cites compromise the first two fundamentals, and the division between the divine and the human in Africa often involves a theological dualism that makes Satan appear more active in ordinary lives than God the Creator. Since dualism is not Trinitarian, then doubt is cast upon such beliefs being Christian. Similarly, emphasizing the difference between the divine and the human poses problems for conceiving the incarnation of Jesus.

There are then a myriad of permutations of tradition and belief in Africa even where is Christ is honoured. Thus Christians are better described by their ethnicity than by their denomination when it is found that just one African people have plural expressions as Gikuyu "Christianities" (Lonsdale 1999, 2002). Anglican, Methodist, and Presbyterian missions among the Gikuyu were

Liberal in their Evangelicalism, so it should not be assumed that they spawned conservative churches, whether directly or as a reaction. Christian Africans have distinct cultural bases and various responses to the different Christian traditions that were brought to them. It cannot be claimed in general that witchcraft accusations are a common feature, let alone leading to hundreds of murders at one place in a short time (Jenkins, 2002, p.124f). Depending on one newspaper article for such sensational information does not convince when he dismisses many such over the Kanungu millenarian deaths in Uganda (Jenkins, 2002, p.244). In this matter Jenkins (2002, p.249) favours press reports of organized murder rather than mass suicide, but academic research rather than journalist reportage points to disease (Vokes 2003), which rather spoils the example of "the grossly violent acts" of "fringe African movements" (Jenkins, 2002, p.155). Witchcraft accusations are in any case not merely about religion, but also about society and economy (Meyer & Geschiere 1999; Stewart & Strathern 2004).

Healing like witchcraft gives African religion power for Jenkins. Religion therefore rises or diminishes by attending to the medical aspect of culture: "Today, rising African churches stand or fall by their success in healing" (Jenkins, 2002, p.125). Lack of exposure to African cultures means that the diversity, even in ethno-linguistic phyla, namely Khoisan, Nilo-Saharan and Afroasiatic are not encountered, so typologies are made without them. John Mbiti (1969), seeking to construct an independent integrity for Africa, was obliged by his evidence to write of African religions and cultures, leaving him only his African philosophy with which to posit an inherent unity in the continent. Healing is more common to Bantu religions, and although these cover large portions of Africa, most churches have not brought healing into the centre of their religious practices, since the use of modern medicine has tended to secularize it of course. Contemporary Pentecostalist emphases on miracles are a critique, but not a replacement, of Western medicine which provides the norm for the miraculous healing to be an extraordinary exception. A pattern to culture is discernible when looking at the rule and not just the exception.

Humans identify themselves with a certain group, or as a particular kind of person, by selectively focussing their life in a certain direction (Hardy 1977), for culture is complex and needs to be acquired.[8] The general patterns of their culture are learned by instruction, inference, and symbolic communication. They are enculturated so that, when they encounter novel situations, they are not only equipped to deal with them but can add the experience so gained to the collective knowledge, building up territorial, social, economic, political,

---

8   "Culture is always learned" (Richardson, 2001, p.5) rather than biologically given. "All human societies must educate their young since culture cannot be genetically transferred" (Leis, 1972, p.4).

legal, moral, personal, intellectual, aesthetic, ritual, and linguistic traditions. To select sociality as the organizing category raises a false dichotomy between the social and the economic, while the category of culture eclipses this. There are a number of terms for the acquisition of culture, which describe also the movement of people between cultures.

Acculturation

This term denotes the transmission of culture, but is associated with Malinowski's one-way view of African culture contact (1945, p.15,17): "an impact of a higher, active culture upon a simpler, more passive one . . . the conception of culture change as the impact of Western civilization". Ethnocentric approaches assume all cultures can be considered from the perspective of one's own. It is the view that everyone takes until they learn to see their own culture from a different perspective.

Though seeing religion, as some Christians of the Two-Thirds World view it, is a learning exercise, such a tangential encounter is unlikely to remove all the occidentally ethnocentric lenses. Jenkins (2002, p.161) is careful to draw the misunderstanding of Two-Thirds World religion with the pens of the "Northern media". They will be subject to Orientalism, racial primitivism, and Joseph Conrad's *Heart of Darkness*.[9] The Christian religion emerging from Africa would be seen as "jungle religion . . . alien and dangerous" (Jenkins, 2002, p.161f).

Yet it is Jenkins (2002, p.36), who has made Christian religions in Africa appear overwhelmingly mysterious by taking sources at face value: the Holy Ghost Fathers not establishing there "Italy or France or any such country", but being "Negroes to the Negroes", and AICs making Christ wholly African. Whence, then, the little Italies of mission stations or the Bafrenzi and Baingereza parties in pre-colonial Uganda? The overall effect has actually been for the mainstream churches and the new religious movements to be counter-cultural, sometimes holding out for one old, traditional custom, or asserting indigeneity, while dismantling the power of elders, and in the main mediating change in a telescoped era of crisis. Meanwhile for Jenkins the unenlightened media of the North have rubbished the missionaries for being absurdly counter-cultural, so it is he, and not they, who has set up the "New Christendom" as threateningly alien to the One-Third World. When immigrants "show little sympathy for the rigid American separation of church and state" (Jenkins, 2002, p.194), the American view is at the end of the day, the correct and civilized one. It must be protected by being warned of the dangers to come, so that it must now perceive the dangers of the 10–40 window in two-thirds of the world (Jenkins, 2002, p.72).

---

9   The greatest darkness in Conrad's novel is to be found in the heart of the European central character of Conrad's novel.

From the outset Jenkins (2002, p.7) has depicted Two-Thirds World religion as "very strongly" oriented to the supernatural, when this is itself an
Enlightenment concept shared only by the Western-educated. In traditional
cultures there is no dichotomy between the natural and supernatural for all
things are spirit-infused (Knighton 2005a). A miracle is not a contradiction of
scientific laws, but a sign and wonder of a spiritual creation. Traditional religions are predisposed to be much more friendly to such a world bestowed with
its own life than one prepared to commoditize everything, including beauty, in
sight. The object of this study can only be comprehended it seems, by placing
its otherness in the violent domesticity of European history so that the Two-
Thirds World appears as a reflection of occidental demons.

Examined more carefully, as migrations have been, acculturation is a two-
way process. Assimilation of a weaker culture by a stronger is not the sole possibility for culture contact. Even if domination is assured by an advantage in
one aspect, such as population, technology, or warfare, it is no guarantee that
the dominating culture will not be changed in any aspect. "A very remarkable
people, the Zulu", the British Prime Minister, Disraeli, said in 1879, "They
defeat our generals; they convert our bishops; they have settled the fate of a
great European dynasty".

Inculturation

This term was popularized by the Jesuits, its very first recorded use in a theological context being in 1962 by a professor at the Gregorian University of
Rome in French: "Today there is a more urgent need for a Catholicism that is
inculturated in a variety of forms." (quoted in Shorter, 1988, p.10). Whether he
was coining a word, translating into French, or mis-spelling "enculturated" may
be arguable, but in any case it was an ecclesiastical appropriation of the sociological term, "enculturation". Inculturation was the word that took off in Catholic
theology from 1974, when the first assembly of the Federation of Asian
Episcopal Conferences spoke of "an indigenous and inculturated Church" and
then the 32nd Congregation of the Society of Jesus gave a decree on inculturation (Shorter, 1988, p.10). Aylward Shorter (1988, p.11) of the White Fathers
defined the term as: "the on-going dialogue between faith and culture or cultures. More fully, it is the creative and dynamic relationship between the
Christian message and a culture or cultures". This formulation was in defence
of Pope John Paul II, who had long taught of a dialogue between faith and culture, because of the integration in a person of the material and the spiritual
(George, 1990, p.31, 39). Shorter (1988, p.11) readily recognized, "that the
Christian Faith cannot exist except in cultural form. When we speak of
Christian faith or Christian life, we are necessarily speaking of a cultural phe-
nomenon. It is a distinctive way of life, which can only operate culturally".

The danger is that inculturation only becomes a cover for a core Roman Catholicism. For instance Peter Phan (1998, p.76) notes the deliberate misuse of a Vietnamese proverb by a seventeenth-century Jesuit missionary to undermine the polygyny generally approved there, and calls it inculturation (Phan, 1998, p.78f)! Though the missionary then, Alexandre de Rhodes, attired himself locally, he believed that Hebrew was the only valid language for God's revelation (Phan, 1998, p.76). Now there are several missiologists who want to take inculturation very much further than a musical and aesthetic overlay of a European religious tradition (Bevans & Schroeder 2004, p.285; Bevans 2002).

Christian Enculturation

The fullest exposition of the term "enculturation" has been given by the American cultural anthropologist, MJ Herskovits.

> The aspects of the learning experience, which mark off man from other creatures, and by means of which, initially, and in later life, he achieves competence in his culture, may be called enculturation. . . .

> Every human being goes through a process of enculturation, for without the adaptations it describes he could not live as a member of society (Herskovits, 1950, p.39f).

To enculture somebody is to envelop that body in a culture. The verb also has middle and passive forms: someone, or some innovation, can enculturate, or be enculturated, into a culture.

In sociology and social psychology, the concept of enculturation, or the conditioning of members of society to the fundamentals of that society, has usually focussed on child learning. The wider approach of comparative anthropology is interested in the differences in adult belief and behaviour across societies. Thus, enculturation is not only a common process, but also a life-long one (Hunter & Whitten 1976, p.143; Seymour-Smith, 1986, p.92f). While much social conditioning occurs at the level of the unconscious, adult members who are increasingly sure of their way round society are faced with degrees of choice which vary according to the possibilities for change presented by new factors arising within or without the society. Conditioning is unconscious precisely because its content does not require personal decision: it is generally accepted as "the way things are". It makes sense, because it is common sense, and needs no reflection, as the unwritten and unspoken premises of life. There is an inter-subjective, shared dimension of common understandings which also invades the conscious mind. Thus the personal and the social are firmly held together in the meaning of enculturation (Bernardi, 1977, p.76f, 85). So the apprehension of the meaning of symbolic forms is itself a social event, such as marriage (Geertz, 1966, p.5).

Enculturation also includes assimilating elements, in and into, his culture without intuition, such as new music, dialect, or the habits of younger or older generation. As many members of society take minute decisions in favour of an innovation, so it gradually becomes accepted as a trait of their culture. A new tradition has been accepted and culture changes to fit it in to its dynamic pattern. Christian enculturation is the process by whereby Christian faith, as brought together by a belief in Trinity and Incarnation (Holmes 2006), is recruited by innovation into a culture. It is a cultural act, not completely in the gift of any individual, for the innovation must be actively accepted if the culture is to be changed to fit the new innovation, and many ramifications are possible. From their travels either local innovators or missionaries bring, culture traits or texts which are inevitably far wider than their gospel message. According to the receiving culture's appropriation, or enculturation, of these traits or texts, both it and the previously disengaged trait will be changed. If in this metamorphosis, Trinitarian faith is engendered anew in a God who in Christ was incarnate, then the culture is process of redemption, not just individuals who may be taken out of it. The actors in mission need to trust the Holy Spirit to accomplish this formally unpredictable transformation (Allen 1912; 1927).

Thus Christian enculturation is presented as a missiological model which can foster the confidence and morale of the Two-Thirds World churches to work out their own salvation. It is not only individuals that are enculturated into society, but also religious traditions. Until these are taken in and absorbed by a particular culture, they remain powerless to transform it, except superficially or destructively. Christian enculturation is a way for mission to realize a vernacular church of the people in a vast range of contexts, including the One-Third World that do not depend on swallowing whole a history of Western ideas. The cosmic Christ, who is the ideal pattern of each culture created by the Word of God, will be revealed in the historical encounter with the message of the Galilean.

Global Christian Religions

One of the chief and most evident observations Jenkins might have made on his empirical data is the plurality of Christian expressions around the world. What then is the basis for a New Christendom, which will impose a religio-political hegemony on the world? The increased communication available to the Two-Thirds World allows it more awareness of the military, political, and economic dominance of the One-Third World, offering it possibilities for religious innovation in order to access the blessings of the relatively few. However even this communication is one-sided, with media empires making their take on the world for audiences who will reward advertisers. The television and film producers, the publishing houses, and the print-media are the product of a growing economic inequality that means that Africa will not be able to confront the One-Third World, only penetrate it from the underside of history.

Jenkins' book is a cross between David Barrett's demographic projections, Andrew Walls' southward moving centre of Christian gravity, and Samuel Huntington's geo-politics for maximizing US power. Barrett's figures are indispensable, but they depend on local informers giving rough estimates of proportions of religious adherence in a nation's people-group. These proportions can be contested and even census figures may be unreliable indicators of present base populations. The key variable is population growth, when Christian faith is considered unlikely to surpass it in total. However past growth rates cannot be guaranteed to continue, rendering extrapolations far into the future to be very fragile (Jenkins, 2002, p.80–96). Uganda for instance is unlikely to quadruple its population in little more than fifty years to 83 million. Most of the territory is static in development and Northern Uganda is suffering terribly, yet as an ally of the USA and UK, it has been selected as a success story by the World Bank and Britain's DfID. Yet one-half to three-quarters of the state's budget is funded by external donors. Without infrastructure, or even peace, Uganda will not be able to sustain such population growth or its churches to be so resourceful as to be able to threaten the Western sense of superiority. Drier countries, as most are, will not be able to sustain urban growth around the tropics, because the water supply will be too constrained by sheer unavailability. Jenkins makes a point about water, but does not adjust his figures down. Thus, Jenkins' concept (2002, p.129) of "rising churches" may prove empty. He does not even consider that urban Christians in the Two-Thirds world may tire of the churches for their exclusive claims and failed promises of material blessing.

Andrew Walls' southward marching centre of gravity also considers numbers of heads, not the will and capacity to transform the world. The Two-Thirds World church is far off having the resources and the morale to form and lead a centre for the global Christian faith, when it is often reduced to begging for funds from the One-Third World, inequitable though this position is. Christians in the Two-Thirds World are ambiguous about their position in the world, oscillating between asserting autonomy, seeking assistance, and emigrating to the One-Third World. Since globalization selects certain havens for direct investment and boosts a growing inequality in income and wealth between countries and persons (Knighton 2001b), it will only be certain people in China, Korea, and India who will be empowered to create new structures, and they have governments and states that are highly suspicious of Christian faith.

Samuel Huntington has been a geo-political adviser to the US government, being on the lookout for threats to the security of his state (Jenkins 2002, p.5f,149,189). Jenkins (2002, p.135) sees the New Christendom taking the place of Islam as the enemy of liberal democratic values: "it so directly contradicts every secular assumption, and undermines the values of the world's dominant social order". "Anti-Christianity will become the new anti-Semitism" (Jenkins, 2002, p.177).

Unashamedly Jenkins uses his imagination to sow a scaremongering sensation among his American readers:

> We might even imagine a new wave of Christian states, in which political life is inextricably bound up with religious belief . . . this political dimension will further intensify the enormous cultural gap between North and South, between secular and religious societies (Jenkins, 2002, p.142).

"We can even imagine Southern Christians taking the initiative to the extent of evangelizing the North . . . and exporting cultural traits presently only found in Africa and Latin America" (Jenkins, 2002, p.14).

> We can easily imagine scenarios in religion will indeed decide political action . . . democratic change itself will provoke more aggressive international policies, as countries with swollen populations try to expand to acquire living space or natural resources . . . by the kind of ruthless private armies that have marauded over Liberia and Sierra Leone since the 1990s (Jenkins, 2002, p.186).

If religious rivalries do not raise the spectres, then Jenkins throws in the Malthusian horror of unchecked population growth, macabrely beloved of the Anglo-Saxon right (Knighton 2005b), which will assuredly bring in "the whole train of common diseases and epidemics, wars, plague, and famine" (Malthus, 1826, p.16). How international wars will be "fought by militias made up of une-ducated fourteen-year-old boys", Jenkins (2002, p.186f) does not elaborate, but the "we can imagine a future when in which Muslim and Christian alliances blunder into conflict", and the rising states of Africa and Asia bring about "THE WAR OF THE END OF THE WORLD" (Jenkins, 2002, p.188). China might fight to protect Christian communities in Asia against an alliance of Muslim and Anglo-Saxon powers. Jenkins (2002, p.190) admits that is "pure fantasy", but "the background is anything but speculative" for a New Christendom to unite against the common threat of Islam again. Such eschato-logical flavours make the apocalyptic Hal Lindsey look historical!

Returning to more empirical issues, it has to be said that African Christianity has not "become quintessentially African, Korean Christianity thoroughly Korean" (Jenkins, 2002, p.135). The influence of Western theologians and denominations has not been displaced. Africans are aware of sins of their unmarried priests and are more open to them marrying, or women being spiritual leaders. The churches in the Two-Thirds World, to the detriment of Christian mission perhaps, have seldom been enculturated by local society, yielding original theology.

Jenkins has completely underestimated the staying and growing power of the mainstream churches,[10] which have the greater institutional expression, because their inherited systems of government allow growth to be organized, permitting their church leaders a solid platform from which to speak to the world. It is bishops who are using English language and tradition to challenge the Episcopalians of North America, not wild, revolutionary charismatics. It is true that the new Pentecostalist churches are growing much faster, able for a while to promote social entrepreneurship as a mirror image of American capitalism, complete with the accent, but these are much more counter-cultural than the old mission-churches are now, or ever were (Knighton 2006). Worshippers must dance, but they have to be taught the Pentecostal pew shuffle, not bring in their 'pagan' routines, for such a direction leads not to global pathways to prosperity, but backwards to Satan. AICs, which have incorporated certain elements from African customs into offshoots of mission-churches still tend to be counter-cultural in terms of many pre-Christian practices, yet because of their tendency to avoid Western education and medicine have lost their more ambitious youth. Thus in East Africa adherence to AICs is declining as a new generation of New Religious Movements takes off, polarized into non-Christian ethnic expressions, such as Mũingiki in Kenya, or into unstable charismatic congregations.

African agency has chosen its own destiny then, but so far that is a plural one. Whether to the consternation of missionaries emphasizing the vernacular or Africa nationalists seeking a moratorium on expatriate missionary contacts, Africans have repeatedly chosen to access the modern and postmodern worlds by joining a religion that mediates the external to them, often through a European language. Two-Thirds World Christians are globally integrated more by religion than they are politically, socially, or economically, because the missionary movement was global relatively early. When Christian mission grants time for the leavening necessary for cultural transformation instead of seeking to foreclose it by inventing means by which individuals are required to convert to another culture, will be the time that Jenkins' readership will have nothing to fear. For that will be the time when they will not face the repercussions of their own interventions.

References

Allen, R. 1912. *Missionary methods: St. Paul's or ours? a study of the church in four provinces.* London: Robert Scott.
Allen, R. 1927. *The spontaneous expansion of the church and the causes which hinder it.* London: World Dominion Press.

---

10   Barrett & Johnson (2004, p.25) have Protestants growing around the world at a mean of 1.36 per cent a year, Roman Catholics at 1.24 per cent, and Pentecostals and Charismatics, whom the mainstream currently outnumber by nearly three to one, at 1.87 per cent.

Barrett, D. 1971. *African initiatives in religion: 21 studies from eastern and central Africa.* Nairobi: East African Publishing House.

Barrett, D. & Johnson, T. 2004. Annual statistical table on global mission: 2003. *International bulletin of missionary research* 27 (1): p.24f.

Barthes, R. 1975. *S-Z.* London: Cape.

BBC News. 2006. Archbishop fears church "fupture". Available at: http://news.bbc.co.uk/1/hi/uk/4775446.stm Viewed 5 Mar 2006.

Bediako, K. 1992. *Theology and identity: the impact of culture upon Christian thought in the second century and modern Africa.* Oxford: Regnum.

Bediako, K. 1995. *Christianity in Africa: the renewal of a non-Western religion.* Edinburgh: Edinburgh UP.

Bernardi, Bernardo (ed) 1977. *The concept and dynamics of culture.* The Hague: Mouton.

Bevans, S. 2002. *Models of contextual theology.* Maryknoll, NY: Orbis.

Bevans, S. & Schroeder, R. 2004. *Constants in context: theology of mission for today.* Maryknoll, NY: Orbis.

Bernasconi, R. 1998. Hegel at the court of the Ashanti. (In Barnett, S. (ed). *Hegel after Derrida.* p.41–63.)

Casson, J. 1998. 'To pant a garden city in the slums of paganism': Handley Hooper and the future of Africa. *Journal of religion in Africa.* 28 (4): p.387–410.

Collier, P. 2003. *Breaking the conflict trap: civil war and development policy.* Washington, DC: World Bank/Oxford: Oxford UP.

Comaroff, J. & Comaroff, J. 1991. *Of revelation and revolution.* Chicago: University of Chicago Press.

Fabian, J. 1986. *Language and colonial power: the appropriation of Swahili in the former Belgian Congo, 1880–1938.* Cambridge: Cambridge UP.

Geertz, C. 1966. Religion as a cultural system. (In Banton, M. (ed) *Anthropological approaches to the study of religion.* London: Tavistock. p.1–46.)

George, F. 1990. *Inculturation and ecclesial communion: culture and the church in the teaching of Pope John Paul II.* Rome: Urbaniana UP.

Gifford, P. 1991. *The new crusaders: Christianity and the new right in southern Africa.* London: Pluto.

Gifford, P. 1998. *African Christianity: its public role.* London: Hurst.

Grossberg, L. 2006. Does cultural studies have futures? Should it? (or what's the matter with New York?): cultural studies, contexts and conjunctures. *Cultural studies.* 20 (1): p.1–32.

Habermas, J. 2005. Equal treatment of cultures and the limits of postmodern liberalism. *Journal of political philosophy.* 131 (1).

Hardy, D. 1977. Man the creature. *Scottish journal of theology.* 30: p.111–36.

Herskovits, M.J. 1950. *Man and his works: the science of cultural anthropology.* New York: Alfred Knopf.

Höffler, A. 2001. *On the incidence of civil war in Africa.* Paper presented to the African Studies Seminar, St. Antony's College, University of Oxford, 5 Oct 2001.

Holmes, S. 2006. Trinitarian missiology: towards a theology of God as missionary. *International journal of systematic theology* 8 (1): p.72–90.

Hunter, D.E. & Whitten, P. (eds) 1976. *Encyclopedia of anthropology.* New York: Harper & Row.

Jenkins, P. 2002. *The next Christendom: the coming of global Christianity.* New York: Oxford UP.

Knighton, B. 2001. Globalization: implications of violence, the global economy, and the role of the state of Africa and Christian mission. *Transformation* 18 (4): p.204–19.

Knighton, B. 2004a. *The vitality of Karamojong religion: dying tradition or living faith?* Aldershot: Ashgate.

Knighton, B. 2005b. *Eroding the concept of commons: a history of an idea inapplicable to natural resource management by Karamojong pastoralists.* PENHA 15th Anniversary Conference, County Hall, London 29 Sep 2005. http://www.penhanetwork.org/2.pdf

Knighton, B. 2006: Multireligious responses to globalization in East Africa: Karamojong and Agĩkũyũ compared. *Transformation* 23 (2).

Leis, P. 1972. *Enculturation and socialization in an Ijaw Village.* New York: Holt, Rinehart, and Winston.

Leach, M. & Mearns, R. (eds) 1996. *The lie of the land.* Oxford: James Currey.

Lonsdale, J. 1999. Kikuyu Christianities. *Journal of African religion* 29 (2): p.206–29.

Lonsdale, J. 2002. Kikuyu Christianities: a history of intimate diversity. (In Maxwell & Lawrie, 2002, p.157–97.)

Malinowski, B. 1945. *The dynamic of culture change.* New Haven: Yale UP.

Malthus, T.R. 1826. *Essay on the principle of population, as it affects the future improvement of society.* London: J. Johnson.

Maxwell, D. 1999. *Christians and chiefs in Zimbabwe: a social history of the Hwesa people c.1870s-1990s.* Edinburgh: Edinburgh UP.

Maxwell, D. 2000. In defence of African creativity: review article on Gifford 1998. *Journal of religion in Africa.* 30 (4): p.468–81.

Maxwell, D. & Lawrie, I. (eds) 2002. *Christianity and the African imagination: essays in honour of Adrian Hastings.* Brill: Leiden.

Mbiti, J.S. 1969. *African religions and philosophy.* London: Heinemann.

Meyer, B. & Geschiere, P. (eds) 1999. *Globalization and identity: dialectics of flow and closure.* Oxford: Blackwell.

Peel, J.D.Y. 2003. *Religious encounter and the making of the Yoruba.* Bloomington: Indiana UP.

Phan, P. 1998. *Mission and catechesis: Alexandre de Rhodes and inculturation in seventeenth-century Vietnam.* Maryknoll, NY: Orbis.

Pirouet, L. 1978. *Black evangelists: the spread of Christianity in Uganda, 1891–1914.* London: Collins.

Ranger, T. 1999. Taking on the missionary's task: African spirituality and the mission churches of Manicaland in the 1930s. *Journal of religion in Africa* 29 (2): p.175–205.

Richardson, M. 2001. *The experience of culture.* London: Sage.

Robertson, R. 1992. *Globalization: social theory and global culture.* London: Sage.

Robertson, R. 1994. Globalization or Glocalization? *Journal of international communication.* 1: p.33–52.

Schreiter, R. 1985. *Constructing local theologies.* Maryknoll, NY: Orbis.

Schreiter, R. (ed) 1992. *Mission in the third millennium.* Maryknoll, NY: Orbis.

Sebeok, T. (ed) 1987. *Encyclopedic dictionary of semiotics.* 3 vols. Berlin: Mouton de Gruyter.

Seymour-Smith, C. 1986. *Macmillan dictionary of anthropology.* London: Macmillan.

Shorter, A. 1988. *Toward a theology of inculturation.* London: Geoffrey Chapman.

Stanley, B. 1978. The east African revival: African initiative within European tradition. *Churchman* 92 (1): p.6–22.

Stewart, P. & Strathern A. 2004. *Witchcraft, sorcery, rumors, gossip.* Cambridge: Cambridge UP.

Thiselton, A. 1992. *New horizons in hermeneutics.* London: Harper Collins.

Tylor, E.B. 1871. *Primitive culture: researches into the development of mythology, philosophy, religion, art, and custom.* London: John Murray.

Vokes, R. 2003. *The Kanungu fire: power, patronage, and exchange in south-Western Uganda.* DPhil. Thesis, University of Oxford.

Walls, A. 1998. Africa in Christian history: retrospect and prospect. *Journal of African Christian thought* 1 (1): p.2–15.

Whitehead, C. 1988. British colonial education policy: a synonym for cultural imperialism? (In Mangan, J.A. (ed) 1988. *'Benefits bestowed?': education and British imperialism.* Manchester: Manchester UP. p.211–30.)

Sebastian C.H. Kim

The Future Shape of Christianity from an Asian Perspective

Philip Jenkins' *The Next Christendom* has made a significant impact on discussion of the rise of Southern Christianity and the future shape of Christianity as a whole. However, there are two difficulties in his thesis: first, the term "Christendom" is an unfortunate term in that it implies, at least historically, the dominating nature of a particular form of Christianity. Jenkins' use of "the next Christendom" suggests the churches of the South will influence or dominate others after the same pattern as European Christendom. The second difficulty is that, when it comes to the idea of the "centre of gravity" of the Christian church shifting to the South, the argument seems to rely entirely on the numerical growth of Christian population in this region. Jenkins focuses his study on the demography of these churches, the reasons for the growth of particular denominations, and their socio-political contexts. The question of how we assess the Christianity in a given context needs to include more than its numerical strength and the study of the ways and means of its expansion. One of the vital questions seems to be the question of the *identity* and *mission* of the church—how do Christians themselves understand the purpose of the church and what are the contributions of that church to its society? In addition to analysing Christianity sociologically, observation of the engagement or interaction of Christians with the context is vital to understanding contemporary Christianity in a particular part of the world and to predict its future shape. In my paper, I shall examine the problem of the terms "Christendom" and "centre of gravity". And then I shall argue, by employing some examples of Asian churches, that the *distinctive features* of Southern Christianity lie particularly in their theological approaches to socio-political and religious problems.

> We are currently living through one of the transforming moments in the history of religion worldwide . . . Until recently, the overwhelming majority of Christians have lived in White nations . . . Over the past century, however, the centre of gravity in the Christian world has shifted inexorably southward, to Africa, Asia, and Latin America . . . Christianity is doing very well indeed in the global South—not just surviving but expanding (Jenkins, 2002a, p.1–2).

The above statement is commonly shared by recent scholarship on religions and sociology. The growth of Christian churches in the Southern hemisphere is set to continue and this affects not only the demography within the Christian church but also the pattern of religious groupings world wide (Barrett et al, 2001, p.12–15). There are a number of scholars who have studied this new phenomenon, notably Harvey Cox (2001), Paul Preston (2001), David Martin (1998, 2002), Grace Davie (1994, 2002) and Philip Jenkins (2002a, 2002b). These studies are conducted from sociological, historical and political perspectives. They attempt to give a comprehensive picture of past and present trends of Christian movements and direct us to certain patterns of emerging Christianity. In spite of differences in methodology and research outcomes among these scholars, two features can be said to be common. First, recognition of the numerical growth of non-Western Christianity. The mode and reasons for this growth varies from place to place but Evangelical and Pentecostal (charismatic) movements are playing the major role in this new phenomenon. Second, as a consequence of the first, an acknowledgement that the "centre of gravity" has shifted away from the West and that the new forms of Christianity will inevitably influence the churches in the West, changing the 'traditional' form of Christianity as a whole. The first feature is less ambiguous since the statistics show quite clearly the numerical strength of the Christian church in Asia, Africa and Latin America and this growth seems to set to continue (Barrett et al, 2001, p.12–15).[1] The second feature deserves more attention since scholars do not agree about the mode and outcome of the interaction between traditional Christianity and the more recent forms of Christianity outside the West. There are two schools of thought on this issue: one, represented by Jenkins, that there will be much interaction between Southern and Northern Christianity in the form of confrontational encounter or clashes of different forms of Christianities. The other, represented by Davie, that the rise of Southern Christian will make very little impact on Northern (European) Christianity since the Christianity developed in Europe is unique. What I try to examine is the question of the future shape of Christianity. I shall discuss Jenkins and Davie briefly and then look more closely at the nature of the churches in Korea, India and Europe. I believe the key to our investigation lies in the integrity of the Christian church rather than in the growing or declining numbers of Christians in a particular context, and as a result, would like to suggest an alternative picture of the future shape of Christianity.

Assessing Christianity: a matter of integrity

Professor Jenkins, in his remarkable survey of the shift of the Christian presence to the South, convincingly argues that the churches in the South have developed distinctive forms of Christianity "strictly on their own terms" and that they will inevitably define the features of the "next Christendom" and therefore the shape of Christianity as a whole (Jenkins, 2002a, p.6–7). He observes that the churches

---

1   See also Johnson & Chung 2004.

in the South are "not just a transplanted version of the familiar religion of the older Christian status: the new Christendom is no mirror image of the Old. It is a truly new and developing entity" (Jenkins, 2002a, p.214). He identifies the distinctive characteristics of the Southern Christianity as traditional (not liberal) on social issues, conservative on beliefs and moral issues, and interested in supernatural and personal salvation rather than radical politics. He holds an optimistic view of the future of Christianity, believing that the rise of the South will be instrumental in the sustenance or even revitalisation of the churches in the North.

Although in many ways she shares Jenkins' thesis, Grace Davie, in her survey of the shift of the Christian presence to the South, arrives at a different conclusion. In her book, *Europe—The Exceptional Case: Parameters of Faith in the Modern World*, Davie deals with the close relationship of modernisation and secularisation in Europe and suggests that secularisation will not necessarily accompany modernisation in the rest of the world. In this sense Europe is the exceptional case. The author persuasively argues that examination of the different patterns of Christian activities in the Americas, Africa and parts of the Asian continent supports her thesis. The basis of her argument lies in the unique development of religious patterns in (Western) Europe. Taking the example of Britain, which she characterises as "believing without belonging", she points out that, though church attendance has drastically declined, the British have not abandoned "their deepseated religious aspirations or a latent sense of belonging", but instead "religious belief is inversely rather than directly related to belonging" and, as the institutional disciplines decline, so "belief not only persists but becomes increasingly personal, detached and heterogeneous" (Davie, 2002, p.2–8).[2] She challenges the notion of Europe being a model for the rest of the world and argues that the religious behaviour of Europeans is distinctive and peculiar to Europe.

What I would like to discuss here is the way Jenkins, Davie and others approach the issue and the nature of their investigations—in other words, their assessment of the impact of the rise of Southern Christianity. Jenkins and other commentators mentioned above focus their studies on the demography of these churches, the reasons for the growth of particular denominations, their sociopolitical contexts, and the characteristics of their faith. When Jenkins describes Christianity in the South as "doing very well indeed", one understands, in the light of his whole thesis, that his observations are mainly determined by the numerical expansion of Christianity there. The question I would like to address is how we assess Christianity in a given context.

Kenneth S. Latourette, in his monumental work, *A History of the Expansion of Christianity*, explained the way he interpreted the expansion of Christianity in three perspectives: geographical expansion (according to the numbers of

---

2   See also Davie 1994.

Christians and churches); the vigour of Christianity in any given era (according to new movements and denominations); and the effect of Christianity upon humankind (1945, p.416–8). Most studies—even, I would say, Latourette's work itself—are done from the first two perspectives, and the last perspective is very difficult to assess indeed, if not impossible. However, the question of how we assess the Christianity in a given context needs to include more than its numerical strength and the study of the ways and means of its expansion. I will argue that evaluating the strength of Christianity in any society has more to do with the *integrity* of the Christian church, and this has to be constantly re-assessed, however difficult this may be. In this regard, two vital questions seem to be about the identity and mission of the church—how do Christians themselves understand the purpose of the church and what are the contributions of that church to its society? In addition to analysing Christianity sociologically, observation of the engagement or interaction of theologians and church leaders with the context is vital to understanding contemporary Christianity in a particular part of the world and to predicting its future shape.

The historian, K.M. Panikkar, in his book *Asia and Western Dominance* predicted that after the colonial era the increase of Christianity in Asia would be "a thing of the past" since it was supported by "the unchallenged political supremacy of Europe" (Panikkar, 1953, p.454–6). However, Christianity in Asia has not only grown in terms of numbers, but also continues to be prominent in many areas of the life of the people. In this period of transformation, Christianity has been an active contributing factor not only in political and economic nation-building but also in sociological and ideological changes taking place in this region. The concerns of Christianity in Asia have been quite different from the problems the churches in the North faced in the past century—secularisation and modernisation. Most Asian countries went through complex and overwhelming encounters with poverty and socio-economic and political injustice, on the one hand, and the experience of being minorities in religiously pluralistic contexts on the other. I would like to address the question of how the churches in Asia have not only survived but also grown and sustained their integrity. In other words, what is their distinctive understanding of their *mission* and their *identity*? How do they see the nature of the church—its function, meaning and form in the contemporary world, and secondly, the raison d'être of the church—its role in society and service to the world? Although the importance of sociological analysis of the Christian church is vital to our understanding of religious phenomena, the rise of Christian thinking and formulation of theology is equally, if not more, important to understanding the future of the Christian church. I shall limit my presentation to theological perspectives from two countries—South Korea and India, which are the most familiar to me.

The Korean case: the churches response to injustice and reconciliation in post-war Korea

The churches in South Korea grew along with the modernisation of the Korean society and rapid growth of the economy. The revival movement of seeking eschatological hope and the emphasis on church growth dominated the Korean church in the second half of the twentieth century and, as a result, the church rapidly grew numerically, forming a largely conservative evangelical constituency. However, the problem faced in Post-war South Korea by the church was the problem of economic and political injustice on the one hand and peace and reconciliation on the other. I will argue that its involvement with contemporary problems made the Korean church credible in the eyes of non-Christians and made an impact on Korean society.

The problem of injustice and Minjung theology

After the Korean War in 1953, South Korea went through political turmoil with corruption and dictatorship. Eventually the military took over the government and through a series of coups d'etat military-backed government continued until 1988. High on successive government agendas was overcoming poverty. They legitimised their rule and their oppression of the opposition party by this and disregarded for the civil liberties of the people. So in the process of the remarkable economic growth, there was political injustice and exploitation of the workers and the farmers. The majority of pastors saw this problem as a simply matter of the "process" of development and concentrated instead on church growth. In this period, *jaebol*s (large business corporations) and mega-churches rose in parallel and the church leadership believed the growth of Christian population and the growth of national economy went hand-in-hand. There were large evangelistic meetings, for example the Billy Graham Crusade in 1973 and EXPLO '74 organised by Campus Crusade for Christ, both of which drew more than a million people. This speech of the head of CCC in Korea on "total evangelization of Korea" is typical:

> They [total evangelisation] cover pre-evangelism, evangelization, discipleship, socialization, and the total Christianization of this nation. When they are realized, the amazing blessing promised in Deuteronomy 28:1–4 will apply to us. In Christ all things will be made new (Kim, 1983, p.23).

However, Charles Elliott rightly points out the lack of social ethics regarding achieving material blessings and church growth:

> Those offers—attractive as they are to people deeply troubled by the processes of transition in which they find themselves caught—are, however, predicated on the assumption that nothing can be done to modify the processes. It is at that point that Cho [Pastor Yonggi Cho of the Yoido Full Gospel Church in Seoul] and the great majority of church leaders who think like him are at their weakest (Elliott, 1989, p.38).

In the context of 1970s Korea, there was a need for a new theological paradigm to meet the need of the urban poor who were victims of a highly competitive capitalist market. The problem of poverty was increasingly seen as not just individual matter or to do with a congregation but had to do with the structure of the Korean economy and society. It was in this point, some Christian intellectuals realised that the poor are not just poor in the sense of lacking material things, but they are also exploited and unjustly treated in socio-political reality, and that the gap between the poor and rich and between employee and employer is widening. The *minjung* movement was sparked when Jun Tae-Ill set himself on fire in November 1970 as his protest against the exploitation of fellow factory workers. The incident shook the country and soon Christian leaders took this as a major issue, and stood for and with the poor and exploited. This meant challenging the status quo of the government and the capitalist market economy of the *jaebol*. In 1973, they declared 'The Korean Christian Manifesto' which says:

> We believe in God who, by his righteousness, will surely protect people who are oppressed, weak and the poor and judge the power of evil in history. We believe that Jesus, the Messiah proclaimed that the evil power will be destroyed and the kingdom of Messiah will come, and this kingdom of Messiah will be the haven of rest for the poor, oppressed and despised (Yoo, 1984, p.258–9).

Following this, Suh Nam-Dong, among the most well-known of *Minjung* theologians, presented his thesis in 1975 that Jesus identified with the poor, sick and oppressed and that the gospel of Jesus is the gospel of salvation and liberation, and for him, it is manifested in struggle with those evil powers and that liberation is not individual or spiritual but rather communal and political. Suh systematized his *Minjung* theology in the following years, seeing the *minjung* as subjects of history and the dealing with "*han*" as the key theme for theology in Korean context.

> Let us hold in abeyance discussions on doctrines and theories about sin which are heavily charged with the bias of the ruling class and are often nothing more than the labels the ruling class for the deprived. Instead, we should take han as our theme, which is indeed the language of the Minjung and signifies the reality of their experience. If one does not hear the signs of the han of the Minjung, one cannot hear the voice of Christ knocking on our doors (Suh, 1983, p.51–65).

Ahn Byeung-Moo, another well-known *Minjung* theologian, asserted that Jesus identified in such a way that Jesus is *minjung* and *minjung* is Jesus as he shared his life with *minjung* and the event of the Cross is the climax of the suffering of *minjung* (Ahn, 1990, p.31–37). Therefore Christ is not present when the word preached nor when the sacrament is conducted but when we participate with or in the suffering of *minjung*. Jesus is God becoming flesh and body, which means material being and reality in everyday life not a ideology or philosophy (Ahn, 1990, p.87–128). Therefore he argued that the *minjung* is the

owner of the Jesus community which is fundamentally a "food community"—
community sharing food—and the concept of a worshipping community
comes later (Ahn, 1990, p.156–185).

Ahn and Suh and other *Minjung* theologians were deeply influenced by Kim
Chi-ha, a prominent activist and poet who expressed in poetry this concept of
sharing food in Christian life and theology:

> Food is heaven
> As you can't go to heaven by yourself
> Food is to be shared
>
> Food is heaven
> As you see the stars in heaven together
> Food is to be shared by everybody
>
> When the food goes into a mouth
> Heaven is worshipped in the mind
>
> Food is heaven
> Ah, ah, food is
> To be shared by everybody (Suh, 1983, p.64).

Minjung theologians captured the people's imagination and brought the issue
of poverty and exploitation into the church. Here we see *Minjung* theology as a
"protest" theology on behalf of the *minjung* against injustice and exploitation.
Their interpretation of the poor is not in isolation from others but it is "rela-
tional". Poor are poor not necessarily because they are sinners or do not have a
"right" relationship with God, but because of the greediness of some others
and unjust system of modern capitalism. Therefore their main concern was not
dealing with individual poor people but rather with social process and the system which prevents the *minjung* from coming out of their misery. In this
respect, *Minjung* theologians' main concern is with anything anti-*minjung* than
with the *minjung* themselves as they try to deal with economic and political
injustice.[3] *Minjung* theology has made a great contribution to Korean church
and society through their understanding of liberation and justice, and by showing the poor and oppressed that they are not or should not be the objects of
exploitation and that their protest was a legitimate one. In spite of shortcomings, *Minjung* theology has made a vital contribution to the identity of the *minjung* and challenged them to stand and speak. Though Latin American
liberation theology made the point that the poor and oppressed are the ones
who need to be liberated, *minjung* theology further asserts that the *minjung* are
the subjects of this liberation as well as the subjects of the history and culture

---

3   21st Century and Minjung Theology. *Shinhack Sasang* (Summer 2000) p.5–29.

of their particular contexts. This was expressed as in the relationship between Jesus and the *minjung*:

> Jesus proclaims the coming of God's Kingdom. He stands with the Minjung, and promises them the future of God. . . . God's will is to side with the Minjung completely and uncondi-tionally. This notion was not comprehensive within the framework of established ethics, cult, and laws. God's will is revealed in the event of Jesus being with them in which he loves the Minjung (Ahn, 1983, p.138–151).

On the whole, *Minjung* theology has been a major instrument of the *minjung* or civil movement that challenged both the church and society to deal with the prob-lems of socio-economic and political injustice, brought democracy in Korea in the late 1980s, and certainly played a "prophetic" role in Korean history.

Theological quests for peace and reconciliation between two Koreas

The Christian attitude toward the Communist North and the Korean War was that the war was the result of the Communist aggression and this need to be responded to with decisive force and vigour, on the one hand, and with prayer and mission toward the people of North Korea, on the other. This response was particularly common since many of the senior leadership of the churches in the South were those who had escaped from persecution by the communist regime in the North during the war and also because, on this issue, the conservative sections of the Christian church and the military-backed government shared same attitude toward the communist government in the North. They believed regime change was the ultimate solution for peace and stability, and co-existence with communist North was not an option. So, in this understanding, the evan-gelisation of North Korea was understood as prior to unification.

This rigid and hostile attitude toward the North was soon countered by a more sympathetic acceptance of the people of the North as same-blood rela-tions. This coincided with the rise of the *minjung* theology movement, increasing awareness of Christians' role in peace and reconciliation, and the sustaining support of the World Council of Churches for peace and reconciliation. The initiative was taken by a group of overseas Korean Christians who met North Korean Christian delegates in the early 1980s, and this created fresh new beginnings. However, the declarations after the meetings were heavily critical of the South Korean and US governments and supportive of the North; there-fore they were rejected by the South Korean media and the general public, and did not really make any impact. Meanwhile, in this period, the WCC took an initiative to bring dialogue between the two parties. The most significant direct dialogue was a meeting between representatives from the North and South Korean churches at a seminar on the "Christian perspectives on biblical and theological foundations for peace" in Switzerland in September, 1986. The most emotional moment of this meeting was during the Eucharist, when all the participants were encouraged to greet one another. The representatives of South and North first shook hands but soon embraced each other. By participating in the Eucharist together—the heart of the Christ's gospel of peace and reconciliation—they showed the desire and hope of the people of divided Korea.

Meanwhile, in the midst of a series of WCC meetings, in 1988 the KNCC issued the "Declaration of the Korea National Council of the Churches toward the unification and peace of Korean people", which made a significant impact both within the church and on the whole nation. The KNCC declaration was welcomed by many Christians but also generated a heated discussion among the Christians and brought the issue of peace and reconciliation within the churches, which motivated conservative Christians to participate in the debate. The declaration starts with the affirmation that Christ came to the earth as the servant of peace and proclaimed the kingdom of God, which represents peace, reconciliation and liberation. It claims that, accordingly, the Korean church is trying to be with people who are suffering. In the main thesis, the declaration acknowledges and confesses the sins of mutual hatred, justifying the division of Korea, and accepting each ideology as absolute, which is contrary to God's absolute authority. The declaration, while affirming the three principles expressed in the Joint Declaration (1972), added the priority of humanitarian practice and the participation of the *minjung*, who are the victims of divided Korea, in the process of unification discussions. The Declaration then proclaimed the year 1995 as a jubilee year for peace and unification when Koreans could celebrate the 50th anniversary of the liberation from Japan. It set down practical steps toward the jubilee year including: church renewal, the church becoming a faith community for peace and reconciliation, and working together with all the churches, employing all the necessary means toward peace and reconciliation.

The jubilee principle has several dimensions: sabbatical, restoration of the ownership, and liberation of slaves. When the KNCC declared 1995 as the Year of Jubilee, it focused on the third aspect of liberation and also more on the proclamation than the actualisation of unification in any particular year. Though many sincerely expected and wished that it could be achieved, the important point was that the Jubilee is proclaimed. It is the proclamation of the liberation of the Korean people from the bondage of ideological hegemony and from political systems which hinder the formation of a common community. This theme is also related to the remembering of God's grace in spite of the present situation, so that Christians are called to hold faith in confidence. The Declaration brought the issue of reunification onto the main agenda of Korean Christians and challenged many conservative sections of the church to rethink the traditional approaches toward the North, moving from evangelism or relief to partnership for the common goal of peace and reconciliation. Furthermore, the Declaration has expressed the vital concerns, not only of Christians but also of the whole nation, on the issue, and has set the future direction of the Korean church. In spite of its limitations and shortcomings, the Declaration was a most significant landmark in the Korean Christian attempt to bring peace and reconciliation.

The Christian groups particularly associated with minjung theology and the movement of peace and reconciliation are not in the main stream of Korean Christianity in terms of numbers. The vast majority of the Korean churches are conservative evangelical churches, emphasising revival, personal experience, eschatological hope, exclusive truth in Christ and the numerical growth of the church, as Jenkins and other rightly observed. Of course, I am not saying that these majority Christian groups were immune from social issues nor entirely silent on the issues of peace and reconciliation. I myself am from one of the large churches in Seoul and I do acknowledge the contributions the majority of churches make to society. What I want to highlight here is that the challenge brought by this small group of Christians has made a great impact on Korean society as they took the most pertinent issues ordinary lives of Koreans and played their prophetic role. They help Christian theology and thinking to permeate society and have been instrumental in bringing justice and hope in the context of injustice and division in Korea. This legacy may arguably be more important for Christian integrity in Korea than the spectacular growth in numbers of Christians.

The Indian case: In search of an authentic ecclesiology

One of the major concerns of Indian politics, economy, society and religion is the problem of communalism or sectarianism. The complexity of communal relationships in India is enriching and beautiful and at the same time communalism's destructive power and divisiveness have been demonstrated among the people of India. Indian Christians have been wrestling with the question of what being a Christian and being church in the midst of Hindu-dominated society means. The topic of ecclesiology rose to prominence in Indian Christian theology particularly during the second half of the twentieth century as the strength of Hindu opposition to Christianity became evident in the various attempts to regulate conversion in both central and local states. These provoked strong reactions from Christians on the basis of the fundamental rights guaranteed in the Indian Constitution and the conviction that conversion was at the heart of Christian belief and practice. However, this opposition to conversion also forced Christian theologians to re-think the idea of the church. As a result, there have been several distinctive theological models proposed for dealing with the problem and I shall discuss two of them here—the kingdom model and the secular model in this paper.

Kingdom model: seeking an Indian expression of Christian community

The meaning and practice of the traditional of the church was first collectively challenged by the "Rethinking Group" of Madras. They recognised the problem of the politicisation of mass conversion and raised concern over the Christian community being confined to the church, which they saw as a Western product. They regarded the traditional missionaries' emphasis on conversion to the Christian community—and therefore change of religious affiliation by joining the church—as the root cause of the problem in Christian mission. And they insisted that there must be an alternative model and goal for Christian mission that is either creating an Indian church, radically different from the traditional church structure, or seeking the kingdom of God and rejecting any form of church.

The "Rethinking Group" produced a book, *Rethinking Christianity in India*, just before the Conference of the International Missionary Council at Tambaram, Madras in 1938 (Devasahyam & Sunarisanam). The book was interpreted by many authors as a response to Kraemer's understanding of theology of religions, but careful examination of the book informs us differently. It appears that the authors' concern was not necessarily theology of religions, but the practical problem of the Indian church in relation to the contemporary debate on mass conversion—the problem of proselytism, the need for integration of the Hindu and Christian communities, the problem of Christian communalism, and the search for an alternative model for Christian mission.

In the book, the article "The Church and the Indian Christian" by Pandipeddi Chenchiah questioned the choice of the church as the central theme of the Conference. He asked openly "by what right Christendom has all but jettisoned the kingdom of God which occupies so central a place in the message of Jesus and substituted in its place the Church of which the Master said so little' (Chenchiah, 1938a, p.81–82). Furthermore, in his article, "Jesus and Non-Christian Faiths", he raised the question, "why should Hindu converts join the Church?" He criticised the missionaries' dogmatic view and insisted on the necessity of continuity in the life of Indian Christians in a Hindu context (Chenchiah, 1938b, p.47–49). He went on to discuss the questions, which Kraemer addressed concerning the church, the message and the missionary mandate. First, on the issue of the church, Chenchiah saw that the problem of the church in India was that it had become 'the centre of influence, the source of salvation, the object of loyalty' and it was "identified with the core and acquired as it were the same value as the original nucleus". He rejected institutional Christianity by separating Christ from Christianity, and seeking what he called the "Raw Fact of Christ". His strongest criticism was that "the Church with all its claims cannot lead us to the Christ"; "the Church detracts our attention from the central fact"; "the Church has never been the cradle of new life", but instead "accommodator to the dominant forces of the old life" (Chenchiah, 1938b, p.53–62). In the church's place, he insisted, Indian Christianity needs, "Christ, the Holy Spirit, the Kingdom of God" (Chenchiah, 1938a, p.99).

Second, regarding the missionary mandate, he argued that there are two obstacles to mission in India—communalism and the church, and he hoped that eventually the "social intolerance of the Hindu and excessive zeal of the missionary may disappear in India". In order to achieve this, he argued that conversion should be separated from church membership. That is, he saw conversion as a change of life without insisting on affiliation to the church because he viewed mission as a "movement in the Hindu social fold" rather than the creation of "a solid society outside". He strongly objected to either individual or mass conversion to the Christian church, but supported a Christian mission in India that was "prepared to see the gradual infusion of Hinduism by Christian ideals and above all Christian life" by creating "a powerful Christian atmosphere within Hinduism". He saw the heart of Christian mission as the creation of "new life" as demonstrated in the life of Jesus, which he believed was able to fulfil the "unrealised longing for a life here" of the Hindus (Chenchiah, 1938c, p.44–52).

In similar vein, Vengal Chakkarai, another key figure in the "Rethinking group", asserted that the church had arisen out of the historical setting of Western Christianity and that Indian Christians are not obliged to follow its pattern. Whatever the positive elements of the church might be, they cannot be included in the "revelation of Christ Himself" since they are not eternal and not of "divine essence". Therefore the church should be inspiration not institution, and the institutionalised church, for Chakkarai, is "the tents put up by our Western friends; but they can never be our permanent habitation". Instead, he emphasised that Indian Christians should seek the kingdom of God which the Lord "announced and for which He gave His life" (Chakkarai, 1938, p.119–123).

The theological question of the kingdom of God and the church is important when it comes to the integrity of Christians because it relates to the practical life of the converts in their relationship with their past religious experiences and the wider community. The "Rethinking Group" represented Christians of a higher caste background who regarded the Hindu tradition as part of their heritage, and did not wish to be excluded from the wider Hindu society. They also saw themselves as sharing a common identity with Hindus in their search for the welfare of India and its people in a time of national struggle against colonial rule. These approaches are recurring themes of Indian theologians, and they arise out of their sincere attempt to solve the problems of communalism and proselytism, for which they saw the church in its western pattern and theology as responsible. The debate at Tambaram was the result of a painstaking search to answer the question of what means to be Christian in their seeking to follow Christ who preached the kingdom of God and also shared his life with the community of believers. What is the place of the church and the kingdom of God in Christianity? The Christian church, in spite of its weaknesses, or rather because of its weaknesses can bear witness to Christ, and continue to be a place for worship and sharing. The church as a visible community, rather than a hindrance, can make an impact on the wider community, and more importantly, the Christian community need not be understood merely in a functional way, but as the body of Christ and therefore of the essence of the gospel. On the other hand, the church constantly needs to be shaped and challenged by the kingdom perspective that there is a hope in Christ beyond the boundaries of the exclusive visible community of believers. The kingdom of God is not limited by historical and cultural traditions of religious affiliation, but open to the possibilities in Christ who has called believers to be part of his ongoing "new creation".

Secular model: "Christ-centred secular fellowship"

Toward and after Independence, the concern of Indian Protestant theologians was more to do with the relationship between the Christian community and the Hindu community, particularly the question of whether converts should leave the Hindu community and join the Christian community, and what joining the church entailed. The Protestant debate on conversion in the 1960s and the early 1970s was a part of the wider Christian discussion in the face of the political and social revolutions taking place in many parts of the world and urgent calls for the church to take part in the struggle for humanisation. There was a conscious shift of emphasis in mission from evangelism (leading to conversion) toward social involvement. In India Christian theologians faced increasing challenges from the Hindu nationalist movement, especially as it started to gain support from certain states and pressured the central government for the rights of Hindus over against other minority communities. In search of a solution, some Indian Protestant theologians suggested that the Christian community in India should be part of the wider Hindu community in an apparently rapidly secularising India, for they believed that not only was secularisation an inevitable process of modernity but also that it would gradually overcome communal tensions. They insisted that a "point of contact" between the Christian community and the Hindu community must be established so that Hindus would not need to convert to the Christian community. This point of contact must be located inside the wider Hindu community since the Christian community was either a stumbling block in this process, or an entity that naturally transcended religious divides to produce a secular fellowship.

At the Nasrapur Consultation in 1966 M.M. Thomas, who was a leading theologian on the issue of ecclesiology, developed his thoughts on conversion and raised the question of the 'form' of the Christian community within the human community (Thomas 1966). He argued that the most urgent task for contemporary Christian mission was to participate in the people's struggle for the "realisation of humanity" rather than following the traditional missionary task of conversion. He further insisted that the secular fellowship was the "point of contact" and could be in "partnership in the struggle" and called on the church to break the communal structure and build up a new partnership of

Christians and non-Christians—the "human *koinonia*". Thomas, reflecting on the Uppsala Assembly of the WCC (1968), published a booklet, *Salvation and Humanisation* (1971), which was the outcome of his search for the "point of contact", and perhaps represents his most mature thinking on the issue (Thomas 1971), but it brought about a direct confrontation with Lesslie Newbigin.[4] Thomas insisted that the mission of the church must take into account the "religious and secular movements which express men's search for the spiritual foundations for a fuller and richer human life" in the present "revolutionary" period (Thomas, 1971, p.1–4). In his critique of dichotomic approaches that separated salvation and humanization—concepts he saw as "integrally related"—he alleged the main problems of Indian Christianity were "pietistic individualism", which emphasised dogmatic belief and the inner experience of conversion, and the communal tendency of the Christian community, which isolated and closed off Christians from others (Thomas, 1971, p.4–12). He then introduced the concept of the "Christ-centred secular fellowship outside the Church", a *koinonia* which was the "manifestation of the new reality of the Kingdom at work in the world of men in world history". He perceived that the Indian understanding of Jesus Christ was as the "Divine Head of Humanity" through whom the Holy Spirit brings all men into sonship of the Father, ultimately uniting all their struggles for humanisation. Therefore, "salvation itself could be defined as humanisation in a total and eschatological sense" (Thomas, 1971, p.12–19).

In order to cultivate the fellowship or *koinonia*, overcoming the "form" of the church was of vital importance for Thomas. Therefore he stressed that the church must "move away from being a communal entity to become an open fellowship able to witness, in all religious and secular communities, to Christ as the bearer of both true human life and salvation" (Thomas, 1971, p.40–41). As a result, he envisaged a "new pattern of combining Christian self-identity and secular solidarity with all men" (Thomas, 1971, p.60). Therefore, he insisted that "the Church must be bearer of Christ in all Indian communities" as it "extends" into both religious and secular society, and saw this as the "only way in which the form of church life in India could be renewed" (Thomas, 1972, p.74). Thomas rejected a Christian mission of calling people to convert to Christianity and also saw the limitations of attempting a synthesis by finding a meeting a point between and

---

4   The discussion first started when Newbigin made his critique on Thomas' comments during his 1965 debate with Berkhof—see Newbigin, 'The Call to Mission—A Call to Unity?' in *The Church Crossing Frontiers*, (Uppsala: Gleerup, 1969), p.254–65. In *Salvation and Humanisation*, Thomas was responding to Newbigin's comments. After its publication, Newbigin wrote a review of Thomas' booklet—Lesslie Newbigin, 'Salvation and Humanisation—Book Review', *R&S* XVIII/1 (Mar 1971), p.71–80. The ensuing correspondence between Thomas and Newbigin from October to December 1971 was published as 'Baptism, the Church and *Koinonia*', *R&S* XIX/1 (Mar 1972), p.69–90.

within Christianity and Hinduism. He believed that, by secularising itself, Christianity could meet the needs of the people in India, which were caused by the rapid secularisation of Hinduism. The main concern for Thomas was not the conversion of individual Hindus to Christianity nor creating a "Hindu Christianity", but rather a perceived need for a conversion of both Christian and Hindu faiths into the common ground which he saw as a "human *koinonia*" or as he later called it, "the Christ-centred secular fellowship" outside the church.

It is important to notice that for Thomas, "secular fellowship" does not mean making the gospel secular. What he intended was not for Christians to lose the religious or spiritual aspect of the gospel, nor for Christianity to be absorbed into Hindu religion but for the secularisation of the Christian community in order to bridge the gap with the wider Hindu community and identify with Hindus. Secular for him meant the Christian community becoming "truly religious" without being "communal" (Thomas, 1972, p.88). Thomas wanted to overcome the problem of the Christian community becoming more and more isolated from the main community in India, especially because of the insistence on a radical discontinuity between the gospel and Hindu religion through the means of conversion. This led to the exclusion of Christians by the Hindu majority as "outcastes", which resulted in the fact that the Christian community was no longer able to make an impact on Hindu society—as was plain especially in the case of the Hindu personal laws. He was confident that secularism would override religious differences and shatter the values which Christianity and Hinduism held as religions, but that the "human *koinonia*" would remain as the meeting-point and that since Christ is in all, he is to be found there too.

The struggle of Indian theologians was to find a common identity as Indians and yet keep a self-identity as Christians within the dominant Hindu community. The theological problem was the relationship of the Hindu and Christian communities and the place of individual Christians in the Hindu context. The "Christ-centred secular fellowship" approach relies on the theological presupposition that the spiritual experience of God can be separated from the act of change of religious affiliation; in other words, the inner commitment to Christ need not extend to sociological change for an individual. However, in the case of independent India, particularly in the 1980s and 1990s, Hindus increasingly called for total allegiance from the religious minorities to a common Hindu identity. This necessitated giving up not only their self-identity as a community but also their individual faith as Christians.

The above two approaches are focused on the *identity* of the church and individual Christians in India. The arrival of the Protestant missionaries and colonial advancement to India came together and India underwent modernisation through these encounters. Though Western science, technology and philosophy was absorbed into Indian society and became part of it, the socio-cultural and religious aspects of Indian life remain traditional, partly because of Indian perception of superiority of these and partly because of their intimate nature and the consequences of the change in daily life. Indians—particularly Hindus—reject the Western form of the church and, as a consequence, the Christians struggle to find alternative models for church in India. Indian theologians who rejected the "modern" form of the church and looked for the "raw fact of Christ" advocated the "Indian" church or "Christian ashram". Thomas and others envisaged that the Christian gospel would permeate the society without forming a rigid Christian community, the church. Though the number of Christians may not increase, the influence of Christians, particularly in education and social work in Indian society, is ever present and this makes Christianity credible and attractive to non-Christians. It is a vital aspect of witnessing to Christ and in Hindu-dominated India, with restrictions on conversion, it may be the only viable model.

I have discussed Christianity in the contexts of South Korea and India, focussing on church's theological approaches to society. Though these approaches have their limitations and problems, they represent sincere searches for the answer to the problems of mission and the church. I would argue that the churches in these countries have made an impact on society not because of their growth in numbers but because of Christian principles, initiated by the church, which shaped the direction of the church and in many cases of the whole society. In this regard, talking about the decline of church attendance may not be as important as formulating and redefining the identity and mission of the church. The place of the church and its role in society may not depend on its size but on its contribution to the society and its people. With this argument, I shall now turn to Christianity in Europe.

The European case: searching for a new identity and mission

In the 1960s the demography of Christianity in Europe changed drastically, though the decline had been gradual over decades. Hugh McLeod identifies this period as "cultural revolution" and argues that the cause of this change was the search for greater individual freedom, which led to rejection of moral and doctrinal codes and authority. This was aggravated by social changes such as rapid decline in rural cultures, weakening of the sense of "respectability", and loss of association of social identity with the church. As a result, "religious community was ceasing to be a necessary source of identity and support" to the people of Western Europe (McLeod, 1997, p.141–3). This idea is taken further by Callum Brown, who insists that though Christianity endured the challenge of the Enlightenment and modernity, the decisive decline in church attendance in the 1960s was because "respectability" was supplanted by "respect", the traditional moral code was replaced by toleration and greater individual freedom and, crucially, women stopped attending church and send-ing their children to Sunday school. In Brown's words, "it took several cen-turies to convert Britain to Christianity, but it has taken less than forty years for the country to forsake it" and, controversially, he claims that in the "death of Christian Britain", "Britain is showing the world how religion as we have known it can die" (Brown 2001). In a similar argument, about the issue of the impact of modernity on religion in Britain, Steve Bruce observes that moder-nity changes the world view of the people, bringing "rationality" and "subtly altering the way we think about the world so as to make religious beliefs and rituals ever more irrelevant". He further argues that the pre-industrial form of the church was challenged by sects, which encouraged individualistic religious-ity (Bruce 1995). The sociologists are in agreement that changing socio-cultural contexts in Europe, particularly modernity and economic affluence, played the major role in the decline of church attendance in Western Europe.

However, perhaps we need to go further than looking at church attendance and the decline of church membership. Grace Davie has made a significant contribution to identifying and mapping the situation of contemporary Christianity in Europe to the extent that Europe is exceptional in terms of its secularisation, the decline of Christianity, and its religiosity as a whole. As her table on "religious belief" shows, there is still a remarkably high percentage of people who have an awareness of the presence of God and an interest in mat-ters of faith. In the foreseeable future it is unlikely that the statistics of church attendance will rise, nor is there any reason to expect that religious belief will decrease suddenly. Obviously Christian theology needs to deal with this gap between believing and belonging. Europe has developed theologies which have served the need of European context and have affected the life of its people for centuries. Furthermore, they have influenced the religious quest of the rest of the world a great deal. Perhaps the theologies developed in Asia, for example, could in turn help the churches in Europe?

The source of the identity of the church

As I indicated above, the integrity of Christianity in Europe lies, I believe, in two aspects of the church. First, the *identity* of the church and of individual Christians in contemporary Europe: Do we define Christianity or Christians by their attendance at a particular church? What do we mean by being Christian or being church? Indian theologians have wrestled with the meaning of being a minority in society and, though their theological search is unique to the Indian context, the implications of their ecclesiological models are important to con-sider. In the case of the kingdom model, the idea of the ashram is very much pro-moted in Indian Christianity and, though the numbers are not great, the perception of integration into Indian religious patterns and work within the socio-cultural framework is vital to Christianity in India. The Christ-centred secular fellowship model is trying to promote the idea that, rather than being confined by the church and therefore losing influence on society, believers are encouraged to be in Hindu society and permeate it with Christian values. These models could be helpful in the radical reworking of ecclesiology in Europe that is needed in order to form an integrated Christianity. Particular forms of Christianity or church, such as Pentecostalism in Latin America or in Asia, cannot just be imported into Europe as they are, as Davie rightly comments. Creative ways of being church need to be found in European soil to fit the particular time and place.[5]

The question I would like to raise is what is the motive behind this move? If Christians believe the raison d'être of the church is for others,[6] it is not a matter of numbers, but of keeping the integrity of the Christian faith and practice in a given context and permeating society with Christian values. The obsession with numbers has to do with the role of religion in forming the core identity of believers in a given society. Many world religions and indigenous faiths are often entwined with political authority and this reinforces people's identity by absolute doctrines, moral codes, and even law, so that it is not be challenged. This is particularly the case where religion has been integrated into the culture and society for many centuries. We see this pattern in the history of Western Christendom, in Islamic fundamentalism and in the Hindu nationalist movement in India. Religious ideas and faith must be open to critique by both insiders and outsiders; otherwise a religious tradition or community can easily be corrupted and become dogmatic.

We may say that the situation of the Christianity in Western Europe is going through a kind of "reformation". Christianity in Europe has dominated the life and faith of the people for centuries, but the very identity of Christianity is now being questioned. The idea of Christendom is anchored in the integration of religion and politics to the extent that religion maintains absolute power. This is a corrupted version of the vision of kingdom of God presented by Jesus. Religious beliefs as well as believers themselves need constantly to be reformed—and the only way to maintain this is by openness to criticism. Any aspect of religious faith—doctrines, rituals, authority, scriptures, institutions, religious leaders—should be open to scrutiny. It is vital for a healthy society that no individual, community, belief or ideology should stand above the criticism of the public, and religious belief is no exception to this principle. In the post-modern context of Europe, the church authorities are open to the scrutiny of the media and the public. I believe this is not a negative aspect of secularisation,

---

5   See Mellor & Yates 2002.
6   For example, Dietrich Bonhoeffer.

but rather it is God-given opportunity for the church to reflect and respond to the challenge to find its identity in being Christian community. In this regard, the decline of church membership is not the issue. Rather than lamenting the situation or trying to win back the lost numbers, the search for integrity is the most urgent task of the church in Europe.

The mission of the church as public engagement of theology

Second, the *mission* of the church in the society: What is the role of the church in contemporary Europe? What is the function of the church in secular and post-modern Europe? What are the problems which the church needs to attend to? Socio-political injustice and the problem of the division, which were the main problems for the church in Korea, are not great issues in Europe nor are the particular approaches—*minjung* theology and theology of unification—prevalent there. Nevertheless the active engagement of the Christian church in the problems of the people is vital for the mission of the Christian church in Europe. The problems of Korean society became opportunities for the church as they took up the challenge to bring hope and justice. In Europe, as Davie points out, the churches are seen as "public utilities" rather than as competing firms and, particularly in the case of the English Church, there is a strong connection between religion and respectability (Davie, 2002, p.44). This means the church can still play an active role in society without being intimidated by secularists' critique of the church.

Throughout the history of western Christianity, Christian theology has shaped and challenged the course of societies in various ways. Christian theology has always tried to be relevant to the context and society, and now, with the privatisation of Christian faith, public theology has emerged as theological discourse. As John de Gruchy points out, theologians tend to fall into one of two extremes: either believing that theology makes more of a contribution and a difference than it actually does or underestimating the significance of its public role (de Gruchy 2004). This is due to the fact that the language and audience of the Christian theology has been largely confined to church circles. Public theology is to do with seeking to engage in dialogue with those outside Christian circles on various issues and urging Christians to participate in the public domain. It seeks to converse with citizens on issues wider than religious matters. The question public theology is eager to address has less to do with the decrease of regular church-going, or with possessing the higher moral ground. Rather, there is an urgent need for Christian theology to be actively engaged in conversation on public issues with the understanding that it can offer complementary or supplementary approaches, and even alternative solutions, to the very complex issues facing society today. Christian theology does not have all the answers to these issues, but it can offer moral, ethical and spiritual insights which are vital for forming a comprehensive approach to problems in modern society.

This public engagement of Christian faith is apparent when Hugh McLeod insists that, in spite of the privatisation of religion in Europe, religion continues to play vital part in motivating and shaping the convictions of public figures in the areas of education and welfare, and in the areas of government policies and moral scrutiny. More recently Christian involvement in public issues has been demonstrated in the "Jubilee 2000" campaign, which was, by and large, initiated and carried out by Christian churches and organisations. In 1998 participants assembled along the main streets of Birmingham, forming a huge human chain around the city, which they then broke to demonstrate the breaking of the bondage of the people of the poorest nations to the burden of debt. Christians took the one of the most pertinent (and yet perhaps most unimplemented) symbols of justice from the Scripture and applied it to the contemporary context of global injustice. The Christian church played the role of prophet in the society and raised her voice in a collective and ecumenical way. Toward the end of the campaign there were 24 million signatures from 60 countries around the world and the campaign established the debt issue as one of the most important items of the global political agenda.

The significance of the "Make Poverty History" campaign, which succeeded Jubilee 2000, has been the successful cooperation of over 500 organisations, which included secular NGO's and organisations of various other religions. The initial campaign permeated into the wider society and the different interest groups were then integrated so that the whole Make Poverty History campaign could be owned by many ordinary people and a wide variety of organisations. Make Poverty History gained momentum in Trafalgar Square in February, when the keynote speech was given by Nelson Mandela, and reached a climax in Edinburgh in July 2005, when a quarter of a million people thronged the streets. What I appreciate about this campaign is how the biblical concept of jubilee has inspired the mobilisation of millions of people to support the cause. It has influenced political leaders to listen to the voice of people who are concerned for those of other continents, nations and cultures. This is indeed the demonstration of a mature society, where people are not only showing their concern for their immediate family, relatives or friends but for those who are far removed from them. Among the participant organisations in Edinburgh, most of them were Christian denominations, local churches, church-related organisations and other religious communities. Furthermore, the initial campaign was not claimed as Christian or by any exclusive group, but encouraged the participation of others and raised awareness among the general public. It is important that Christians did not shy away from policy-making but actively engaged in and contributed to the public discussion. It is equally important that, though Christians and churches are a leading part of the movement, they have not asserted their own agenda but been facilitators of the campaign. The campaign highlights the way in which Christians can contribute to society by creatively and actively engaging with policies not out of concern for ourselves but for the sake of others. The church, without holding an attitude of occupying the moral high ground, can and should play an active role in society. The Jubilee campaign has demonstrated that biblical concepts are still very relevant to the post-modern society of Britain, Europe and beyond.

I have given an example of the church's involvement in public issues to show that the integrity of the Christian church does not depend on the size of the church but on how the church understands itself—its identity—and how it engages in public concerns—its mission. Therefore when Callum Brown asserts the "death of Christian Britain", one has to question his understanding of Christian-ness in the context of history and contemporary society. Yes, "Christian Britain" as the dominance of Christendom—with great numbers, authority and power—has passed, but Christianity as permeated into the lives of the people not only persists but is more vibrant than ever before, and this state of affairs is more in line with the teaching of the founder of Christianity. Furthermore, this understanding of the mission and identity of Christian faith might determine the future shape of Christianity in Europe, despite the decline of church attendance. As Jenkins rightly points out, "whether we look backward or forward in history, we can see that time and time again, Christianity demonstrates a breathtaking ability to transform weakness into strength" (2002a, p.220).

The future shape of the church: bringing colour to society

When sociologists discuss the relationship between modernity and the decline of religion (Christianity, in the case of Europe), the underlining assumption is often that the challenge of modernity has been "rationality" (see Steve Bruce). Religion does not fit into the category of scientific rationality. Modernisation, in the process of bringing rationality, pushed people into certain modes of thinking and conformed their views to facts and rules. In modernity there is less room for imagination and the metaphysical dimensions of life—it forces us to look at the world through a single lens. In Europe, rationality has replaced the 'respectability' enjoyed by the church for many centuries. Now it is respectable to be rational—talking about facts and figures and it is not respectable to be religious—talking about religious experiences and faiths of any kind. Sometimes it seems one can be enthusiastic about any area except religion! The most damaging effect of the European version of secularisation is the deprivation or lack of awareness of spirituality in the life of the people. We may say that they are "poor in spirit"—a very European version of poverty.

William Meissner has observed, the "man without imagination, without the capacity for play or for creative illusion, is condemned to a sterile world of harsh facts without color or variety, without the continual enrichment of man's creative capacities" (Meissner, 1984, p.187). The churches in Europe can bring hope in the midst of these "harsh facts without color" and the church is called to respond and provide this colour in the life of the people. As Davie has shown, modernity takes very different shapes and the challenge of rationality has not threatened religion in the same way in other modern countries such as North America and Singapore. It is possible to be modern and practise "irrational" religion, just as it is possible to embrace modern science while appreciating art, music and literature.

This aspect of bringing richness of life can also be applied to our discussion of the relationship between the churches in the North and the South, which is the main theme of this volume. Here I would like assert my disagreement, with all due respect to his thesis, of Professor Jenkins' employment of the term the "next Christendom" to describe the rise of Southern Christianity. This is neither appropriate nor accurate. His observations that Southern Christianity is traditional (not liberal) on social issues, conservative in beliefs and moral issues, and interested in the supernatural and in personal salvation rather than radical politics are very pertinent, and I am in agreement with his assertion of the influence of Southern Christianity on its Northern counterpart, but not in a way he perceives it. I note that, in the year following the publication of his book, he preferred to use the title "The Next Christianity" in an article (Jenkins 2002b). Many criticisms of the term "Christendom" have been made, for example, Peter Phan (2005) in an article in *Mission Studies* and also Raimundo Panikkar's classic article (1987) on the difference between "Christendom", "Christianity" and "Christianness". The concern with the "centre of gravity" and of "Christendom" undermines the ethos of the Christian faith as being salt and light of the world, but relies on the mechanics of numbers and dominance, as we have seen in the history of Christianity. Despite the "success" stories of church growth in Africa, Latin America and some countries in Asia, there are vast numbers of small and struggling churches that can hardly be described as constituting the "centre of gravity" or imagining "the next Christendom". It is these small and struggling churches that exhibit a more accurate picture of the Southern Christianity. That this is the case should not be regarded as uncharacteristic of the Christian community, since it is in line with the message of being in weak in Christ that the Apostle Paul preached. The sentiment of "Christendom" and obsession of "the centre of gravity" is far from the spirit of Christianity; it is a distorted concept of how we understand Christianity and mission. It has been the particular concern of mission theologies to examine how it is that, given the vulnerability inherent in the early Christian mission, in later centuries mission has been carried out with this attitude of seeking of dominance, preservation and expansion of Christian territory.

Most scholars on the subject emphasise the exciting phenomena of churches in the non-European world and the rapid decline of Christianity in

Europe as forming a contrasting picture. However, the future shape of the church needs to be understood in the context of global Christianity as the body of Christ or household of God. As the Christianity of Europe has contributed to the rest of the world through out the centuries to bring a colour—the European understanding of Christian faith to the lives of the many in the rest of the world, so the rise of Southern Christianity has to be seen to bring more colours to the traditional Christianity which are the outcome of their rich Christian experiences in their particular contexts. Nor do I think the European churches have exhausted what they have to contribute to the rest of the world. In the words of David Bosch (1992), "we need new relationships, mutual responsibility, accountability, and interdependence (not independence!)".

The integrity of the church lies not in where majority of Christians are, but in how the church is "salt and light" in the given society, and this does not depend on the number of Christians and churches, and certainly not on the shift of the "centre of gravity". As there is no doubt that the churches in Europe have made vital contributions to the Christianity in the rest of the world, so these contributions should continue regardless of changes in the situation in Europe. The churches in the rest of the world are grateful for what the European churches have offered to their churches and societies, and this cannot just be dismissed as colonial advancement or as church expansion. At the same time we appreciate the rise of non-European Christianity and their contributions to their counterpart in Europe. European churches are finding it hard to get used to the situation of being a minority in society—but this experience is not unusual in the history of non-European Christianity and lessons can be drawn from this experience for Europeans. The lessons learnt by the European churches through their long traditions are important to remember because, though the European pattern of religious behaviour and of secularisation may not be repeated in the same way, most of European experience is not exclusive to Europe and the churches in other parts of the world may still find a great deal of commonality with their situation and historical instances from which to draw lessons. In the household of God and in a globalised world, we all are inter-dependent and are influenced by one another, and perhaps this is the most exciting aspect of the church's new *identity* and *mission*.

Coming back to the question of the future shape of Christianity, my thesis has hinged on the question of the integrity of the Christian church. As I see it, the future shape of the church will not be a series of confrontational encounters or clashes of different forms of Christianity, as many have predicted. Nor will it be the situation that the North and South will exhibit such distinctive characteristics that there is little in common between the two. I do not regard these two notions as in line with the spirit of Christianity or as an accurate assessment of ground reality, at least in the case of Asian Christianity. Rather, the different traditions and expressions of faiths will form a mosaic of Christianity as a whole, as each contributes their own distinctive colour to the wider community. This notion is not merely an ideal vision or a theological assertion of how global Christianity ought to be. The sharing of theological insights and findings is already taking place between the North and the South; in fact this has been the case throughout the history of Christianity as a whole. Reflecting the diversity of and vibrant inner interaction between different Christian communities within Southern and the Northern Christianities, the future shape of Christianity can be imagined as a mosaic within a mosaic, with a greater variety of colours added into the whole Christian community.

References

Ahn Byung-Mu. 1983. Jesus and Minjung. (In Kim Yong Bock (ed) *Minjung theology: people as the subjects of history.* Maryknoll, NY: Orbis.)

Ahn Byung-Mu. 1983. 1990. *The story of Minjung theology.* Seoul: Korea Institute of Theology.

Barrett, D., Kurian, G. & Johnson, T. 2001. *World Christian encyclopaedia, 2nd ed.* New York: Oxford UP.

Bosch, D. 1992. *Transforming mission: paradigm shifts in theology of mission.* Maryknoll, NY: Orbis.

Brown, C. 2001. *The death of Christian Britain.* London & New York: Routledge.

Bruce, S. 1995. *Religion in modern Britain.* Oxford: Oxford UP.

Chakkarai, V. 1938. The church. (In Devasahyam, D.M. & Sunarisanam, A.N. (eds). *Rethinking Christianity in India.* Madras: Hogarth Press. p.119–123.)

Chenchiah, P. 1938a. The church and the Indian Christian (In Devasahyam, D.M. & Sunarisanam, A.N. (eds). *Rethinking Christianity in India.* Madras: Hogarth Press.)

Chenchiah, P. 1938b. Jesus and non-Christian faiths. (In Devasahyam, D.M. & Sunarisanam, A.N. (eds). *Rethinking Christianity in India.* Madras: Hogarth Press.)

Chenchiah, P. 1938c. The Christian message in a non-Christian world: review of Dr. Kraemer's book (appendix) (In Devasahyam, D.M. Sunarisanam, A.N. (eds). *Rethinking Christianity in India.* (Madras: Hogarth Press. p.44–52.)

Cox, H. 2001. *Fire from heaven: the rise of pentecostal spirituality and the reshaping of religion in the twenty-first century.* Cambridge, MA: Da Capo.

Davie, G. 1994. *Religion in Britain since 1945: believing without belonging.* Oxford: Blackwell.

Davie, G. 2002. *Europe—the exceptional case: parameters of faith in the modern world.* London: Darton, Longman & Todd.

Devasahyam, D.M. & Sunarisanam, A.N. (eds.) 1938. *Rethinking Christianity in India.* Madras: Hogarth Press.

Elliott, C. 1989. *Sword and spirit: Christianity in a divided world.* London: BBC Books.

Freston, P. 2001. *Evangelicals and politics in Africa, Asia, and Latin America.* Cambridge: Cambridge UP.

Gruchy, J. de. 2004. From political to public theologies: the role of theology in public life in South Africa. (In Storrar, W. & Morton, A. (eds) *Public theology for the 21st Century.* London & New York: T & T Clark. p.45–62.)

Jenkins, P. 2002a. *The next christendom: the coming of global Christianity.* New York: Oxford UP.

Jenkins, P. 2002b. The next Christianity. *The atlantic monthly.* 290(3) (October, 2002). p.53–68.

Johnson, T. & Chung, S. 2004. Tracking global christianity's statistical centre of gravity, AD 33-AD 2100. *International review of mission.* April: p.166–81.

Kim Joon-Gon, 1983. Korea's total evangelization movement. (In Ro Bong-Rin & Marlin L. Nelson (eds) *Korean church growth explosion.* Seoul: Word of Life Press.)

Latourette, K. 1945. *A history of the expansion of Christianity,* Vol VII. London: Eyre and Spottiswoode.

Martin, D. 1990. *Tongues of fire: the explosion of Protestantism in Latin America.* Oxford: Blackwell.

Martin, D. 2002. *Pentecostalism: the world their parish.* Oxford: Blackwell.

McLeod, H. 1997. *Religion and the people of western Europe 1789–1989* (Oxford & New York: Oxford UP.

Meissner, W.W. 1984. *Psychoanalysis and religious experience.* New Haven & London: Yale UP.

Mellor, H. & Yates, T. (eds) 2002. *Mission and spirituality: creative ways of being church.* Calver, Derbyshire, UK: Cliff College Publishing.

Panikkar, K.M. 1953. *Asia and western dominance: a survey of the Vasco da Gama epoch of asian history, 1498–1945.* London: George Allen & Unwin Ltd.

Panikkar, R. 1987. The Jordan, the Tiber, and the Ganges: three kairological moments of Christic self-consciousness. (In Hick, J. & Knitter, P. (eds) *The myth of Christian uniqueness: toward a pluralistic theology of religions.* Maryknoll, NY: Orbis. p.104–7.)

Phan, P. 2005. A new Christianity, but what kind? *Mission studies.* 22 (1): p.59–83.

Suh Nam-Dong. 1983. Toward a theology of Han. (In Kim Yong Bock (ed), *Minjung theology: people as the subjects of history.* Maryknoll, NY: Orbis. p.51–65.)

Thomas, M.M. 1966. The struggle for human dignity as a preparation for the Gospel. *NCCR* 86 (9): p.356–59.

Thomas, M.M. 1971. *Salvation and humanisation: some critical issues of the theology of mission in contemporary India.* Madras: CLS.

Thomas, M.M. 1972. Baptism, the church and koinonia. *R&S* 19 (1): p.69–90.

Yoo Dong-Sik. 1984. *The mineral vein of Korean theology.* Seoul: Jun Mang Sa.

Frans J. Verstraelen

Jenkins' *The Next Christendom* and Europe

Philip Jenkins' *The Next Christianity* is not the first book dealing extensively with global Christianity. For example, David L. Edwards published *The Futures of Christianity: An Analysis of Historical, Contemporary and Future Trends within the Worldwide Church,* while I myself produced *Christianity in a New Key: New Voices and Vistas through Inter-continental Communication.* Since Jenkins' book, Scott M. Thomas has launched *The Global Resurgence of Religion and the Transformation of International Relations: The Struggle for the Soul of the Twenty-First Century.* It would be interesting to compare these publications which cover a crucial period of developments in religion. Though I will refer to these publications, my main aim is to have an in-depth look at Jenkins' *The Next Christendom,* in particular his evaluation of the status of European Christianity within global Christianity. I will do so as a Christian European, more precisely as a European missiologist with forty years of contact and experience within Africa, especially Ghana, Zambia and Zimbabwe. I have researched and published on contemporary issues of Christianity in both Africa (e.g. Verstraelen 1975, 1998, 2002) and Europe (1987, 1996).

The significance of a publication can be judged from the impulses and challenges it provides to its readers, in particular those who are working within the same field of study. Philip Jenkins' book is such a stimulating publication. Its challenge in my case is that I have come to an evaluation of Christianity in secularized Europe that is quite different from his. I will further reason upon a subject that is, understandably, absent in Jenkins' study, namely that European Christianity not only is surviving, but also has a significant contribution to make to the future of global Christianity. I will deal with the topic in four parts: 1. Jenkins' view of European and Southern Christianity. 2. Christianity in Europe: an evaluation from a European perspective. 3. Christianity in Europe: influenced by Southern Christianity? 4. Epilogue: Interaction between European and Southern Christians.

Jenkins' View of European and Southern Christianity

Christianity in Europe in relation to Southern Christianity

There is much in Jenkins' study that is correct regarding the status of Christianity in Europe. For instance, that rates of church membership and religious participation have been declining precipitously (p.94). His main thesis is that Europe is secular while the South is religious, and that salvation for Europe depends on its opening up to the influence and evangelizing contribution by Southern Christianity (p.96, 112). There are in his view two options for salvation of Europe's Christian character: either remain Christian but then with a powerful Southern cast, or it will entirely lose its Christian character (p.191). Jenkins sees the Christian faith in Europe as a kind of inculturation, albeit an old-established example (p.109). During a visit to the centre of Amsterdam "which is the heart of the world's most secular societies" he could hardly detect any religious activity of the autochtonous population, while in a working-class quarter he saw a swelling stream of individuals heading towards an African church: "That one congregation probably represents, in miniature, the future faith of Christianity in West Europe" (p.98).

Jenkins asks how feasible it is that Black and Brown Christians are evangelizing Whites? At any rate, new churches like the Black successful London's Kingsway International Christian Centre (KICC) will have to treat White habits and worldviews with due respect and sensitivity: to practice inculturation in fact (p.207). How such an adaptation will work out for Southern evangelizers themselves has not been mentioned. While traditional Christianity is weakening in large sections of the North it is, in Jenkins' view, indeed being reinforced and reinvigorated by Southern churches by means of immigration and evangelization. The type of Christianity spread by such means has a predictably Southern caste, conservative and charismatic. The success of the "prophets of Africa", Asia and Latin America, will determine what kind of North will be confronting a rising South (p.192).

Developments within Southern Christianity

Jenkins' *The Next Christendom* presents a lively picture of the impressive expansion and dynamic forms of Christianity in the Southern hemisphere (Latin America, Africa and to a lesser extent Asia).[1] It is a varied picture since Jenkins uses a broad concept of being a "Christian": if you call yourself a Christian he accepts it at face-value (p.88). He, however, mentions as central characteristics of the newer churches, including the most expansionist movement, Pentecostalism: preaching deep personal faith and communal orthodoxy, mysticism, all founded on clear scriptural authority, with prophecy as an everyday reality, as

---

1   Jenkins has no reference to the interesting and inspiring form of Christianity in Oceania and the Pacific. In this respect he follows most writers on *global* Christianity who totally ignore the countries in Oceania and the Pacific. (See Verstraelen 1996 on "Visions from Oceania: on mission to and from *peripheral* peoples, p.145–194). Jenkins refers only to countries "at the Pacific rim".

well as faith-healing, exorcism, and dream visions (p.8). It is good to note, with Jenkins, that Southern Christianity encompasses, besides Pentecostal and Independent churches, also Southernized former mission (so-called established) churches. These taken together form the New Christianity, about which Jenkins predicts, "On present evidence, a Southernized Christian future should be distinctly conservative" (p.8).

Yet, *The Next Christendom* has also a few references to possible secularizing inroads into Southern Christianity:

- "As Southern Christianity continues to expand and mature, it will assuredly develop a wider theological spectrum than at present, and stronger *liberal* and *secularizing* tendencies may well emerge" (p.8; emphasis added).
- "African and Asian societies might undergo the *same kind of secularization* that Europe experienced in the eighteenth century" (p.138; emphasis added).
- Southern religious organizations will become more formal and churchlike (losing their sectarian character) "and just possibly more *skeptical* towards claims about healings and prophetic visions" (p.138).
- "A growing Pentecostal community tends to create a larger public base for growth of democratic capitalism and, in the long term, perhaps for greater *secularism"* (p.138).
- ". . . it is likely that as the rising churches mature, their *social positions* will become quite as *diverse* as those of their Northern counterparts" (p.209). As regards these "social positions" Jenkins refers to women's rights and equality, and to alternative expressions of sexuality, gay rights and blessing the marriages of homosexuals (p.201, 202, 209).
- To the point is Jenkins' question concerning religious loyalties of the children (and grandchildren, etc.) of immigrant Southern Christians living in Europe who, in Jenkins' view, will become the evangelizers of secular Europeans: "how far they will adopt the *laxer* and more *"modern" thought ways of Europe"*, with the possibility that "the next generation might conceivably be as *religiously lukewarm* as their White neighbors" (p.99).

Jenkins, however, asserts that regarding Southern Christians in Europe, "the process of secularization is not yet that advanced" (p.99). Regarding secular and liberal tendencies within the New Christianity in the South, Jenkins is confident that "all these changes are likely to occur over generations" (p.138).[2]

---

2   The study on *Secularism in Africa. A Case Study: Nairobi City* (Nairobi 1997), undertaken by Aylward Shorter and Edwin Onyancha, shows that a secularizing influence is not something of an eventually distant future, but is already taking place in the Southern hemisphere.

Christianity in Europe: an Evaluation from a European Perspective

Preliminary remarks and questions

To contrast Jenkins' evaluation of Christianity in Europe with my own evaluation I am adding to Part I a few more statements concerning Europe in relation to global Christianity as expressed in his *The Next Christendom*:

> In one possible scenario of the world to come, an incredibly wealthy although numerically shrinking Northern[3] population espouses the values of *humanism*, ornamented with the vestiges of *liberal* Christianity and Judaism. Meanwhile, this future North confronts the poorer and more numerous masses of ascendant Christianity and Islam[4] . . . one crucial difference is that the have-nots will be inspired by the *scriptures* and the language of *apocalyptic*, rather than by the texts of Marx and Mao" (p.160–1).

In other texts Jenkins refers to the North/Europe as largely secular or secularized, that confronts a South in which religion thrives and expands (p.96 and passim).

The problem is that Jenkins, in relation to Europe/European Christianity, does not clarify concepts like secular, secularization (he even uses "secularism", p.138), liberal, humanist, except that he leaves one with a feeling that, from a Christian perspective, we have to consider these things as negative if not bad. Another point of consideration, in relation to Southern Christianity's "inspiration by the scriptures" is that Jenkins nowhere refers to the need of exegesis and hermeneutics of biblical texts, for instance regarding the preference in some Southern churches of the Old Testament above the New testament, called Hebraism (p.131–132), and the (mis)use of Rom.13:1–7 by Independent and

---

3   "Northern" includes both North America and Europe. I do exclude North America (USA/ Canada) which have their own religious history and situations, and limit myself to Europe.

4   Jenkins has many references to Islam, including a special chapter (Chapter 8) on The Next Crusade. Though Jenkins disagrees with Huntington's statement that Christianity will numerically be supplanted by Islam and Huntington's understanding of Christianity being 'Western Christianity' (p.5–6), his main expectation seems to be in concord with Huntington's *The Clash of Civilizations* when he foresees a future clash between Christianity and Islam. Though there are many uncomfortable issues in the relationship between Christians and Muslims, I prefer the viewpoint of Buruma and Margalit's *Occidentalism* (London, 2005, p.147): "Although Christian fundamentalists speak of a crusade, the West is not at war with Islam. Indeed, the fiercest battles will be fought inside the Muslim world. That is where the revolution is taking place, and where it will have to be halted, preferably not by outside intervention, but by Muslims themselves". In my view, Muslim immigrants living in Europe and enjoying at least freedom of religion, ha[4] The study on *Secularism in Africa. A Case-Study: Nairobi City* (Nairobi 1997), undertaken by Aylward Shorter and Edwin Onyancha, shows that a secularizing influence is not something of an eventually distant future, but is already taking place in the Southern hemisphere.

Pentecostal churches when obeying political leaders who oppress and exploit people (p.153). It is of crucial importance for both Southern and Northern churches to have a proper biblical interpretation of "obeying authority" because, if this obedience is interpreted as absolute, the mission of Jesus (see Luke 4:16–22), which the Church has to continue, will be impeded in cases when governments are not "serving God".[5]

It even seems that Jenkins dissociates himself from any exegetical and hermeneutical interpretation of biblical texts as liberal (=bad?) when he writes, "Northern *liberals* demand that church texts and traditions be viewed in the context of the cultures that produced them, so that it is legitimate and necessary for churches to change[6] in accordance with secular progress" (emphasis added). Jenkins has anyway a denigrating remark about liberals, when he refers to Northern liberals as "practicing a dilettantish kind of cafeteria religion" (p.197); he perhaps aims at certain individuals, but as a general remark it is a cheap sneer that could act as a boomerang.

Perhaps my remarks seem wide of the mark and as "rational" regarding Jenkins' *The Next Christendom* which gives such a shining picture of the vitality and dynamism of Southern Christianity. His strong conviction seems to be that salvation for a dying Christianity in Europe will come from a healing and energizing influence of Southern Christianity, especially from its thriving congregations and communities already present in most countries of Western Europe.

How bad the situation of Europe is in the mind of Jenkins follows from two labels he has given to it:

"Heart of Darkness": "Originally applied to Central Africa, the experiences of the twentieth century suggest that the label more justly belongs to Europe, the region somewhere between Berlin and Moscow" (p.161–162). My comment to this is: the twentieth century in Europe, indeed a time of 'deep darkness' because of racial and anti-human totalitarian regimes, was above all a time of intense suffering of European people, not only the Jews. That is now past, though not forgotten. "Heart of Darkness", in the perception of many contemporaries in different parts of the world, refers nowadays rather to the powers that rule and control the United States of America which with national pride and military might tries to defend its political and economic interests by all means, even at the cost of human lives.

"Babylon": "In this world, the West will be the final Babylon". This second label is mentioned as conclusion of the one possible scenario mentioned above

---

5   For an example of a church leader in Zimbabwe who misuses Rom. 13:1–7, and a proper exegesis of this text, see Verstraelen 1998, "Church-State Relations in Pre-and Post-Independence Zimbabwe", p.73–75.

6   "Interpret" would have been here the appropriate term.

(p.160–161). It is not (made) clear what Jenkins means by applying this second label to the West, Europe.

"Babylon" evokes the story of the exile and captivity of Jews in Babylon (eighth and sixth century CE). The interesting thing, not without consolation and inspiration for today's European Christians, is that the Jews of the time gained something from their trying experience in the form of a new understanding of their past and new forms of worship. Another question is: are Southern Christians in Europe also receiving something from living in Europe-Babylon? Is Europe the final Babylon for (Christian) immigrants, and if yes, in what sense? At any rate, in contrast to the Jews who were deported from Jerusalem to Babylon, the contemporary immigrants have come to Europe voluntarily, mainly for economic not religious reasons.[7]

Christianity in Europe: perspectives from within Europe

Jenkins in his *The Next Christendom* rightly points to Europe as secular or secularized in the sense that many Europeans are losing their Christian faith. This has been confirmed by the authors mentioned in Part I: Edwards has a chapter on the future of Christianity "In Secular Europe" (Edwards, 1986, p.285–356), Verstraelen has a chapter on "perspectives from Europe on the future of mission in a secular context" (Verstraelen, 1996, p.15–208). The latter quotes Bishop Karl Lehmann, president of the Catholic Bishops' Conference in Germany, as saying that proportionally, since Boniface, there have not been as many pagans in Germany as in our days. A similar picture can be given of other European countries. Christians are not only leaving their churches but losing their Christian identity (Verstraelen, 1996, p.197–8, 201).

While Jenkins seems to concentrate his attention on Europe as exclusively secular, a closer look shows that, besides a *secular* Europe, there is also a *religious,* and indeed a *Christian,* Europe. To understand these three types of Europe and to compare their interconnection, we have to delve briefly into Europe's history.

Secular Europe. Something radical happened in the thinking of many Europeans, caused by a scientific revolution in the 17th century that ushered in a new world view during the eighteenth century: the Enlightenment. This world view was characterized by two central concepts: reason and progress, which obscured if not eliminated the previous world view that was based mainly on faith. The Enlightenment—though carried in its origins by the intellectual elite—has

---

7   The reference to Marx and Mao (p.161) in the same 'possible scenario' was applicable to some 'revolutionary' youth in the 1960s but is presently out-of-date in Europe. To find the contemporary influence of these communists one has to move to the South: Cuba in Latin America, and North Korea in Asia and, of course, China.

had, and still has, profound repercussions on secularizing European society, including Western Christianity. Think of an issue like "reason against revelation" and the influence of Immanuel Kant's philosophy and theology.

The secularization process in Europe has been evaluated in different ways: one way was to see it as a legitimate form of emancipation from too much interference of the church in human affairs; another way, to see it as liberation from religious imposition, leading to laicization and a decline of religious involvement; finally as a real crisis in faith itself, a threat of a total eclipse of God, transcendent or immanent. Eight Dutch and Belgian philosophers, all related to the Catholic tradition, explain the eclipse of God among citizens of especially North-West Europe, because God has been repressed by four obsessions: power, money, nature, and health (Vosman 1990).

When Jenkins considers Europe as secular, he apparently sees secularization primarily as a crisis of the Church, which manifests itself in a precipitous decline of church membership and church participation.[8] From an inside, European, perspective the actual religious crisis has a deeper dimension. According to Bishop Lehmann it is a crisis of God, a loss of "experience of transcendence", and he accepts that the secularization process will result in churches becoming a minority in society (Verstraelen 1996, p.197–8).

Religious Europe. While it is obvious that there is a secular Europe, there is also a Europe that is religious. For a long time secularization was considered an inevitable part of modernization: with economic and educational progress the salience of religion in public social and political life was supposed to decline. There is, however, nowadays a global resurgence of religion taking place throughout the world that is challenging our interpretation of what it means to be modern. This resurgence takes place also in the developed world witness New Age spiritualists, Western Buddhists, Japanese traditionalists, but also charismatic Catholics, evangelicals and Pentecostals.

The resurgence of religion is part of a larger *crisis of modernity* in the West. It reflects a widespread disillusionment wit a modernity that reduces the world to what can be perceived through reason, science, and technology, leaving out important values of the sacred, religion or spirituality. Many scholars identify the global resurgence of religion with extremism, terrorism or fundamentalism, and interpret this phenomenon as a fundamentalist revolt against modernity. In

---

8   Jenkins' view is perhaps due to an American perspective. Scott M. Thomas has an interesting observation saying that "the US model shows that political secularization (separation of church and state) does not have to imply social secularization, and so the American experience can be contrasted with the decline of religion in Europe. A variety of surveys have shown that American patterns of religion are closer to those found in the Islamic world, and in much of the developing world" (Thomas 2005, p.216).

fact it has been influenced by the impact of globalization on a wide-ranging cultural revolt against *secular* modernity. The global resurgence of religion does, however, not signal an end to a belief in reason, but it does indicate the end to a belief in an exclusively secular reason. The great reversal, according to Thomas, took place in the 1970s, when faith in science and technology, along with modernity and progress in the *West* and the modernizing mythology adopted in *developing countries,* "lost their totemic power and started to go in the reverse" (Thomas, 2005, p.43 references the global resurgence of religion in ibid., p.2, 10–11, 39, 42–3).

A good number of European people, especially among the younger generation, are disillusioned with Western science and technology; they are searching for doors into the interior, psychic and spiritual, of human existence. Though in Europe Christianity may be in a serious crisis, religiosity in the sense of looking for a deeper meaning and value of life, is certainly not. From a Christian perspective there are, however, different evaluations of this new religious consciousness. Bishop Lehmann considers it as "a vagabonding religiosity that becomes regressive due to lack of community and social control".[9] A more positive evaluation can be found in a publication of Peter Spink, Canon Emeritus of Coventry Cathedral, *A Christian in a New Age* (London 1991). He takes the new religious consciousness with its desire to break free from the paternalistic shackles imposed by traditional secular and religious institutions, as a serious challenge for developing a new Christian spirituality that answers the religious needs and aspirations of people living in a secularized world (see Verstraelen, 1996, p.199–200).

Christian Europe. Jenkins somewhere mentions that recent critics have agreed that Christianity's days in Europe might be numbered though he himself says, seemingly somewhat skeptically, that modern Europeans imagine that Christianity will survive on their continent (p.192). If one have put so much emphasis on numbers and statistics like one can find in *The Next Christendom* (see p.86), than it will, indeed be difficult to discover traces of living Christianity because it has become like a minority gulf in a sea of secularism. Let us try to discover Christianity, an exercise I myself am confident will be successful, although success will not be the appropriate label.

First we will look at history how Christians in Europe responded to the process of secularization and secularism, to the resurgence of religion, and what type of Christianity has survived—before a new approach began to take shape, there were serious attempts in the West to "modernize" Protestantism. This led to the creation of liberal Protestantism which tried to help Protestant Christians to come to terms with the Enlightenment and to adapt it to the modern world.

---

9   Interview in *Evangelische Kommentare,* quoted in the Dutch daily *Trouw,* 01-03-1995.

Similar serious attempts to "modernize" Catholicism, liberal Catholicism, took also place in the 19th and beginning 20th century, but it was vigorously resisted by Pope Pius IX and Pope Pius X. The idea behind these attempts at Christian modernism was the recognition that religion had come of age, and had to come to terms with the fact that science, technology, and progress had created a new form of life, modernity, which was now the global home of us all. However, a collapse in the faith of modernizing religion has resulted in the global resurgence of religion, which motivated people of different faiths and cultures to rethink and re-evaluate how religion and modernity are related (Thomas, 2005, p.42–3).

There have been in Europe's history some forceful reactions to the impact of the Enlightenment worldview on the Christian faith through a conscious return to revelation by, for instance Soren Kierkegaard (1813–1855) and Karl Barth (1886–1968). However, after Kant, a return to revelation can no longer consist in a simplistic return to earlier theological positions and formulations. The European mind has been shaped too much by rationality, science and technology, than that it easily surrenders its rational mindset. Yet in more recent times the experience of two consecutive World Wars, together with the nuclear threat of complete annihilation of our planet, and the apparent impotence—notwithstanding a theoretical capacity to eliminate persisting dire poverty—have demonstrated the limits of reason and progress.

An important catalyst in stimulating rethinking and re-evaluating the relationship of Christian faith and modernity has been Bishop Lesslie Newbigin, a former long-term missionary in India and after his retirement, a missionary in secularized Britain. He has made his ideas and approaches known through books—*The Other Side of 1984, Questions for the Churches* (Geneva 1983), *Foolishness to the Greeks, The Gospel and Western Culture* (Geneva 1986)—and by meeting people concerned about the crisis in faith and church.[10] Newbigin challenged both a purely rational worldview and the mission of churches in a secularized environment. Without denying the positive fruits of a scientific and rational approach to many aspects of human life like education, health, communication etc, he makes it clear that the interpretative framework of the Enlightenment does not provide an answer to total reality. He, henceforth, invited the churches to denounce the shortcomings of the Enlightenment thinking and acting (and one would like to add their own shortcomings),[11] on the basis of the Christian "fiduciary framework" (Newbigin, 1983, p.17–27).

---

10   For instance, in the Netherlands: a meeting with Newbigin was held in Amersfoort, September 22, 1986; the missiological Journal *Wereld en Zending* published reviews of his books; the first issue of the Vandaar-reeks published Dutch reactions to Newbigin's ideas about the Gospel in the West (see Brinkman/Noordegraaf 1990).

11   See "The secularization of Christendom and the blunders of Europe's churches", in Edwards 1987, p.285–312.

Newbigin has pointed out that Europeans, as heirs of the Enlightenment, tend to reduce everything to "problems" for which they seek "solutions" on the basis of scientific analysis. There are, however, apparently "problems" in life for which there are no obvious "solutions". This is an indication that a new frame of reference would be needed. Inverting Marx' eleventh thesis on Feuerbach, Newbigin states, "Our (Western) culture has been confident during the last two centuries, that it could change the world. Perhaps we may now have to insist that the point is to understand it" (Newbigin, 1983, p.18).

The Church must once again clearly and courageously take the stand that it is a community to which has been given a frame of reference which primarily is based on faith, a "fiduciary framework". In the thought world of the Enlightenment "doubt" was glorified as the first principle of knowledge, while "faith" was considered a bad word. Now it is suggested that "faith", the act of "expectation" and "receiving" should be put first, and to consider "doubt", the critical ability to question every belief, an essential but nevertheless secondary activity when interpreting reality. The horizon of Christian activity in the world is not just an earthly utopia but a heavenly city, God's new creation. This eschatological vision and expectation is not an escape from real life here and now. It supports the hope and perseverance in the struggle for healing and wholeness in this world. The reductions and distortions of God's intentions for his creation, that affected people and churches in Europe, have to be denounced on the basis of the Christian "fiduciary framework". The healing of modern Western culture and of European Christianity will have to come about from within this same "fiduciary system" (Newbigin, 1983, p.17–27; see also "reflections on Salvation as 'wholeness' in European Christianity" (Verstraelen, 1996, p.82–88).

A comparison with Jenkins' viewpoints

I have given an analysis of Europe as being not only secularized but also religious and Christian. Historically the sequence should rather be: Christian, secular, and religious. In fact, these qualifications are present in today's European countries simultaneously, though in different proportions. I limit myself to the situation in the Netherlands, without knowing the exact numbers and percentages of each category, while concentrating on conscious Christians.

Visions and reflections. People who have remained or have become conscious Christians have seen and experienced an enormous change during the last half century. They experienced so to speak Psalm 91:7, "A thousand may fall at your side, ten thousand close at hand", because in a short time Christians became a minority group. Church buildings had to be closed, often converted into supermarkets or even mosques. However, the continuation of the Psalm verse, "But you it shall not touch", did not exactly express what many Christians experienced. They too were heirs of the Enlightenment ideology with both its positive and negative impact. They adhered to a rational mindset but saw the ratio as a gift from God to be put to good use, but at the same time—within a swelling see of increasing secularism around them—they were not immune to doubt.

The global resurgence of religion has given to Christians more rational confidence that secularism does not provide the absolute and complete answer to the meaning of life, and that consequently there is room for alternative inter-pretations. They could even score among rationalists if they knew of Pascal's Penséés, "Les incrédules, les plus crédules" = those who do not believe, believe most (Pascal, Les Penséés, ed. 1933). How European Christians can move beyond the interpretative framework of the Enlightenment and live out of the Christian "fiduciary system" is a secret bound to personal history and grace. The life-story of Alister McGrath is an example of somebody to whom intellectual wan-derings in a "wilderness period" of being confronted with the immense agenda of liberalism at both Oxford and Cambridge, served to bring home how spir-itually and intellectually *satisfying* evangelicalism is:

> My belief is that evangelicalism will gain the intellectual and spiritual ground within Western Christianity during the next generation - but it will do so only after a thorough shake-out, in which some of its less desirable and theologically dubious aspects have been purged, and the necessary attention paid to some of its emerging weaknesses. Evangelicalism needs to shed its ghetto mentality and become involved in the real world as it prepares to expand still further (McGrath, 1988, p.3–50).

But it is perhaps just as much a secret —rationally seen— why the majority in the Netherlands apparently feels *satisfied* with a life without religion, without God. Peter Berger did remark from a sociology of knowledge perspective:

> While it is questionable whether modern science and modern technology are intrinsically and inevitably inimical to religion, it is clear that they have been perceived in this way by large numbers of people. . . . The final consequence can be put very simply (though the simplicity is deceptive): modern man has suffered from a deepening condition of 'homelessness . . . a metaphysical loss of 'home' (Berger, 1974, p.84).

Reflections on concrete conditions of conscious Christians in the Netherlands show that their religion or Christian faith is not something self-evident. Titles of Dutch publications indicate the tension among Christians between the Enlightenment-ideology and the Christian "fiduciary framework". One example (in translation) is *To believe becomes uneasy. Towards a second primitivism?*[12] I will deal with the second part of this title later. Another example (again in translation): *Enthusiasm or diffidence in religion: a missionary orientation.*[13] The

---

12   Okke Jager, *Geloven wordt onwennig. Naar een tweede primitiviteit?* (Baarn: Ten Have, 1987).
13   "Weelderig of verlegen omgaan met religie? Een missionaire plaatsbepaling", in a special issue of the Dutch missiological Journal, *Wereld en Zending*, 1991 no.1.

latter publication clearly indicates that "diffidence" almost exclusively applies to Christians in Europe and their churches. It also demonstrates a way to go beyond diffidence so that the last verse of Psalm 91:7 can be experienced: "His truth will be your shield and your rampart"

Christians on the Ground

Going beyond interpretations (Newbigin) and reflections (Jager and *Wereld en Zending*), I have to say something about Christians on the ground. The practical conditions of Christians can be deducted from a Handbook prepared for congregations vis-à-vis the crisis they are experiencing. This book, entitled (in translation) *Forty words in the desert: Handbook for the Christian community facing the crisis of church, faith and culture* (The Hague 1989),[14] is based on the idea that we, Dutch Christians, at least in some respects, are living in a desert. Signs of the desert are the continuing erosion of the church and the experience of emptiness and confusion, which many faithful experience within themselves. They live in a kind of no man's land between crumbling tradition and a future with still no steady form. The title of the book suggests that Christians have to wander through the desert before a renewal of faith, church and culture can take place.

I quote from this handbook "Oases of Hope" where a number of positive aspects of the crisis are mentioned:

–   Remarkable, for instance, is that in the big cities, where the desertification of the church has advanced most, one can find everywhere small enthusiastic oases of church life.
–   Jenkins, when visiting Amsterdam, did not discover any of these oases, he only noticed an (imported) African church; unfortunately he did not meet the author of the Handbook who, as a pastor for university students in Amsterdam, could have guided him.
–   Notwithstanding much confusion in matters of faith which no longer are taken for granted, there is as never before a serious search for what the Gospel really contains, in "leerhuizen" (literally "learning houses", modeled after the Jewish synagogue-school), in courses, discussion groups, conferences, etc. Also remarkable is that, despite minimal church attendance, the market of religious literature has maintained itself.
–   Although we apparently live in a time of eclipse of God, other signs of hope are signals of people intensely seeking and waiting for God. Remarkable in this connection is the book of Kushner, "When bad things happen to good people", which deals with God in relation to evil, has been, for more than a

---

14   Bernard Rootmensen, *40 woorden in de woestijn. Werkboek voor de gemeente bij de crisis van kerk, geloof en cultuur.* s'Gravenhage: Meinema 1989, fourth edition.

year, among the top-ten of the book market. Secularization has for many Christians been an almost necessary process of being liberated from all kinds of infantile images of God and of reality.

— More examples are new forms of meditation and prayer, involvement of Christian groups in work for refugees and new Netherlanders, in Dutch often called "medelanders" (Rootmensen, 1989, p.197–200).

I myself add some more positive signs of Christian life in the Netherlands:

— Mission of presence among drug-addicts, prostitutes and other marginalized people by small bands of religious groups (especially nuns) who have left their bastions of monasteries and now live close to people.

— Greater involvement of lay-people in the Catholic Church in keeping parishes viable, even without the presence of a priest. When Jenkins speaks of "a massive and growing imbalance between the Catholic faith and their pastors" and speaks of "dreadful consequences for parish life" (p.213) he is rather fixed on an understanding of the church as mainly a clerical institution. However, in Catholic mission history the church developed particularly under leadership of laypeople, catechists and teachers, with only the occasional presence of a priest. A similar situation is emerging in many places in the Netherlands which, far from weakening, can in fact re-vitalize a Christian community.

— The crisis in church life has led to impulses and new initiatives for ecumenical cooperation. When, for instance, the city of Leiden in the 1970s expanded with a new neighbourhood called the Merenwijk for about 25.000 people, the local Christian Council raised the question of how to make the church present there: Should each major church—the Netherlands Reformed Church, the Reformed Churches, and the Catholic Church—build its own church centre? Taking into account diminishing church attendance, the Council opted for one church centre, in which the three churches together with some smaller groups like the Lutheran Church, would participate. What the biblical imperative of unity among the followers of Jesus Christ could not achieve, the crisis within Dutch Christianity did! A common church centre was built, symbolically called "de Regenboog" (the Rainbow), services were held in common on the understanding that, when a Protestant pastor was leading worship it was understood to be a Protestant service, when a Catholic priest led the service it was considered Catholic. For people attending these services and taking part in all kinds of common activities, it was a refreshing experience of a new Christian community, to which each church stream contributed from its own tradition.[15]

---

15   For the story (the problems with the different central church authorities, the challenges of integrating different traditions and the achievements), see the publication of one of the leading pioneers of this new ecumenical community, Father Jan van Well, *Oecumene metterdaad* (Van Well 1996).

The fact remains that in the Dutch desert of secularism, Christians are present as a minority, but they are alive in scattered small oases. The Handbook *Forty words in the desert* concludes saying:

> Little can be said about the future except that, in faith, it will come about in hope. We may be confident that the desert will not be the end. Reason enough to move trough the desert with hope of a blessing and where possible to push back the desertification. At any rate reason also to continue singing of a blooming desert (cf. Isaiah 43:18–21). . . . It is remarkable that oases do appear unexpectedly, often in times when we have given up a sign of hope for something good (Rootmensen, 1989, p.200).

Christianity in Europe: Influenced by Southern Christianity?

In this part we will see how feasible an evangelization of the North by the Christian South will be, and what the implications are for Southern Christians themselves, since proper evangelization means "to treat White habits and world-views with due respect and sensitivity: to practice inculturation, in fact" (Jenkins, p.207).

Preliminary remarks and question

There is a significant difference between Jenkins and myself when interpreting the way Christianity in Europe not only survives but also finds a new vitality.

- Jenkins sees traditional Christianity of the North being reinforced and reinvigorated by Southern churches by means of immigration and evangelization (p.192), and to him the immigrant (for instance African) churches probably represent the future face in Western Europe (p.98). This opinion, in my view, resembles very much the foreign phase of implanting Christianity we know from the history of missions.
- My view is expressed above in part that deals with a diminishing group of European Christians, who wander through a secularizing desert, but who also find ways of living and developing a new type of faith and church. These new ways can be characterized as post-secular Christianity and, in fact, a New Christianity, a label—as we have already noticed—to Jenkins reserves exclusively for Southern Christianity. One should take note that in the part that evaluates European Christianity, there is no reference to any influence of Southern Christianity. The small minority group of conscious Christians can be likened to the Holy Remnant in Israel's history: it denotes a small group through which in anticipation the existence of Israel as a nation would be renewed. This expectation of Israel's renewal became more and more intense during the Babylonian captivity, a situation which has a resemblance to the desert-experience of today's Christians in Europe.

Indeed, the revival of Christianity in Europe is primarily a local challenge and task, exercised by people who have been exposed to the temptations of secularism but have remained loyal to the Christian faith by realizing the short-comings of an absolute rationalist interpretation of reality, and by finding truth and peace in the fiduciary framework of the Gospel of Jesus Christ. European Christians have to be foremost "missionaries to themselves", analogous to what pope Paul VI told African Christians when he visited a meeting of African Bishops in 1969 at the shrine of the Holy Martyrs of Uganda in Kampala (Pope Paul VI, 1970).

Having stressed the primary local call for mission by locals does, however, not exclude the possibility of influence and inspiration from outside, in our case the influence of Southern Christianity on European Christian life and prac-tice. Before looking at some instances, it is good to be reminded that "Southern Christianity" does not form one coherent body and also, that not everything it does represent can be called "Christian". It consists of a great variety of commu-nities, Independent, Pentecostal, mainline Churches, in different forms and out-looks. Consequently their influence capability will also greatly vary. Since I cannot enter here into detail, we have to deal with the issue in more general terms.

– First of all, Northern Christianity had to readjust itself to the new constel-lation of Christian history, caused by the clear and massive emergence of a Southern type of Christianity. Instead of considering itself as central, it had to learn to see itself as part of a polycentric global Christianity.
– Jenkins refers to Christianity in large sections of the North as "traditional" (p.192) without explaining it. At any rate, European Christians have come to realize that much of their ways were too rational, too institutionalized, and above all, too spiritualized. European Christians, by merely looking at immigrant Southern communities in their midst, and how they understand and express being Christian, do more clearly see the shortcomings and limi-tations of their Northern type of Christianity: a reduction of religion to the private sphere, an extreme confidence in rationality even in religious mat-ters, and a tendency to overlook the importance of the Gospel for daily life and for justice and love in the world.
– For Southern Christians the Bible is the great inspiration and orientation for life. Jenkins closes his *The Next Christendom* with an illuminating sec-tion on the Bible in the South. Biblical stories do correspond to the experi-ence and worldview of Southern Christians: persecution, exile, martyrdom, struggle for survival while viewing life as a spiritual warfare (p.217–220). For Christians in the North, it is, however, not so easy to recognize the Bible as an authoritative guide for life, in both the private and public sphere. But modern Biblical interpretation, developed in the West, has contributed to unmasking biased and sectarian explanations as well as a naïve Biblicist

and fundamentalist-literal use of the Bible.[16] Nevertheless, the Bible is not a book of science that has to be analysed rationally, it is a manifesto written in faith to evoke faith; it deals with the most fundamental questions regarding the origin, meaning and purpose of life. European Christians are discovering this and can be inspired by Third World readings of the Bible without following them in all respects. It is therefore good to heed in this connection the critical observation made by the Sri Lankan theologian Wesley Ariarajah about faith of the South in his Postscript "From the 'other side'" in Newbigin's *The other side of 1984*:

> In most countries of Asia, Africa and the Middle East. . . . faith perspectives do in fact provide the overall basis for society. But there is so much distortion, injustice and misery, that people look upon science and technology as the force which can combat superstition, ignorance and conditions of servitude. (Newbigin, 1983, p.68; see also Ariarajah 1985).

Some instances

Jenkins expects that, under influence of Southern immigration and evangelization, Christianity of the North will obtain a predictably Southern cast, conservative and charismatic (p.92). While Southern Christian communities have a strong charismatic attraction and influence on European Christians, many of the latter groups strongly oppose certain conservative aspects of the South. I explain:

Charismatic influence. People of the North are generally reserved in their feelings and stiff in their expressions. A French musicologist has made the observation how strange it is that people listening to music in a concert hall in Europe sit still without any movement, while elsewhere not only music but other aspects of life are accompanied by dance—music is *ars bene movendi,* it appeals to all the fibres of body and soul (Chailley, 1967, p.74–5). See, for instance, how Zimbabwean parliamentarians, mostly middle-aged men, react with dancing when their votes have passed a law. In Europe there would perhaps a modest clapping of hands, in Africa people express their emotions through dancing. Southern ways of expressions in worship reflect a Southern cast: they use traditional music and instruments, encourage emotional expressions of dance, of spontaneous praise and thanksgiving (Jenkins, p.102). More lively expressions are introduced into worship and meetings of European Christians. They recognize a model in Southern Pentecostal and Charismatic communities. However, the influence of European youth—culture and music—that has been used in special church services for young people, may also have (had) an influence.

---

16   See my remarks above on exegesis and hermeneutics in relation to the use of certain biblical texts by Southern Christians.

Conservative aspect of a "Southern cast". One can think especially of the position of women and their rights. Jenkins speaks of "preaching a traditional role for women" by Southern churches (p.199). But what is preached is rather a confirmation of the traditional role of women which, in Africa, is not always commendable: for instance, a widow is often chased out of her home which is claimed by relatives of her late husband. There is little support forthcoming from leaders of Southern churches to improve the plight of girls and women. Improvement of women's rights has a greater chance for Southern Christians immigrating to Europe, stimulated also by laws in European countries which, to a great extent, have been formulated under influence of Western humanist and Christian principles.

– Jenkins has references to "Western standards of the world" (p.202) which he contrasts with the "own standards" of Southern churches (p.209). In my view, the Western standards of the world will erode and, in the end, abolish the own standards of Southern churches regarding human rights especially of women[17] and other Southern practices which block genuine freedom of humans. The former, secular, kind of standards are, in fact, often more in line with the Christian gospel than the latter ones. Europeans will on the basis of their laws support and uphold women's rights, and European Christians will do the same on the basis of laws as well on the basis of the Christian gospel. Jenkins too expects that Southern churches will probably not remain so staunch on these social issues as they evolve and diversify (p.202), but he does not indicate what are the factors that influence that change.

– Jenkins speaks of allegedly "primitive" attitudes towards the spiritual world found in Africa and Asia which acquire steadily growing credence among White Western evangelicals and Pentecostals, with their belief in spiritual warfare (p.136). The reference to allegedly "primitive" attitudes brings me to reflections developed in the Netherlands about a new approach to faith, called a "second primitivity" or a "second naivety". This thinking has been developed, among others, by the Nijmegen professor Han M.M. Fortmann and the French philosopher Paul Ricoeur (see Jager 1987). The discussion centers on the tension between critical analysis of religion and trustful sur-render to religion, a tension between an intelligent skeptic and a reflective believer: the former is aware of the rationality of the believer and starts doubting his doubt, while the latter experiences the same but in opposite direction. To compare both positions, Jager uses the metaphor of the

---

17   There are also groups of European Christians who, on the basis of a fundamentalist-literal interpretation of certain biblical passages defend a submissive position of women in society, family and church.

"anthropologist" and the "missionary". The aim is to arrive at a condition
of tested innocence or childlikeness as fruit of a conscious reflection: "By
passing through criticism it appears possible to arrive at a non-naïve childlikeness;[18] this childlikeness then becomes a critical power against the
myth of scientific thinking" (Jager, 1987, p.179; translation FJV)

Charles Taylor refers to an insight on religion expressed in William James' *The
Varieties of Religious Experience,* "that in certain domains love and self-
opening enable us to understand what we would never grasp otherwise, rather
than just following on understanding as its normal consequence" (Taylor, 2002,
p.47, quoted in Thomas, 2005, p.44). Erik Erikson's psychiatric investigations
support childlikeness as an essential quality of a mature adult who, in his view,
must admit into his life a religious dimension (see Hoare, 2002, p.145ff). And, of
course, it is Jesus who told his disciples, "I tell you this: unless you turn round
and become like children, you will never enter the kingdom of heaven" (Mt.18:2;
Mk. 9:36; Lk. 9:47). This critically tested childlikeness is called a second primitivity or a second naivety. These concepts are quite different from Jenkins' reference to allegedly "primitive" attitudes (p.136). A critically tested childlikeness,
qualified as "second primitivity" or "second naivety" applies to Christian believers who have been challenged by and have overcome the absolutizing Enlightenment ideology.[19] The faith of most Southern Christians has not (yet) been critically
tested as was the case with the faith of many European Christians. But that testing time will come also for Christians from the South, and it has already started.
     Thus, the answer to the question whether Southern Christianity influences
European Christianity is "yes" and "no". Yes, because of charismatic impulses for
more lively and dynamic forms of worship and because of new ways of con-
necting the Gospel to daily life, for instance through the healing power of faith.
No, regarding the basic process of keeping the faith within the trying challenges of an a-religious or even anti-religious environment of pure rationality.

Epilogue: Interaction between European and Southern Christians

It seems that Jenkins, when dealing with Christianity in Europe, is impressed
above all by the churches of the New Europeans, immigrants who have brought
with them Southern Christianity. He apparently did not have eyes to discover

---

18   The term "non-naïve" refers to making use of one's intellect.
19   Jager, however, admits that " many people have not yet found that possibility. They still find
      themselves in the tunnel of the critical period of criticism. They live "as erstwhile the first
      disciples, in the time between Good Friday and Eastern, the interim-period of suspicion. Also,
      then it is possible to walk *together* as the disciples on their way to Emmaus" (Jager, 1987,
      p.179; translation FJV).

and value the oases of autochton Christian presence, which he calls the "Old Christianity" but who, because of their desert experience through which they have found a new understanding of Christian faith, deserve also the qualification of New Christians.[20] One of the reasons why Jenkins has overlooked the oases of Europe's New Christianity, is perhaps his interest, if not obsession with numbers. He states, "much of this book concerns numbers and focuses on present and future religious statistics" (p.86); Though Jenkins is not uncritical concerning valid evidence numbers provide, he, while improving David B. Barrett's *World Christian Encyclopedia* as regards Asia (p.223, note 3), presents an abundance of impressive numbers especially regarding the expansion of Southern Christianity. The diminishing numbers of what he calls Old Christianity seem not to fit well in the set-up of his story.

Yet, in biblio-historical perspective numbers are of relative importance. When Abraham pleads with the Lord to save Sodom from destruction, he first thought to be able to find fifty good men, but he had to count down that number to forty-five, then to thirty, finally to ten. And the Lord responded: "For the sake of the ten I will not destroy it" (Gen. 18:16–33). Jesus does not wait for big numbers to find it worthwhile to appear: "Where two or three are gathered together in my name I am among them" (Mt. 18:20).[21]

I sometimes ask myself to which place Christ would go when he would come to visit his faithful. I fancy that his first visit would not be to the Easter celebration of the Zion Christian Church where "more than a million ZCC pilgrims gather for several days", nor to the crowd "which greets the Pope in St. Peter's square on Easter morning" (Jenkins, 2002, p.68–9) or on any Sunday as I saw recently myself. I like to think that his first visit would possibly be to a small band of four Christians, including a Catholic Priest and a Protestant pastor, who recently settled down in IJburg, a new section of the city of Amsterdam. They don't have a congregation, let alone a church building. They gather in a common house for meditating on the Scriptures, to pray and breaking the bread, while welcoming any body who visits them out of whatever reason. They gather in the name of Jesus with hope and conviction that their witness of Jesus' presence, "the Lord will add to their number" (Acts 2:42–47). It is a Christian oasis, the beginning of a new Christian community.

---

20   Jenkins reserves the term New Christians/New Christianity to Southern Christians/ Christianity. See his chapter 5: The Rise of the New Christianity.

21   The relativity of numbers in this verse becomes even clearer by starting with "three," then followed by "two", thus: "Where three or even two are gathered in my name, I am among them". This sequence is expressed in one of the new hymns created by the Netherlands' New Christianity.

Let us make some concluding remarks. Jenkins' firm statement that "*Northern views* on religious matters should become *less and less* significant as the new century develops" (p.119) has been clearly refuted because:

1. First of all, Christianity in Europe is fully alive, but in new ways compared to before, though numerically in a minority position which is not necessarily experienced as negative.
2. Christianity in Europe has, above all, survived the onslaught on religion caused by an almost dictatorial secularism.
3. It has obtained confidence in faith through a critically tested childlike trust in God and in the Gospel of Jesus Christ.
4. Southern Christianity, which is rapidly expanding and will soon become the majority in global Christianity, is already experiencing the challenges of secularization and secularism.
5. The experiences and insights, won by European Christians in their testing period, can assist Southern Christians when they have to go through similar secular challenges, in other words, when they have to turn from a first to a second naivety.
6. Especially the points 4 and 5 strongly justify my refutation of Jenkins' statement mentioned above, which rather should read, "*Northern views* on religious matters should become *more and more* significant as the new century develops".
7. Jenkins' view on the relationship of Northern with Southern Christianity is that the re-invigoration and re-vitalization of the former depends on the influence of the latter.
8. In fact, both types of Christianity contribute to the life of global Christianity: Southern Christianity by revitalizing the understanding of Christianity as related to the totality of human life and to celebrate it, European Christianity by showing the way how to keep the faith when faced with the onslaught of secularism.
9. European Christians nowadays have to accept and find their place within the new constellation of global Christianity which soon will numerically be dominated by Southern Christianity. Southern Christians should, however, not look back in resentment to past mistakes and shortcomings of Northern Christianity, but look at common present and future challenges to bring the Gospel to an at the same time secularizing and religiously sensitive world.
10. Finally, a quotation from David L. Edwards' *The Futures of Christianity* which I wish to make my own:

    I am prejudiced because I am a European, but I cannot ignore the faith that has survived this acid-throwing by European modernity. It has survived the unromantic agony of doubt and the humiliation of the need to change one's mind. . . . I believe that a faith tested and purified in these fires still has something precious to contribute to (other) continents. . . . But if the rest of the Christian world wants to receive from Europe's churches and other Christian movements in the years to come anything but messages of guilt and defeat, it will be to its own advantage if it can build a new relationship based on mutual respect (Edwards, 1987, p.356).

References

Ariarajah, W. 1985. *The Bible and people of other faiths.* Geneva: World Council of Churches.

Berger, P., et al. 1974. *The homeless mind: modernization and consciousness.* New York: Random House.

Brinkman, M. 1990. *Het evangelie in het westen: Nederlandse reacties op Lesslie Newbigin.* Vandaar-reeks no. 1, Kampen.

Buruma, I. & Margalit, A. 2005. *Occidentalism: a short history of anti-Westernism.* London: Atlantic Books.

Chailley, J. 1967. *40,000 jaar muziek.* Utrecht/Antwerpen: Het Spectrum.

Ecclesia in Africa. 1995. Nairobi: Pauline Publications.

Edwards, D. 1987. *The futures of Christianity: a analysis of historical, contemporary and future trends within the worldwide church.* London: Hodder & Stoughton.

Hoare, C. 2002. *Erikson on development in adulthood: new insights from the unpublished papers.* Oxford: University Press.

Jager, O. 1987. *Geloven wordt onwennig: naar een tweede primitiviteit?* Baarn: Ten Have.

Jenkins, P. 2002. *The next Christendom: the coming of global Christianity.* New York: Oxford UP.

Mbiti, J. 1969. *African religions and philosophy.* London: Heinemann.

McGrath, A. 1993. *Evangelicalism and the future of Christianity.* London: Hodder & Stoughton.

Newbigin, L. 1983. *The other side of 1984: questions for the churches.* Geneva: World Council of Churches.

Newbigin, L. 1986. *Foolishness to the Greeks: the gospel and western culture.* Geneva: World Council of Churches.

Pascal, B. 1933. *Les Pensées. Nouvelle Edition annotée par Adolphe Espiard,* agrégé de philosophie. Tome II. Paris: Bibliothèque Larousse.

Paul VI, Pope. 1970. *Discourse at first all Africa Episcopal symposium in Rubaga Cathedral at Kampala (1969).* Kampala: Symposium Dossier, Gaba Pastoral Papers.

Rootmensen, B. 1988. *40 woorden in de woestijn: werkboek voor de gemeente bij de crisis van kerk, geloof en cultuur.* S'Gravenhage: Meinema.

Sanneh, L. 1989. *Translating the message.* Maryknoll, NY: Orbis.

Shorter, A. 1991. *The church in the African city.* London: Geoffrey Chapman.

Shorter, A. & Onyancha, E. 1997. *Secularism in Africa: a case study, Nairobi City.* Nairobi: Pauline Publications.

Taylor, C. 2002. *Varieties of religion today.* Harvard: Harvard UP.

Thomas, S. 2005. *The global resurgence of religion and the transformation of international relations: the struggle for the soul of the twenty-first century.* New York: Pallgrave Macmillan.

Verstraelen, F. 1975. *An African church in transition: from missionary dependence to mutuality in mission. A case study on the roman Catholic church in Zambia.* Leiden: Interuniversity Institute for Missiological and Ecumenical Research (IIMO).

Verstraelen, F. 1987. The future of mission: a western perspective. (In *International review of mission* 1: p.42–47.)

Verstraelen, F. 1991. Religieuze verlegenheid en missionaire uitdaging: een samenvattende beschouwing. (In *Wereld en zending* 2: p.75–86.)

Verstraelen, F. 1996. *Christianity in a new key: new voices and vistas through intercontinental communication.* Gweru: Mambo Press.

Verstraelen, F. 1998. *Zimbabwe realities and Christian responses: contemporary aspects of Christianity in Zimbabwe.* Gweru: Mambo Press.

Verstraelen, F. 2002. *History of Christianity in the context of African history: a comparative assessment of four recent historiographical contributions.* Gweru: Mambo Press.

Vosman, F. 1990. *God en de obsessies van de twintigste eeuw.* (Thomas More Academie). Hilversum: Gooi & Sticht.

Well, J. Van. 1996. *Oecumene metterdaad: de geloofsgemeenschap in de Merenwijk te Leiden.* Kampen: Uitgeverij Kok.

Wereld en Zending, 1991. Verlegen of weelderig omgaan met religie? Een missionaire plaatsbepaling. 20 (2): p.1–86. (Ed. Jaap van Slageren)

John Chesworth

Challenges to the Next Christendom: Islam in Africa

The paper seeks to examine a present challenge to the development of Africa as a major part of the next Christendom. In the "Cold War", Africa was the centre of an ideological struggle between the Communist East and the Capitalist West. Africa is now at the centre of a spiritual struggle between Christianity and Islam. The centre of Christianity is moving south and the spread of Christianity in Africa is rapid. At the same time Islam is also spreading rapidly. Both Christianity and Islam are missionary religions using evangelism and *da'wa* to bring about growth. The paper seeks to explore how both religions are advancing within Africa. Islam regards Africa as a continent that should be Muslim and as such is determined to Islamise Africa. This is a direct challenge to the view that Africa will be a significant part of the next Christendom. The paper will explore the strategies being used by Muslims in order to spread Islam in Africa and will compare and contrast them with the methods of evangelism being used by Christians. The role of external agencies in aiding both Muslims and Christians will also be examined. The polemics used by both groups will be analysed and their effects on harmonious relations will be assessed. The conclusion will attempt to assess the long-term outcomes. The question still remains will Africa be the heart of the next Christendom or the base for further expansion of Islam?

In the "Cold War", Africa was the centre of an ideological struggle between the Communist East and the Capitalist West. A proxy war in Angola, for example, was fought between the two ideologies. Now Africa is at the centre of a spiritual struggle between Christianity and Islam. In 1993 Samuel Huntington published an essay "The Clash of Civilisations?" and he proposed that with the collapse of Communism in the East, ideological issues had ceased to be the *casus belli* and that culture rather than politics and economics would be the reason for strife. He posited that the basic differences between the ways of thinking of different civilisations mean that clashes are inevitable and that the two most significant "civilisations" in Africa are the West and Islam.

"A Clash of Monotheisms"

With the increase in tensions between different groups in various parts of Africa on ethnic and religious grounds, the need for a theoretical model in order to understand the continent becomes increasingly necessary. Huntington outlines his own thesis, saying:

> The balance of power among civilizations is shifting: the West is declining in relative influence. . . . Islam is exploding demographically with destabilizing consequences for Muslim countries and their neighbors. . . .The West's universalist pretensions increasingly bring it into conflict with other civilizations, most seriously with Islam . . . (Huntington, 2002, p.20).

Religion is a characteristic of civilisations and often is one of the foundations of a civilisation. Huntington sees that as disillusion set in about these ideological battles, there was a global resurgence in religions. "That resurgence has involved the intensification of religious consciousness and the rise of fundamentalist movements. It has thus reinforced the differences among religions" (Huntington, 2002, p.65): "Muslims feel the need to return to Islamic ideas, practices, and institutions to provide the compass and the motor of modernization" (Huntington, 2002, p.116).

How have others responded to Huntington's ideas? Tariq Ali, in *The Clash of Fundamentalisms*, provides a critique of Huntington's views:

> This simple but politically convenient analysis provided an extremely useful cover for policy-makers and ideologues in Washington and elsewhere. Islam was seen as the biggest threat because most of the world's oil is produced in Iran, Iraq and Saudi Arabia (Ali, 2002, p.273).

Ali states that "the world of Islam has not been monolithic for over a thousand years" (2002, p.274). Islam has been influenced by the cultures of host nations, which have changed it. Regarding the intra-Muslim wars and Muslims versus the rest, Ali argues that they were often the result of manipulation by the West and the Communist bloc:

> In a [December 2001] essay [Huntington] defines the post-Cold War conjuncture as one of 'Muslim wars', arguing that 'Muslims fight each other and fight non-Muslims far more often than do people of other civilizations'. . . . Either we are seeing an 'age of Muslim wars' or a 'clash of civilisations'. It can't be both. In fact it is neither (2002, p.281–282).

Ali sees that Huntington is in fact undermining his own theories in the light of the events of the present day.

Philip Jenkins provides a useful critique of Huntington:

> [Huntington] believes that the relative Christian share of global population will fall steeply in the new century, and that this religion will be supplanted by Islam. . . . [His] analysis of the evidence is misguided in one crucial respect. While he rightly notes the phenomenal rates of population growth in Muslim countries, he ignores the fact that similar or even higher rates are also found in already populous Christian countries, above all in Africa (Jenkins, 2002, p.5).

Further, Jenkins argues that by "2050, there should still be about three Christians for every two Muslims worldwide" (Jenkins, 2002, p.5).

Reza Aslan refers to a "clash of monotheisms" (Aslan, 2005, xv); essentially this is what is being played out in Africa. Both Christianity and Islam are

TABLE ONE: Population of Africa's regions, with totals for Christians and Muslims

	Population	Christians	Expressed as a %	Muslims	Expressed as a %
AFRICA	**887,963,657**	**410,973,132**	**46**	**358,028,349**	**40**
Eastern Africa	282,268,572	173,427,447	**61**	60,901,689	**22**
Middle Africa	106,240,870	86,542,016	**81**	9,739,161	**9**
Northern Africa	190,493,739	17,177,489	**9**	167,247,315	**88**
Southern Africa	52,039,833	42,712,086	**81**	1,122,363	**2**
Western Africa	256,920,643	91,114,094	**35**	119,017,821	**46**

(Source: WCD 2005)

missionary religions, using evangelism and *da 'wa* (call) to bring about growth. The centre of Christianity is moving south and the spread of Christianity in Africa is rapid. At the same time, Islam is also spreading rapidly. We ask the key question: Will Africa be at the heart of the next Christendom or the base for further expansion of Islam?

The World Christian Database indicates that the difference in the numbers of Muslims and Christians for the whole continent is only 50,000,000 out of a total population of 890,000,000. This small difference becomes significant when we consider that "Christianity spreads primarily by conversion, Islam by conversion and reproduction" (Huntington, 2002, p.65f).

Having considered these numbers, we need to ask how committed are these vast numbers of individuals who are counted as being Christians and Muslims? For how many of them is their faith just a superficial veneer? Reflecting on this question, out of an experience of over twenty years in East Africa, often conversion comes quickly, but for many the roots remain shallow. To illustrate this: each year an anti-corruption group *Transparency International* ranks the most corrupt nations, Kenya which is stated as 65–80% Christian, consistently appears as one of the most corrupt nations.

The "Abuja Declaration" and all that . . .

We now explore how both religions are advancing within Africa. Islam regards Africa as a continent that should be Muslim, and therefore is determined to Islamise Africa. This is a direct challenge to the view that Africa will be a significant part of the next Christendom.

What strategies are Muslims using in order to spread Islam in Africa? In order to examine this, we shall use the Islam in Africa conference held in

Abuja, Nigeria, in November 1989 as a starting point. The conference led to the foundation of the Islam in Africa Organisation, (IAO) formally constituted in July 1991. At the conference, a number of distinguished Muslim academics presented papers, setting out the situation of Islam in Africa. As we explore the spread of faith in Africa, we will examine two of the papers presented at Abuja and how they present the spread of Islam.

Ali Mazrui, in his paper "African Islam and Comprehensive Religion: Between Revivalism and Expansion" states:

> In Africa, since independence, two issues have been central to religious speculation—Islamic expansion and Islamic revivalism. Expansion is about the spread of religion and its scale of new conversions. Revivalism is about the rebirth of faith among those who are already con-verted. Expansion is a matter of geography and population—in search of new worlds to con-quer. Revivalism is a matter of history and nostalgia—in search of ancient worlds to re-enact. The spread of Islam in post-colonial Africa is basically a peaceful process of persuasion and consent. The revival of Islam is often an angry process of re-discovered fundamentalism (Mazrui, 1993, p.247).

Mazrui further sets out what he terms the Imperative of Expansionism for Islam, by listing some of the factors that slowed down the spread of Christianity in post independence Africa:

> The post-colonial decline of the prestige of Western civilization in Africa and the decline of [Africa's] fascination with it.
>
> The post-colonial decline of the influence of Christian missionaries within [Africa]—including the reduced role of mission schools in . . . education.
>
> The post-colonial change of focus of Christian missionary work in Africa as a whole—the shift *from the mission of saving souls* to *the mission of saving lives.*
>
> Post-colonial atheist[s] in Africa are more likely to be former Christians than former Muslims. This is partly because atheism is in itself an alternative form of Westernization.
>
> The post-colonial prosperity from oil-rich Arab countries has given Islam resources for mis-sionary work in Africa which are unprecedented in modern Islamic history. Islam is beginning to be economically competitive with Christianity in the rivalry for the soul of Africa.
>
> With regard to the natural increase of population, the figures are hard to interpret. But, at least at the level of elites, Christian elites in Africa are more likely to favour smaller families than Muslim elites (Mazrui, 1993, p.252–253).

Mazrui also sets out what he sees as the differences between Revivalism and Expansion:

> [R]evivalism in the Horn of Africa and the Sahel was in part the product of hardship and des-peration, revivalism in Libya was partly the product of new wealth and its attendant self-confidence. . . . the outcome of a convergence of oil-wealth and the threat of a Western hegemony. . . . As for the geographical expansion of Islam, it is more modest in eastern Africa than in western Africa. . . . European colonization of West Africa earlier in the [last] century never really arrested the spread of Islam, although European colonization did considerably help the spread of Christianity. . . . By contrast, Islam in eastern Africa was seriously harmed by the advent of European colonial rule. . . . During the European colonial period, Islam in eastern Africa continued to be *Arab*-led—whereas the leadership of Islam in West Africa had

already been deeply indigenised. In eastern Africa it appeared as if Arab missionary activity was in competition with European missionary effort—two rival foreign forces (Mazrui, 1993, p.262–263).

The ideas presented are perceptive; it is of particular interest to note the difference between the development of eastern and western Africa, especially in terms of indigenisation. In more recent writings, focussing on the situation in Kenya and the Constitutional review process, he has called for a return to the former pattern of rule on the "Coastal strip" of East Africa (*Daily Nation* 11/08/01 & 17/11/01), which was ruled by the Mazruis, this could arguably go against the way in which he had previously portrayed Revivalism, as matter of "history and nostalgia" (Mazrui, 1993, p.247).

The second paper, by Tijani el-Miskin, "Da'wa and the challenge of Secularism: A Conceptual Agenda for Islamic Ideologues", sets out some interesting ideas, especially emphasising the problem Islam has with secular states, which are seen as favouring Christianity. Using Nigeria as the example he demonstrates the anti-Muslim stance of secularism:

> In predominantly Muslim countries like Nigeria, secularism has taken a specifically anti-Muslim dimension. Officially, secularism is viewed as a way of avoiding privileging one religion over another. However, the essentially Christian character of Western heritage (which is privileged over Muslim heritage) is generally ignored. The contradictions in the Nigerian conception of secularism are also manifest in other respects. Among the fanatical exponents of secularism in Nigeria are the lobby groups like CAN (Christian Association of Nigeria) (el-Miskin, 1993, p.269).

Having demonstrated the dangers of a secular form of government for a Muslim community, he further emphasises that the value system in use is suspect:

> The myth of secularist neutrality in Nigeria is also clear in the fact that the Christian community's only political, economic and social heritage is the one inherited through Western colonization which brought Christianity to the country. The only other value system that possesses alternatives is Islam (el-Miskin, 1993, p.270).

El-Miskin then presents the two central programmes of expansion of Islam:

> Contemporary *da'wa* in Nigerian [*sic*] or anywhere in Africa or the Muslim world must make the critique of secularism its conceptual starting point. This is a very necessary theoretical prelude to *da'wa* in a place like Africa all of whose Muslim populations are under secular states. . . . [T]he two central programmes of all *da'wa* activities around the world must be instituted in its organization. These . . . are . . . expanding the demographic zone of Islam through large-scale conversion and consolidating the existing constituency of Islam through mobilization of the *Umma* to be conscious of and live according to the Islamic alternative. . . . Four . . . challenges: The challenge of political models, of evolving Islamic alternatives to dominant secular ones, spiritual challenge, rhetorical challenge (el-Miskin, 1993, p.270–271).

The two methods: demographic expansion and conscientizing the *Umma* are vital if Islam is to expand.

The establishment of the Islam in Africa Organisation shows that Islam has a new seriousness in establishing its identity in Africa, with an increase in "Islamic pride" and a commitment to enable both development and *da'wa* in Africa.

The communiqué, issued immediately after the conference, became known as the "Abuja Declaration". In 2004, Hope FM, a Christian radio station based in Nairobi, criticised Islam and offered to distribute copies of the "Abuja Declaration" to any who applied. Hasan Mwakimako reports it in this way:

> [Starting 29th] March 2004, I listened to Hope FM, a Christian run radio station that invited Pastor David Oginde, [to speak on the Constitutional review] . . . Throughout three days [the host] Tina [Mukenya], Pastor Oginde and another castigated Muslims as intolerant and conspirators. Their guest introduced another pet subject in Christian-Muslim relations . . . details of the so called 'Abuja Declaration' were 'revealed' to the Christians. . . . [T]he 'Abuja declaration' was argued as the genesis of Muslim demands for the Kadhi Court, the evidence was an out of context quote by Usman Bugaje, the Secretary-General of the Islam in Africa Organization that 'Islamization, is a process that starts with the Kadhi's Court arbitrating on matters of personal laws, next comes the extension of jurisdiction to cover all civil matters, and eventually ends with the *sharia'*. After reading this statement . . . [Tina] posed the question: 'It's a conspiracy isn't it?' The response was the expected, yes! (Mwakimako, 2004, p.34–35).

When this writer discussed the Islam in Africa conference with Muslims who attended it, they all denied that such a declaration was issued. But, reading the official Communiqué, published as an Appendix to the proceedings in 1993, and comparing it with a copy purported to have been issued immediately after the conference in 1989, raises some issues concerning the approaches for propagating Islam in Africa. Some of the purposes of the IAO are stated as:

> To encourage the teaching of Arabic language which is the language of the Qur'an as well as the lingua franca of the continent and to strive for all restoration of the use of Arabic script in vernacular.
>
> The conference salutes and highly commends the efforts which the Muslim youth are making in the service of Islam and pledges its full support for them in this worthwhile endeavour.
>
> To urge Muslims to establish strong economic ties between African Islamic countries and other parts of the Muslim world in order to facilitate mutual assistance and cooperation in commerce, industry and finance with a view to evolving a sound economic system based on Islamic principles.
>
> The conference notes the yearnings of Muslims everywhere on the continent who have been deprived of their rights to be governed by the *Shar'ia* and urges them to intensify efforts in the struggle to re-instate the application of the *Shar'ia* (Alkali, 1993, p.433, Appendix Six).
>
> To establish Islamic Tertiary and Vocational Centres which are designed to train Da'wah workers who will be trained to acquire trades and skills which will equip them to be self-employed and productive.
>
> To support, enhance and co-ordinate Da'wah work all over Africa on Islamic matters and publicize the research findings;
>
> To support the establishment and application of the *Shar'ia* to all Muslims; (Alkali, 1993, p.435–436, Appendix Seven).

This extract is from the official 1993 communiqué and it shows that there was a desire to propagate Islam within Africa particularly through *da'wa* and Islamic literature in various vernaculars. Some of the statements appear contentious to non-Muslim readers, notably the emphasis on *shari'a*. However, it is some of the terminology and phrases that are only found in the 1989 document that are of real concern:

- To ensure the appointment of only Muslims into strategic national and international posts of member nations.
- To *eradicate* in all its forms and ramifications *all non-Muslim religions* in member nations (such religions shall include *Christianity*, Ahmadiyya and other tribal modes of worship unacceptable to Muslims).
- To ensure the declaration of Nigeria [as] a Federal Islamic Sultanate at a convenient date, . . . with the Sultan of Sokoto enthroned the Sultan and Supreme Sovereign of Nigeria.
- To ensure the ultimate replacement of all western forms of legal and judicial systems with the Sharia before the next Islam in Africa Conference. (Communiqué 1998:4–5)

It is unclear whether these statements (referred to as the "Abuja Declaration") are a deliberate attempt to discredit the IAO, or if they reflect the actual sentiments of the conference.

The statements from both documents reveal something of the desires of the Islamic world: that Islam should be spread throughout the world; that Muslims should "call" others to the faith; that states with a Muslim majority should be ruled in an Islamic way, with Muslims in key government posts and that other religions are seen as inimical to the progress of an Islamic community.

Currently the IAO website states that:

> Of all the continents, Africa is the only one with an absolute Muslim majority. In effect this makes it the only continent that can be said to be Islamic. And this should not be surprising; contact between the continent and Islam had been on for a long time (IAO Website 8 Oct 2005).

The data given by the IAO does not adequately demonstrate that Africa has a majority of Muslims. A comparison of the percentages of Muslims and Christians in a selected number of African countries, using the statistics available on the Islam in Africa Organisation website and the World Christian Database website, is informative:

What is perhaps surprising is that, with the exception of Ethiopia and Nigeria, the percentage for Muslims is virtually the same for both sources. However the differences in the reported percentages for Christians is more marked, with a difference of over 10% for Ethiopia, Kenya, Nigeria, South

TABLE TWO: The percentages of populations of Christians and Muslims as
reported by IAO and WCD in Selected African Countries

SELECTED COUNTRIES	Christians		Muslims	
* indicates Member states of the IAO committee	IAO	WCD	IAO	WCD
DR Congo	NA	95	NA	1
Ethiopia	35–40	55	45–50	34
Gambia*	NA	4	NA	87
Kenya	66	80	6	7
Libya*	–	3	97	96
Malawi	NA	77	NA	16
Mauritania*	0	0.2	100	99
Niger*	20	0.5	80	90
Nigeria*	30	47	60	42
Senegal*	NA	6	NA	87
South Africa	68	82	2	3
Sudan*	5	16	70	70
Tanzania*	NA	53	NA	30
Tunisia*	1	0.5	98	99

(The figure for Niger the 20% is stated as consisting of a mix of Christians and those with
indigenous beliefs.) (Sources: WCD 2005; IAO 2005)

Africa and the Sudan. (See Appendix for a further set of comparative percentages from the CIA World Factbook).

Strategies for Muslim and Christian expansion in Africa

It is not possible to go into detail as to how Islam is being spread through
da'wa, nor the methods that Christians are using to evangelise in the whole of
the continent. A number of examples of methods found in East Africa will suf-
fice to illustrate this. Research in Tanzania and Kenya recorded a number of
methods used by Muslims, including:

- *Mihadhara* (Public Debates) mainly using the Comparative Religions
  Approach; this continues to be very popular with Muslim Preachers using
  the Bible to demonstrate the truth of Islam.
- Tracts and Pamphlets: Many are in circulation, written to challenge
  Christians to question their faith. Titles include: *Uislamu katika Biblia* (Islam
  in the Bible); *Mafundisho ya Yesu kwa nuru ya Qur'ani* (The teachings of

Jesus in the Light of the Qur'an); *Maisha ya Nabii Isa* (Life of the Prophet Jesus); *Sikumkana Yesu bali Mtume Paulo* (I did not deny Jesus, rather the Apostle Paul); *Injili ya Barnaba* (The Gospel of Barnabas). Several of these titles were written by former Christians.

- Newspapers: One is particularly provocative: *An-Nuur* (The Light), which the Supreme Muslim Council of Tanzania distances itself from it. It is worth noting that some Christian newspapers are also as provocative, notably: *Msema Kweli* (Truth Teller).
- Radio Stations: *Iqra FM 95.1* based in Nairobi is building up a following.
- Internet: Such as Islam in Tanzania (www.islamtz.org). This site has the texts of various articles and links to an on-line edition of *An-Nuur*. Articles written by, amongst others, Mohamed Said, the leader of *Warsha*, and a Zanzibari, M. Rajab (who sees the ruling party, CCM, as a Christian led anti Muslim party). In addition it has a chat-line and links to further information about Tanzania and about Islam.
- Cassettes and Videos: These are readily available in shops and on the streets. They include material from Deedat and recordings of *Mihadhara*, some of which are extremely offensive.
- Mosque Building: Often large Mosques are constructed in areas where there were few or no Muslims, thus giving a visible Muslim presence. An example is from Monduli Loryondo where a large mosque was built with external funding, to spread Islam amongst the Maasai. A "trick" denounced by the then MP, Lepilal ole Moloimet (Machapula, March 2000). Also, large new mosques have been built in the main cities, usually in prominent locations. Whilst on a visit to Dar es Salaam in November 2004, two new mosques were observed in the central business district, both beautifully finished in marble, with tall minarets.
- Financial Support: such as Bride Price, higher than usual to encourage families of Christian girls to let their daughters be married to Muslims. An example from Ujiji: Christians will pay 80,000/= –150,000/=; Muslims will pay to Christians 150,000/= –250,000/=; but Muslims amongst themselves will either pay no Bride Price or no more than 60,000/=. All figures refer to the Tanzanian Shilling (Katoto, March 2000).
- Employment and Trade: Work and accommodation are offered to jobless young Christians by Muslim traders. In Iringa a Transport Company is reported as only employing Muslim drivers, leading unemployed drivers to opt to become Muslims, in order to obtain work (Mbangwa, March 2000). Provision of cheap accommodation, particularly in Dar es Salaam, for young people coming to work in the city.
- Schools: Muslim-run Secondary Schools are offering places to Christians and in some cases then influencing the Students to become Muslims.
- Scholarships: Offered to the youth to study abroad, in a Muslim university.

- Health Services: Hospitals and Dispensaries are being run by Muslims, in some cases service will include active propagation of Islam.
- Relief Services: Various Islamic agencies are becoming involved in providing relief.

Frans Wijsen and Bernadin Mfumbusa, in their 2004 study *Seeds of Conflict: Religious Tensions in Tanzania*, have given similar examples. In addition they add "Securing Political Power" and "Influencing Manners" (Wijsen & Mfumbusa, 2004, p.53). They also note that "most of the strategies mentioned . . . have been used by Christian missionaries" (Wijsen & Mfumbusa, 2004, p.55).

Hamza Njozi (2000) and Lawrence Mbogoni (2005) have both written books on the situation in Tanzania. Njozi writing from a Muslim perspective gives a useful overview of the issues that have frustrated the Muslim community since independence. Mbogoni examines many similar issues from a Christian perspective, especially *mihadhara* and Hijab.

Having looked at the strategies used by Muslims, it is necessary to also examine how Christians are operating. Both regionally and internationally, Christians are active in working to evangelise Muslims. Some groups can be regarded as specifically aiming their evangelism at Muslim communities, such as Life Challenge Africa, Sheepfold Ministries and *Njia ya Uzima* (Way of Life). Other groups are aiming at evangelising anyone, including those who are already Christians. Some of the groups who are active can be seen as aggressive. From the mid-1980s Christians regularly began to organize outreach in the form of public rallies. Frieder Ludwig reports on the growth of one organization:

> Since 1986, at least one 'crusade' a year has taken place in Dar es Salaam. In order to organise a 'crusade', representatives of Assemblies of God, Lutherans, Anglicans and other churches work together in the 'Big November Crusade Ministries'. This organisation was officially registered in 1989/90. In 1990, it began to work outside Dar es Salaam and in 1991 there were 'crusades' in not less than twelve regions (Ludwig, 1996, p.223).

These "crusades" usually take the form of rallies held on open ground in an easily accessible part of the city. Meetings are held daily—in the late afternoon—for up to two weeks. They usually have several choirs and a well-known speaker, either from within the country or from abroad. Groups involved in similar outreach include Christ for All Nations (CfAN). Its leader, Reinhard Bonnke, a German who is a regular visitor to Tanzania and Kenya, has frequently stated "Africa shall be saved" (Whittaker, 1998, p.113). Ludwig comments on this approach "[it] does not leave much room for dialogue with other religions. In Tanzania [Bonnke] has to refrain from direct attacks, but nevertheless he uses a 'powerful' militant language" (Ludwig, 1996, p.223).

These examples highlight the "rivalry" between Christians and Muslims in reaching people. As Mazrui stated in his paper given at Abuja, "In Africa Christianity and Islam have often been in competition for the soul of the continent. Rivalry has sometimes resulted in conflict" (Mazrui, 1993, p.248). Jenkins also acknowledges the tensions brought about by rivalry:

> Rivalry is troublesome enough when both sides are competing for converts among followers of traditional indigenous religions, but in some situations, Christians are seeking to convert Muslims, and vice versa (Jenkins, 2002, p.168).

The approach used by Christian evangelists such as Reinhard Bonnke has led to outbursts of violence between different communities. This has been more the case in West Africa but is also present in East Africa, when rivalries can also be motivated by politicians wishing to show their power. This is being demonstrated yet again in Kenya as the referendum on the proposed new Constitution is being used by politicians to divide the country on ethnic and religious grounds.

Sadly, both Muslims and Christians are using polemical attacks on the other faith in propagating their own beliefs and this is leading to an increase in tensions as the faith communities become increasingly polarised.

Islamdom or Christendom?

In conclusion, an attempt is made to assess the long-term outcomes. The question still remains: Will Africa be at the heart of the next Christendom or the base for further expansion of Islam?

Both Christians and Muslims can legitimately regard Africa as a mission field and both groups will continue to expand through various methods of outreach. The methods that are becoming increasingly prominent are those that refer back to the basics of the faith, as Jenkins mentions:

> The more Western media penetrate a Third World nation, the more people stress their traditional values to avoid being submerged by these alien standards. The consequence is a revival of faiths providing straightforward moral teachings, including both fundamentalist Islam and traditional minded Christianity (Jenkins, 2004, p.21).

But, whilst Islam is in general presenting one model of faith to the world, that of Sunni Islam, albeit with a range of interpretations, Christianity continues to present a widely divergent set of "truths" and a great deal of internal rivalry and "sheep stealing" which could well lead to fragmentation rather than expansion. The ways in which Christianity is presented in any African country today must lead to confusion amongst potential converts.

El-Miskin states the view held by Muslims, that in the end Islam will succeed, ". . . when the Islamic movements gain the upper hand" (1993, p.272–273).

This reflects the opinion given fifty years ago by Leslie Harries, writing about Islam in East Africa, "Islam is not in a hurry. Islam has survived ruder shocks in East Africa than the present loss of political supremacy" (Harries, 1954, p.30–31).

Islam may not be in a hurry, but slowly and surely it is getting there, to achieve its goal. This is seen in the IAO communiqué, which stated some clear aims; when we reflect on these, certain trends become apparent: in particular, spreading Islam, encouraging Muslim youth and the re-introduction of *sharī'a*.

We have already explored some of the methods being used to spread Islam. There has also been an increase in activism by Muslim youth, especially those who have studied in Muslim countries. Kahumbi Maina states that they:

> Have brought back an intellectual orientation that is generally at variance with the traditional Shafi view of certain religious practices. Wahhabism, in its puritanical, uncompromising and aggressive form has been imported into East Africa by many of these recent graduates (Maina, 1995, p.172).

This has led to youth who desire to raise awareness amongst the Muslim community as to what being a Muslim involves. They are seen as being inspired by Wahhābī and Tabligh ideals, while others are influenced by al-Qaeda and the desire to return Islam to its rightful place within society and to remove the perception that they are second class citizens.

The re-introduction of *sharī'a* in many of the northern states of Nigeria has increased an awareness of *sharī'a* and the call for its implementation elsewhere in Africa. Modupe Oduyoye records the events in Zamfara State in October 1999:

> [The] State Governor . . . rose up and declared the Islamic legal system operational. He said: it has become pertinent that we wake up from this sorry state and live up to our responsibility to the Almighty (Oduyoye, 2000, p.1).

Frederic Mvumbi commenting on this says that "most of these ideas originate from the Arab world and Pakistan and are then exported to Africa. [Where] . . . African Muslims embrace them and live with them" (Mvumbi, 2005, p.81).

The re-introduction of *sharī'a* has led to an increase in violence and a greater sense of polarisation between the two faith communities. Ida Glaser reports on the events in September 2001 in Jos: "Christian and Muslim youths set up road blocks and stopped cars. Only if people were from the 'right' religion were they allowed through. [They were asked either to recite John 3:16 or the *shahāda*]. Those who failed were killed" (Glaser, 2005, p.14).

The situation in Nigeria is significant for the whole continent, especially as the proportion of Muslims and Christians is almost equal. There have been many studies of Christian-Muslim relations in Nigeria, recent studies by Patrick Udoma (2002), Osman Kane (2003) and Umar Danfulani (2005) are helpful in setting the present situation in an historical perspective as well as recording the present situation.

Both Islam and Christianity are meeting success in Africa with Reformist and Traditional "back to basics" approaches. For Islam, this is helping Africans to regain pride in their sense of identity, and an increased desire to create Islamic states, often at the cost of good inter faith relations. For Christians, an increased sense of African identity has been achieved by the rejection of the "Mother Church" of the missionaries who brought Christianity and established the church in Africa. This is illustrated by Presbyterians in Kenya rejecting the Church of Scotland and Anglicans in Nigeria disassociating themselves from Canterbury (Ashworth, 2005, p.7). This has been at the cost of distancing themselves from the world wide church and potentially the loss of Christian unity.

Muslim expansionism in Africa is a challenge to Christendom world-wide. Unless Christians in Africa develop a deeper personal commitment and churches agree to work together, Islam may indeed gain the upper hand in Africa, as they themselves confidently expect.

References

Alkali, N. et al. (eds) 1993. *Islam in Africa—proceedings of the Islam in Africa conference.* Ibadan: Spectrum Books.

Ali, T. 2002. *The clash of fundamentalisms: crusades, jihads and modernity.* London: Verso.

Aslan, R. 2005. *No god but God: the origins, evolution, and future of Islam.* New York: Random House.

Ashworth, P. 2005. Nigerians distance themselves from Canterbury. *Church Times* 23 Oct 2005: p.7.

Barrett, D.B. et al. 2005. Missiometrics 2005: a global survey of world mission. *International bulletin of missionary research* 29 (1): p.27–30.

Chesworth, J.A. Fundamentalism and outreach strategies in East Africa: Christian evangelism and Muslim *Da'wa.* (In Soares, B. (ed) *Proceedings of the third international colloquium Muslim/Christian encounters in Africa.* Brill, Leiden (Forthcoming).

Daily Nation 2001a. Commentary: Don't say Majimbo, say Federalism. 11 August.

Daily Nation 2001b. Central Kenya MPs now back Majimbo. 17 November.

CIA World Factbook. 2005. http://www.cia.gov/cia/publications/factbook Viewed 1 October 2005.

Danfulani, U.H.D. 2005. *The sharia issue and Christian-Muslim relations in contemporary Nigeria.* Stockholm: Almqvist & Wiksell International.

Glaser, I. 2005. *The Bible and other faiths: what does the Lord require of us?* Leicester: IVP.

Harries, L. 1954. *Islam in East Africa.* London: UMCA.

Huntington, S.P. 2002. *The clash of civilizations and the remaking of world order.* London: Free Press.

Islam in Africa Organisation. 2005. www.islaminafrica.org Viewed 8 October 2005.

Jenkins, P. 2002. *The next christendom: the coming of global Christianity.* Oxford: Oxford UP.

Jenkins, P. 2004. After the next Christendom. *International bulletin of missionary research.* 28 (1): p.20–22.

Kane, O. 2003. *Muslim modernity in postcolonial Nigeria.* Leiden: Brill.

Katoto, E. 2000. Interview with the author in March 2000. Kongwa, Tanzania.

Ludwig, F. 1996. After Ujamaa: is religious revivalism a threat to Tanzania's stability? (In Westerlund, D. (ed) *Questioning the secular state.* London: Hurst & Co. p.216–236.)

Machapula, F. 2000. Interview with the author in March 2000. Kongwa, Tanzania.

Maina, K.N. 1995. Christian-Muslim relations in Kenya. (In Bakari, M & Yahya, S.S. (eds) *Islam in Kenya.* Nairobi:ISP. p.116–141.)

Mazrui, A.A. 1993. African Islam and comprehensive religion: between revivalism and expansion. (In Alkali, 1993, p.247–265.)

Mbangwa, F. 2000. Interview with the author in March 2000. Kongwa, Tanzania.

Mbogoni, L.E.Y. 2005. *The cross versus the crescent: religion and politics in Tanzania from the 1880s to the 1990s.* Dar es Salaam: Mkuki na Nyota Publications.

el-Miskin, T. 1993. Da'wa and the challenge of secularism: a conceptual agenda for Islamic ideologues. (In Alkali, 1993, p.266–275.)

Mvumbi, F.N. 2005. Islam in Africa today: some observations. *Chakana* 3 (6): p.65–83.

Mwakimako, H. 2004. Christian-Muslim relations in Kenya: a catalogue of events and meanings. Paper presented at Woodbrooke, Birmingham. 23 April.

Njozi, H.M. 2000. *Mwembechai killings: and the political future of Tanzania.* Toronto: Globalink Communications.

Oduyoye, M. 2000. *The Sharī'a debate in Nigeria.* Ibadan: Sefer.

Udoma, P.L. 2002. *The cross and the crescent: a Christian response to two decades of Islamic affirmation in Nigeria.* London: St Austin Press.

Whittaker, C. 1998. *Reinhard Bonnke: a passion for the Gospel.* Eastbourne: Kingsway.

Wijsen, F. & Mfumbusa, B. 2004. *Seeds of conflict: religious tensions in Tanzania.* Nairobi: Paulines Publications.

World Christian Database, 2005. www.worldchristiandatabase.org Viewed 8 October 2005.

APPENDIX

The reported Populations of selected African countries from various sources

SELECTED COUNTRIES	Population		
*Member states on the IAO Committee	IAO (1998 est.)	WCD	CIA (July 2005 est.)
DR Congo	NA	56,079,226	60,085,804
Ethiopia	59,680,383	74,188,932	73,053,286
Gambia*	NA	1,499,176	1,593,256
Kenya	28,337,071	32,849,169	33,829,590
Libya*	NA	5,768,469	5,765,563
Malawi	NA	12,572,372	12,158,924
Mauritania*	NA	3,039,802	3,086,859
Niger*	9,671,848	12,872,813	11,665,937
Nigeria*	121,800,000	130,235,642	128,771,988
Senegal*	NA	10,587,234	11,126,832
South Africa	42,834,520	45,323,008	44,344,136
Sudan*	33,550,552	35,039,802	40,187,486
Tanzania*	NA	38,364,837	36,766,356
Tunisia*	9,380,404	10,041,690	10,074,951

(Sources: IAO: 2005, WCD: 2005 & CIA: 2005)

John Chesworth

Comparison of the Reported Percentages of Christians and Muslims from a range of sources

SELECTED COUNTRIES	Christians			Muslims		
*Member states on the IAO Committee	IAO	WCD	CIA	IAO	WCD	CIA
DR Congo	NA	95	70	NA	1	10
Ethiopia	35–40	55	35–40	45–50	34	45–50
Gambia*	NA	4	9	NA	87	90
Kenya	66	80	78	6	7	10
Libya*	–	3	–	97	96	97
Malawi	NA	77	80	NA	16	13
Mauritania*	0	0.2	0	100	99	100
Niger*	20	0.5	20	80	90	80
Nigeria*	30	47	40	60	42	50
Senegal*	NA	6	5	NA	87	94
South Africa	68	82	80	2	3	1.5
Sudan*	5	16	5	70	70	70
Tanzania*	NA	53	30	NA	30	35
Tunisia*	1	0.5	1	98	99	98

(Sources IAO: 2005, WCD: 2005 & CIA: 2005)

Karel Steenbrink

Realistic Perspectives for the Christian Diaspora of Asia

More than anything in his book, Jenkins is following in chapter 8 Samuel Hunting-ton's *Clash of Civilizations and the Remaking of World Order*. This is not only clear from the title of the chapter (The Next Crusade) but from the apocalyptic and warrior language. This paper wants to question his analysis. It focuses on the difference between social-political versus religious analysis in the colonial period and shows that it is to Asian Christians to decide which way they want to go. Anyhow, Christianity in Asia and in other parts of the world will have to cope with the growing power of Islam, Hinduism, and perhaps also Buddhism, and old and new manifestations of Chinese religions like Confucianism and Taoism. Christianity will have to come to terms with the remnants of a colonial past and learn how to behave as a minority religion, as a small player in a diaspora. It must be a prophetic voice, joining efforts together with all positive elements in Asian societies.

There have been quite a few contradicting visions on the future of religion in Asia during the last century. Some spirited Protestant leaders at the beginning of the 20th century spoke about "the world for Christ in this generation". They were succeeded by the not much less grandiose views of someone like Arend Th. Van Leeuwen who in the 1960s predicted the spread of a secular spirit all over the world, beginning with Western Christianity, but to be continued in the great Asian religions. This was not effectuated. Instead, since the 1970s the Wrath of God (Gilles Kepel, 1989: *La Revanche de Dieu*) has spread over most parts of the world and religion is again one of the major social powers to be reckoned with.

In chapter VIII of *The Next Christendom: The Coming of Global Christianity*, Philip Jenkins discusses the possibility of a "next crusade". More than anywhere else in his book, Jenkins is here following Samuel Huntington's *Clash of Civilizations and the Remaking of World Order*. This is not only clear from the title of the chapter (*The Next Crusade*) and the apocalyptic content of the opening text (suggesting that on the Day of Judgment Jesus will obey the command of the Quran). It is also clear from the warrior language from the first paragraph onwards: this is a vocabulary of "civil wars, political violence, battle, blood-shed, persecutions, murder, massacres" all within the first twenty lines. As if we are reading a story of horror and anguish, misery and utmost fear.

In this contribution I want to question his analysis. I will focus upon the difference between social-political versus religious analysis in the colonial period and show that it is up to us to decide which way we want to go. Anyhow, Christianity in Asia and in other parts of the world will have to cope with the growing power of Islam, Hinduism, and perhaps also Buddhism, and old and new manifestations of Chinese religions like Confucianism and Taoism. Christianity will have to come to terms with the remnants of a colonial past and learn how really to behave as a minority religion, as a small player in a diaspora. It must be a prophetic voice, joining efforts together with all positive elements in Asian societies.

In the common descriptions of Asian religions, as also the case in the 8th chapter of Jenkins' *Next Christendom*, there are clear boundaries between the big players in the global religions. Giants divided, because only with clear divisions between friends and foes, between antagonistic parties, can a true battle be fought. It is from the beginning clear where the dividing line must be seen: in the rhyming couplet of Cross versus Crescent, the Battle Fronts are found in Nigeria, in Pakistan, Indonesia, the Philippines, the Balkans. All these territories have known conflicts between Muslims and Christians during the last decades. Hinduism, of course, must be reckoned with, but Islam seems to be the great enemy. Something like an Antichrist fighting the true returning Christ. This is the apocalyptic mood of the last section of this chapter where a curious scenario is depicted:

> A similar conflagration [like in 1914] might evolve from an Asian struggle between (say) a vigorously Christian Philippines and a resolutely Muslim Indonesia, especially if each nation offered clandestine support to secessionist groups in its neighbor's territory (Jenkins, 2002, p.190).

This is the end of the chapter. It has some reservations: the conditional "say", "if", "might". Indonesia is further mentioned on p.175–6 where the Maluku wars of 1999-2002 and other violence with inter-religious aspects is mentioned. In a few sentences there is a balance: as to Maluku the number of 5000 people killed (for both sides together) is mentioned. But the rest of the page is a list of other incidents with only a rather one-sided enumeration of Christian victims. The section of the book reads as if Christians are mostly victims and suggests that Muslims are the aggressive party. As if the enthusiasm of the beginning of the 20th century when there was a hope that Asia and the rest of the world would be won for Christ in that century has turned into the anguish that a religious war between the religions would start in Asia and most of all between Muslims and Christians with dramatic and damaging effects for the Christian minorities in this continent where about half the human population of the world lives. What is the realistic perspective for Christians as minorities among the population of Asia?

Scholars versus Soldiers

Western statements and analysis about the non-Western world have been very critically scrutinized by Edward Said in his *Orientalism* (1978) and more specifically in his *Covering Islam: How the Media and the Experts Determine how we see the Rest of the World* (1981). The books need no further explanation or recommendation. But still, their basic guidelines still need implementation.

Matters are even more complicated when we look at the global situation from the other side. In the 1980s the Indonesian Prof. Abdul Mukti Ali already promoted the idea of "Occidentalism" as the study of Western culture. In the 1990s the Arab scholar Hasan Hanafi wrote a book that in translation reads as: *Occidentalism. How We React towards the West.*[1] Only recently the term has become common also in western writings, among others in the book by Ian Buruma and Avishai Margalit: *Occidentalism: The West in the Eyes of its Enemies* (2004). Analysis, writing of history, is never part of a really and fully detached collection of facts and compilation of a picture, on both sides it is a mixture of facts and ideology.

Although we still can speak of two sides, the Western and the non-Western, the two are not absolutely separated. Not only, like in the 19th century, western scholars do research about non-Western societies, or soldiers and colonial officials develop their methods to control and regulate these societies. Nowadays the Hindus and Muslims, Chinese, Indonesians and Indians react to the books and articles written about them. In early 1994 the first issue of the new Indonesian Journal for Islamic Studies, *Studia Islamika* had a 30 page article "Dismantling Cultural Prejudices: Responses to Huntington's Thesis in the Indonesian media" (Prasetyo 1994). This contribution summarised eight reactions in the Indonesian media to the first article by Huntington in *Foreign Affairs*, Summer 1993. The same Indonesian journal published in 1999 a long article on the perceptions of Indonesian Muslims (Ropi 1999).

One of the possible ways of giving structure to the difficult topic of mutual perceptions is the disparity between the academic study of a religion and the political observation of the colonising power. Max Müller (1823–1900) is quite often seen as the scholar who invented the religions of the East as scriptural giants. His name will for ever be connected with the great series in 50 volumes of the *Sacred Books of the East*. His quest was the wish to study the basic text: the original sources, the great commentaries, to show the way to the basic idea of a comprehensive world religion. His quest was in smaller fields carried out be a large number of 19th and 20th century scholars. Dutch studies of Indonesian

---

1   I have come across this book through the Indonesian translation: *Oksidentalisme, Sikap kita terhadap Tradisi Barat*, (Jakarta: Paramadina, 2000).

Islam had a long tradition of work in the manuscript rooms of the greater libraries. Writing dictionaries, grammars, catalogues of manuscripts, editions of Javanese and Malay texts with introductions, references to Arabic, Persian, Tamil, when possible also Buddhist and Hindu sources. That is one of the ways Islam was also studied with respect to Indonesia. In comfortable armchairs in Oxford and Leiden scholars reconstructed the original doctrine of Hinduism and Islam. They drew their conclusions often from more distinguished doctrines and rituals than the distorted and poorly practised religions of their own times. They often even did not deem it necessary to go to these far countries to see concrete modern faithful of these beliefs. Marshall Hodgson sees in this "Arabistic and philological bias an interest in the word rather than the substance, where data for Egypt and Syria easily are taken for Islamdom as a whole" (Hodgson, 1977, p.39–40). Much of this research, however, came to interesting and sympathetic studies about Islam, especially in its mystical expression. The Jesuit priest Piet Zoetmulder wrote in 1935 a doctoral dissertation on various streams of Islamic mysticism and even took a position in a debate about the orthodoxy of al-Hallāj, who was executed when he was accused of heretical doctrines: "This union could best be compared with the indwelling of God in man by his *gratia sanctificans*, as in the Catholic doctrine which preserves fully the divine transcendency" (Zoetmulder, 1935, p.37).[2]

Much different from these armchair scholars were the colonial officials and soldiers. They had to deal with the concrete modern representatives of the religions. Since the beginning of the full colonial era in the 19th century they took Islam as the most dangerous and strongest enemy. As to Indonesia we have the testimony of Raffles as Governor General in Batavia during the British interregnum of 1812–1816:

> Every Arab from Mecca as well as every Javanese who had returned from a pilgrimage thither, assumed on Java the character of a saint and the credulity of the common people was such that they too often attributed to such persons supernatural powers. Thus respected it was not difficult for them to rouse the country to rebellion. The Mohammedan priests have almost invariably been found most active in every case of insurrection (Raffles, 1817, p.3).

So it has been often in colonial history. To give just one further example: in 1888 the Dutch minister of Colonial Affairs, Levinus Keuchenius, rejected the idea of subsidizing Islamic schools because he feared "that the involvement of the colonial government and the financial sacrifice required for the sake of those schools would eventually only lead to the promotion of a type of religious education that would surely be of little profit to our authority and our influence" (Steenbrink, 1993, p.87). Islamic education in the Dutch East Indies was thus

---

2   Zoetmulder quotes here also Asin Palacios who declared the doctrine of Hallāj "not pantheistic but Christian".

forced to go its own way, without any connection to the colonial government. On the contrary generous subsidies were given to Christian mission that considered (government sponsored) education as a major means to spread its religion.

The Cowboy versus Sindbad

On 4 November 2004 the prestigious Erasmus Prize for exceptionally important contributions to European culture, society or social science, was awarded to three Muslim scholars: Moroccan sociologist Fatima Mernissi, Syrian philosopher Sadik al-Azm and Iranian Abdulkarim Soroush. By far the most sparkling and original speech at that occasion was delivered by Fatima Mernissi with the title: "The Cowboy or Sindbad? Who will be the Globalization Winner?"[3] In this speech Mernissi played with two concepts in the best tradition of symbolic anthropology. Sindbad stands for the trader, adventurer, who travels with good humour, no weapons other than the ability to make communication and solidarity, and is able to address all kind of people. Sindbad is, to judge from his name not an Arab, but originating from the Indo-Pakistani subcontinent, from Sind. He must—from a trader in a Hindu or Buddhist environment—have become an Arab of Baghdad through the intermediary of Persian storytellers.

> The only thing predictable in the seven trips Sindbad undertook, was that to communicate with strangers, be they humans or even birds and sea-monsters, made him richer and happier. Communication with the stranger who manifests God's cosmic capacity to manifest itself in diverse images is one of the strong messages which runs through Sindbad's tales and explains why, among all the '1001 Nights' stories, only this one became a universal heritage, enchanting European and American children alike.

Sindbad was a hero for the 9th century of the Arab world and has remained not only a feature for entertainment but also a cultural ideal since then. In sharp contrast to the ideal of Sindbad there is the prototype of the cowboy, as a film hero, adapted to the American or even global culture of the 20th century. The cowboy

> expressed the twentieth century Hollywood world economic vision, just as Sindbad reflected that of the ninth century Baghdad, and the difference between the two lies in the very concept of what constitutes wealth: cattle for the first and travel for the second. Often, the cowboy did not own the herds he was tending, yet his job was to protect the fortune already existing on his territory even though it belonged to the ranch master. The cowboy did not have to travel because his wealth was under his very eyes and only one role was left to the stranger to play: that of the cattle thief.

---

3   A Dutch translation of the article by Fatima Mernissi, 'De Cowboy of Sindbad: Wie zal de winnaar zijn in de globalisering?' in Max Sparreboom (ed) *Religie en moderniteit*, Breda: De Geus, 2004, p.17–55. An English summary in http://www.mernissi.net/books/articles/sindbad. html, viewed on 20 March 2006. Quoted sections are from this extract.

When looking at this opposition one of course is easily lured to see in George W. Bush and his crusader ideology the cowboy and the "war against terror" as the ultimate symptom of the narrow-mindedness and fear of the other of the cowboy. But we should not too easily apply the opposition to the people we love or like. Mernissi does not naively glorify Muslim cultural tradition. She praised the first generations of the Islamic empire, especially the caliphs Al-Mansur and Al-Ma'mun (between 754–833) as the golden age of Baghdad and Muslim culture. She blamed Caliph Al-Mu'tadid (1042–1068) for relying on the sword not on the pen as his weapon. In the same way the USA trusted big investments in new broadcast programmes for the Arab world instead of providing money for a good research of the existing ones.

For Mernissi globalisation is a process that was already going on for many centuries. In the 9th century, the time of the imaginary Sindbad, a Jew or any trader could safely travel from Cordoba in Spain to China. Unfortunately, the Islamic empire could not continue this openness and positive attitude towards the stranger.

Missionary, Merchant and Military

As a parallel to the pair of Sindbad and cowboy we may discuss the triad of the three M's, the merchant, military and missionary. The three were in diverse combinations represented in the Christian history of Asia. It was Nestorian merchants, sometimes accompanied or followed by the religious specialists, who established small Christian communities along the trading lines: the silk road and also along the south-western coast of India where the Syro-Malabar Thomas Christians became sociologically something like a caste of their own: with exclusive marriage within the own community but good relations in the field of trade to outsiders.

Later arrivals of Christians were less peaceful. In 1498 the Portuguese conquered Goa, followed in 1511 by Malakka, and in 1522 by Ternate. The spread of Asian Christianity was not a matter of a marching order as was the case in Central and South America. Asian countries and communities were too strong to be included into a *corpus christianum* by just commanding them to accept a new religious system. With the notable exception of the Philippines it was mostly in the marginal regions of Asia, sociologically and geographically, where Christianity could gain a strong following. It was among the mountain peoples of India, Burma, Indonesia, among the lower class of India and China that we find most converts.

Under colonial rule the missionary was often in a problematic relationship with the merchant and the military. He often had to rely upon them for safety and facilities. Sometimes he was seen in one line, especially when in the 19th and early 20th centuries European superiority took the colonial enterprise as a *mission civilatrice* and identified economic with cultural and religious superiority. One after another, the Asian Christian communities had problems in defining their identity after independence. They all stated then that to be a Christian could go hand in hand with being a 100% Indian, Indonesian, Japanese. It is not mere coincidence that movements towards a (Protestant) contextual theology or (Catholic) inculturation started in the 1960s.

In the 1970s and even more strongly in the 1980s we may notice a decrease in the efficiency of the Western ideologies (communism, socialism) and a return of the religious identities. This was most clearly visible in India where the Bharata Janata Party was established in 1980. It exploited a Hindu identity as a political weapon against the secular Congress Party. It was first of all the Muslim community of India that suffered most under this rise of Hindu fundamentalism, but also many difficulties rose for the Christians.

After the Asian Synod of 1997, Pope John Paul II came to India for a visit in November 1998. In a speech he expressed his observation about the weak position of Christianity in Asia. But he expressed also his hope for 'a bountiful harvest in the coming millennium'. In another speech the Pope talked about 'a Christian spring for Asia in the Third millennium'. This was the start of what now already has been labelled 'the conversion debate' in India. Numerous articles have been written on the theme and we can only give some aspects of the debate.[4] In March 1999 there were cruel attacks on Christian villages in Gujarat, that even made some give the comment that, "the attention of militarised Hindu sects has now turned from Muslims to Christians" (John, 2000, p.26). The principal of the New Delhi Jesuit college Vidyajyoti, T.K. John, a true Indian notwithstanding his name, blamed the Christian fundamentalists:

> Christian fundamentalists too, it has to be acknowledged, have been going round the towns and villages, marketing religiosity, like vendors of cheap goods, making facile promises, issuing threats, project a god that is as narrow as their world, and promise rewards that are of the same kind (John, 2000, p.28).

But John also blamed radical Hindus:

> A close scrutiny of the writings of the early protagonists of Hindutva (Savarkar, Hedgewar..), the recent 'Quit India' order served on the missionaries in Maharashstra, the slogan and campaign to make Banswara district of South Rajasthan 'Christian-free by the year 2000', the inclusion of Christians among the 'foreigners' in class 9 'Social Studies' text books in Gujarat, and what was accomplished in Dangs to exterminate Christianity from the district point to one thing: the sponsors and promoters of Hindutva reject Christianity totally (John, 2000, p.29).

---

4   A special issue of *Jnanadeepa*, the journal of the Jesuit led Pontifical Institute of Philosophy and Religion in Pune, Vol 3 (2000) no 1 has 13 contributions on the theme. Two important articles were published in *Vidyajyoti*, the Journal of the New Delhi Jesuit school, Vol 64 (2000) no 1. See also Steenbrink, 2003.

What are the motives behind the modern Hindu protests against proselytism, conversion and even against presence in their country of the small Christian minority? It certainly is not the result of thorough comparisons between Hindu and Christian doctrines. It is quite striking that the poor in the small villages are targeted now: because the rise of the suppressed (the poor, the *dalit*, the women) must be resisted. Why are Islam and Christianity unacceptable, while conversion to Buddhism or Jainism are accepted! Is it the fear that as an international organised religion Christianity can smother Hinduism that for centuries has lived as a "non-organized religion"? In fact the number of Christians is small (2.3%) and is not growing during the last decades. Many Hindu religious leaders have condemned the attacks on Muslims and recently also on Christians in India. They identify the recent call to "cultural nationalism" as a veiled expression of fundamentalism and seek mostly non-religious political factors behind the protests.[5]

In this discourse and heated debate it looked as if Christianity in India is one community. Also in the debate about the general communalism, it is often stated as if the Muslim community could be treated as one, united community. Unfortunately (or should we say: thank God!) this is not the case. Indian Christianity is an extremely divided group, related to so many foreign missions, so many spirited Indian individuals who interpreted Christianity in their own way. And the same is true for all Asian Christianities, perhaps with the exception of majority Catholic Philippines. But even there the 8% charismatic not-yet-dissident El-Shaddai group causes a serious threat to this majority feeling.

Weak States and Strong Religions

It was not only Islam and Hinduism that increased in the period of "God's Revenge", from the late 1970s on. It was also Christianity that saw a proportional increase in membership and sometimes also in prestige and political influence, albeit modest in most Asian countries. We may notice a process of globalisation in the religious field: the "Big Five" (Hinduism, Buddhism, Islam, Protestantism, Catholicism) are growing everywhere at the cost of the smaller traditions. In fact, many religious movements have protested against globalisation.[6] But in my view, the religious protesters against globalisation have often forgotten that they themselves are also representatives of global institutions. The world religions are even the longest lasting of civilization's primary institutions (Hefner, 1993, p.34). They have brought freedom and enlightenment to many people, but also oppression of local and deviating streams.

---

5   For the figures see D'Mello, 2000, p.5–22.
6   One of the first was the Tamil theologian Felix Wilfred in various articles, put together in his *Sunset in the East?* Madras: Chair in Christianity, University of Madras.

The country where this movement has become strong is Indonesia. Since the defeat of communism in 1965, it has become common law that everybody must become a member of a universal religion. Even Confucianism is not acknowledged in Indonesia because it is restricted to one country alone. Tribal religions have to seek an umbrella under one of the major religions. There were local groups, secessions from Islam, who first fled to Catholicism, then to Protestantism, and now are in a stage of loose membership to Hinduism, a quite broad-minded and not so clearly defined religious tradition. But also in other countries we can see this development. Korean shamanism is more or less crushed between various Christian churches and a revival of formal Buddhism.

The most corrupt countries of Asia, according to Transparency International, are either Christian or Muslim: Bangladesh ranking highest as most corrupt, followed by Indonesia and the Philippines. Singapore – a Chinese but not so religious state – is the cleanest one. What could be the role of religion in this matter? It is quite striking that there are inter-religious NGOs who fight against globalisation of economy, corruption and in favour of women's rights, while it is mostly people who are close to the official religious leadership of Islam who promote the implementation of *sharia* law.

In such a weak state it occurs quite often that local conflicts can be used by the local elite to make profit, strengthen their position and take revenge on their enemies. In the long period of unrest and conflicts that started in Indonesia in 1995, preceding the fall of Soeharto and only calmed down in 2002, it was not a national civil war of Christians versus Muslims, but rather a long chain of local conflicts where the opponents used the opposition between Christians and Muslims to give a somewhat more national and even international banner to local conflict. To mention just one example, we want to give some details of the North-Halmahera conflict of 1999–2000, part of the Maluku Wars of 1999–2002.

The violence in North Halmahera became probably the worst in the whole region for the period under discussion. Some claim at least 2500 dead between 18 August 1999 and the end of that year. The centre of riots and fighting was on the eastern coast of North Halmahera. The most serious conflicts in the (mostly Protestant) Kao-Tobelo-Galela region are related to migrations after several volcanic eruptions on the island of Makian (between Tidore and Bacan, off the West Coast of Halmahera between 1975–1980. Some 17,000 (mostly Muslim) inhabitants of Makian, many of them traders, were resettled amongst the small communities on the eastern coast of north Halmahera, mostly farmers and fishers. In November 1999, after rumours that Makian-Muslims had attacked a Kao village, the Christians started to set mosques on fire, whereupon many Makian settlers fled to the island of Ternate and killed a number of Christians in revenge. On 26 December massive killings in settlements of Makian-Muslims started, which caused many reactions in other parts of Indonesia. A bloody and nearly complete civil war between Christian and Muslim parties started in Northern Halmahera with only very little presence of the army until a period, when people complained that this whole area was in total chaos and anarchy. A serious complication here was the presence of an Australian gold mine in the highlands of Northeast Halmahera. They preferred the better educated literate Muslim migrants from Makian over the mostly still illiterate Christians of the coastal areas and paid them salaries that were considered rather high in this region.[7]

Also many other studies about local conflicts show that national politics or international religions only play a secondary or even lesser role in the painful and often disastrous conflicts. We should not too easily attribute global or even transcendental dimensions to personal greed and hatred, restricted intrigues and conspiracies.[8]

A Proposal for a Diaspora and the Debate on *fiqh aqalliyat*

We have already mentioned Gilles Kepel, the author of a book published in 1989 under the title *La revanche de Dieu*, describing a (nearly) worldwide trend of a come-back of religion. In 2004 Kepel published another important book with a strong title: *Fitnah. Guerre au coeur de l'islam* (Paris: Gallimard). The book was translated into English with the title *The War for Muslim Minds: Islam and the West* (Cambridge, MA: Belknap). Kepel wants to stress that we should see the Muslim expressions of hate, terrorism and exclusion versus the Western world not as a war between Muslim and the West, but rather as a sign of an internal struggle within the Muslim world itself, looking for a new orientation. The Arab word *fitnah* has the original meaning of temptation, considered as the individual temptation by the devil but also as the terrible trial of mankind at the end of time. This is the same double meaning as the sentence in the basic Christian prayer: "and lead us not into temptation". In later Arabic the word *fitnah* has received the connotation of civil war. According to Kepel a civil war or internal strife among Muslims is going on and the terrorist attacks on Western society are just a side effect of this internal debate and strife.

Until the abolition of the caliphate of the Ottoman ruler in 1923, there was a nominal supreme leader for the majority *sunni* Muslims. Since then the new developments in the Muslim world have lead to many new organisations, brotherhoods, alliances and streams. No dominating organisation or leadership has emerged. Leadership in the Muslim world has become more and more fragmented. The central holy places of Mecca and Medina are since the middle

---

7   More details in Steenbrink, 2001, p.64–91.
8   See the analysis of Indonesian conflicts in Jamal et al 2002; Colombijn 2002, Coppel 2006.

1920s under the control of a sectarian movement, the Wahhabi Muslims, who never succeeded in gaining the hearts of the majority of Islam. The Arab language has lost its dominant position in the Muslim world in favour of English that has become the major means of communication of Muslims worldwide. The Muslim world has become more and more divided. Notwithstanding its unity in the annual hajj-ceremony in Mecca, in most countries a competition is going on between various streams of Islam.

Traditional Muslim ideology divides the world into a *dārul islām*, a House of Islam, and a *dārul harb*, the House of War, territory ruled by the infidels. In the *dārul islam* the dominating religion is Islam. Although minorities have specific rights and protection as *dhimmī*, they are considered second-class citizens. Non-Muslims in this ideal Muslim state have to pay the *jizya* or special poll-tax, and are not allowed to show their religion in public (no processions, no magnificent church buildings, no church bells ringing). This mediaeval construction has been challenged by the modern ideal of democracy, and equal rights for citizens. Besides, more and more Muslim live as minorities in Western countries. There is a debate on the duties and rights of these Muslims, called the *fiqh aqalliyāt*, the rules for Muslims living as minorities.

Not only in Western countries, but also within the Muslim world itself, there is more and more diversity among Muslims themselves. In countries like Pakistan, Bangladesh and Indonesia, just to mention three of the larger Muslim countries of Asia, there is a deep gap between champions of the implementation of *sharia* law and the supporters of secular law, between traditionalists and reformists. The "crusade" is not between Islam and the West, but rather it is an internal strife within the Muslim world and only some minorities would like to consider it as a fight against outside enemies. We should not join this ideology but rather join the debate on how to live in a religious community that is a minority.

The same can be seen in the world of Hinduism. The *Ramraj* movement of the BJP, Bharata Janata Party, wants a united Hindu state in India instead of the secular product of British colonialism as founded by Mahatma Gandhi and Jawaharlal Nehru. But this constructed neo-Hinduism only can be promoted when it stimulates the fear of the other, for enemies outside this Neo-Hinduism through attacks on Muslims (culminating in the demolition of the Babri-mosque in December 1992) and on Christians. Like Islam, Hinduism also has problems with living in a plural society where Hindus are a minority or at least not a dominant religion. Still, it is possible. The history of Hinduism in the Caribbean can give here interesting examples, but this would lead us too far away from our major subject.[9]

---

9   For a study of another Hindu minority see Bakker 1993. Bakker is now working on a com-
      parative study of Hinduism in the Caribbean.

What about Asian Christianity? It has for a long time lived in dreams of the final conquest of the whole world for Christ. The diaspora situation was considered by foreign missionaries but also by many of the new believers as a temporary situation. In the colonial period this could be easily cherished, because in so many Asian countries political power was still in Christian hands. The process of decolonisation involved the support of Christians for the nationalist movement. This was also the time of contextualisation of theology, of inculturation in local culture. The slogan of the first Catholic bishop of Indonesia (1940), Albertus Soegijopranoto, has been repeated again and again: 100% Catholic, 100% Indonesian. But how to live as a minority? We want to elaborate here some thoughts on the subject by the late priest Yusuf Bilyarta Mangunwijaya (1929–1999).[10]

Diaspora minority as the reality of most Asian Christians

In 1995 and 1996 some two hundred Christian churches, schools and convents were burned down in riots on the Indonesian major island of Java. These incidents were often interpreted as inter-religious conflicts, where Muslims were blamed for attacks on Christians, but they were also interpreted as signs of social unrest, where a majority of Muslim poor attacked shops, schools and churches, owned by Chinese and other minorities. Amidst this unrest the priest, social activist and architect Mangunwijaya rather cynically remarked: "When our churches are set on fire, we Catholics say: do not be afraid, we will build them again and in a more sumptuous style.... But the essence of our faith is not in magnificent buildings or in prestigious institutions."[11] The two patrons of the Catholic mission were contrasted by him: Saint Francis Xavier was the model for the earlier centuries of mission, when missionaries went hand in hand with the military and merchants. Twentieth century mission received as its patron Saint Theresa of Lisieux, a modest young lady. Indonesians should not try to become big as an institution, not lobby for more Catholic ministers in the government or pray that "Gus Dur" [the common name for the well known Muslim leader Abdurrahman Wahid, president from 1999–2001] would receive baptism. True Christian faith is best expressed in a minority and diaspora situation.

There were a number of critical reactions to this "diaspora-gospel" of Mangunwijaya. Some said that he blamed the victims of the church fires, rather than the diehards, fanatics, bandits and criminals, who caused the inferno of these buildings. Small groups and dispersed Catholic congregations should not be exalted, as in the case of the Chinese Catholics, who really live

---

10   For this section see also Steenbrink 1998.
11   *Hidup Katolik*, 24 November 1996.

in an unwanted situation. Besides, especially in the big cities of Java, such as Jakarta, Bandung, Surabaya, the Catholics and the Christians in general live dispersed amongst an overwhelming majority of Muslims and meet many restrictions in expressing their faith in public.

Notwithstanding these criticisms, Mangunwijaya was asked to design the *Pastoral Letter of the Catholic Bishops for Easter 1997*, together with the Jesuit Franz Magnis Suseno. In this letter the unrest of the previous years was not interpreted as an inter-religious conflict, but as the result of social and economic oppression. Moral depravation was seen in the manipulation of political parties, the ban on trade unions and the increasing corruption. These crimes created a situation, where religious leaders could no longer control their communities. These crimes also created the situation, which resulted in attacks on shops, economic, cultural and religious buildings.

The publication of this pastoral letter, signed by Cardinal Justinus Darmaatmadja, was certainly not an official approval of the idea of a Diaspora Church, but it provided support for Mangunwijaya's ideas. In a series of seven articles in the Catholic Weekly *Hidup Katolik* [March–April 1997] these were elaborated and became subject of a general debate. Writing about the 16th and 17th century, Mangunwijaya stressed even more than in his novels that the Portuguese and Spanish of this period "were champions of fanaticism and cruelty, compared with the Protestants and Muslims and certainly when considered beside the Hindus and Buddhists."[12] Discussing the structure of the parish, he sketched the system of the Dutch missionaries in Indonesia since the 19th century as an effort to imitate the situation in their home country, where some Catholic areas segregated themselves from a liberal and protestant majority. Also in Indonesia the strategy of the Catholic Church had been too much concentrated on the creation of a separate community, with its own schools, political party, newspapers and hospitals. The inner heart of the church still was considered to be the clergy, the religious women and men, with the lay people mostly as consumers only. Life in a modern metropolitan city is a nomadic life: people migrate for work, for living, for recreation. In this hectic world the basic unit for living is the family. The church should try to heighten the quality of the family rather than its own institutions. A missionary church should only operate institutions which are really functional for its main purpose, the arrival of the Kingdom of God. In this way a diaspora church should also become a flexible and accommodating church.

Philip Jenkins opens his chapter 8 with a quote from the *hadith*, here related by Abu Huraira, not the most reliable transmitter of traditions and by some even seen as a notorious inventor of false ones. It tells the final victory of Islam, but

---

12   *Hidup Katolik*, 23 March 1997, p.30.

only on the day of judgment. There is a good and practical alternative reading for the theme of this chapter. It is from the basic source, the Koran: "If God had pleased He would have made you all a single people, but that He might try you in what He gave you, therefore strive with one another to hasten to virtuous deeds" (Koran 5:48, similar texts in 6:35, 11:118, 13:31, 32:13, 10:99). For the time being we have to accept the diversity, to deal with it in peace and to compete in goodness. Is this a naïve alternative for the next crusade that is predicted by the political scientists? Taking into account not only the external diversity of the religions, but most of all their internal differences, this seems much more realistic than the crusade of whole civilizations, marked by different world religions. Let the scholars, the missionaries, but most of all Sindbad be the guide for this mission.

References

Bakker, F. 1993. *The struggle of Hindu Balinese intellectuals: development of Hindu thinking in modern Indonesia.* Amsterdam: Free UP.

Buruma, I. & Margalit, A. 2004. *Occidentalism: the West in the eyes of its enemies.* New York: Penguin Press.

Colombijn, F. & Lindblad, J.T. (eds) 2002. *Roots of violence in Indonesia. Contemporary violence in historical perspective.* Leiden: KITLV.

Coppel, C. (ed) 2006. *Violent conflicts in Indonesia.* London: Routledge.

D'Mello, J. 2000. Letting the converted speak. *Jnanadeepa.* 3: p.5–22.

Hefner, R. (ed) 1993. *Conversion to Christianity: historical and anthropological perspectives on a great transformation.* Berkeley: University of California Press.

Hodgson, M. 1977. *The venture of Islam. Vol. 1.* Chicago: University of Chicago Press. p.39–40.

Jamal, M. et al (eds) 2000. *Communal conflicts in contemporary Indonesia.* Jakarta: Pusat Bahasa dan Budaya IAIN.

Jenkins, P. 2002. *The next christendom: the coming of global Christianity.* Oxford: Oxford UP.

John, T.K. 2000. The call for a debate in conversion. *Vidyajyoti* 64.

Prasetyo, H. 1994. Dismantling cultural prejudices: responses to Huntington's thesis in the Indonesian media. *Studia Islamika.* 1 (1): p.133–164.

Raffles, T. S. 1817. *The history of Java.* 1978 reprint. Kuala Lumpur: Oxford UP.

Ropi, I. 1999. Depicting the other faith: a bibliographical survey of Indonesian Muslim polemics on Christianity. *Studia Islamika.* 6 (1): p.77–111.

Said, E. 1978. *Orientalism.* New York: Vintage Books.

Said, E. 1981. *Covering Islam: how the media and the experts determine how we see the rest of the world.* London: Routledge.

Steenbrink, K. 2003. Problems and perspectives of conversion in recent Catholic theology. (In Heller, D. (ed). *Bekehrung und Identität. Ökumene als Spannung zwischen Fremden und Vertrauten.* Frankfurt: Otto Lembeck. p.134–151.

Steenbrink, K. 2001. Interpretations of Christian-Muslim violence in the Moluccas. *Studies in Interreligious Dialogue* 11. p.64–91.

Steenbrink, K. 1998. Y.B. Mangunwijaya's blueprint for a diaspora church in Indonesia. *Exchange* 27 p.17–36.

Steenbrink, K. 1993. *Dutch colonialism and Indonesian Islam.* Amsterdam: Rodopi.

Zoetmulder, P. 1935. *Pantheism and monism in Javanese suluk literature.* Leiden: KITLV. 1995 edition translated by Merle Ricklefs.

Joop Vernooij

Religion in the Caribbean: Creation by Creolisation

The Caribbean region is a unique part of the world with its mixed peoples, cultures and religions, a melting pot or callaloo. The region is an *in between* of East and West, North and South, the region of indigenous peoples, ex-enslaved, indentured labourers of Asia, Lebanese, Chinese. All of them experienced the challenges of a multi- and intercultural society. The peoples created for themselves new worlds, cultures, and religions. The meeting or confrontation with colonial Christianity led to new features of religion like voodoo (Haïti), santería (Cuba), winti (Suriname), and orisa (Trinidad). Also, Hinduism and Islam from Asia adapted to the new context. Writers, theologians, and philosophers in the French Caribbean launched the concept of creolisation, the dynamic process of creation of culture and religion. For them, *tout monde* (everybody) has to create life by creolisation. This concept can be a vehicle for the analysis of developments of religion(s) in the world. Philip Jenkins does not mention the Caribbean in his *The New Christendom* (2002).

Philip Jenkins' book *The Next Christendom: The Coming of Global Christianity* (2002) makes no mention of religious issues in the Caribbean. He does not refer to the unique and particular world of the Caribbean. The Caribbean region is an *in between* of North and South, East and West. The region has been called a melting pot, a *callaloo*, a pepper-pot, a salad bowl, in social as well as in religious affairs. It is a seedbed of cultures and religions.

As a long-time resident of the region, I would like to describe the specific situation and special function of religion in the Caribbean. Specifically, I will concentrate on the concept of *creolisation* of religion and of theology in the region. Such an approach can lead to new concepts, attitudes and perspectives, both for people inside as well as outside the region. The history of the Caribbean has been on of a search for identity and integrity. People have achieved their survival and liberation through the process of creolisation. This contribution will focus mostly on the Christian religion in the Caribbean. The Caribbean, or the West Indies, is not only a geographical or strategic notion, but has meaning in the field of culture, economics and politics, as well as religion. The picture is a complex one. For 500 years the region has been a site of violence, begun by the European powers with their introduction of red and black slavery, neo-colonialism, and fragmentation as a variety of population groups, languages, religions, and lifestyles were brought in for "development" of the region (Premdas 1999).

Before the Caribbean became Spanish, French, English, and Dutch, it had its own indigenous culture. In the course of five centuries it developed its own identity, that of a new humankind. The Dominican friar Bartolomé de las Casas described the history of his time as one of destruction and dehumanisation of land and people (de las Casas 1578). The European powers created this situation as their own colonising development project.

Historical characterisation of the region by scholars from abroad, starting in the early twentieth century, focused on the search for African and Asian cultural survivals from the time of black slavery and indentured labour. Later on, a focus on the Indo-Caribbean, the Chinese Caribbean, the Maroon Caribbean and even the indigenous Caribbean histories concentrated on the reshaping of the region's cultures, religions, languages by the newcomers in diaspora. It was at this time that the key concept of *creolisation* was introduced.

By way of beginning I need to explain the subtitle "Creation by Creolisation." What this tries to express is that in the Caribbean the whole world came together, creating its own new world on local level. The history of the development of the idea of creolisation can be useful and fruitful for the whole world today, especially where the main issue was and is creation of new humankind in the midst of inhuman circumstances.

The Religious Panorama

First of all I need to give a brief overview of the complex religious field in the region of the West Indies. The Christian churches in the Caribbean were colonial churches with racism (for example, a baptism day for whites and another day for blacks; the whites seated in front of the church and the blacks in the back benches), and prejudice that led even to the denial of the cultures of the new peoples (Caldecott 1970; Dayfoot 1999; Bisnauth 1989; Lampe 1992, 2001). These characteristics are evident already in the stories of de las Casas and continued into the last century with remnants still present now. The perspectives changed only through the self-conciousness and self-organisation of the peoples themselves (Hurbon 2000; Bebel-Gisler 1975). In the midst of this the peoples created new life styles and religions. We note the religions with a clearly Roman Catholic component such as Santería (Cuba), Vodu (Haiti), Candomblé (Brazil) and the religions with a European protestant component, such as Baptist Shouters (Trinidad) and Kuminia (Jamaica). There are other new types of religion like Orisa (Trinidad), Kele (St. Lucia), Confo (Guyana), Winti, Kejawen and Inderjaal (Surinam). The well-known Rastafaria is a new model of religion, created in the roots of Caribbean slavery, indentured labour, neo-colonialism, with significant survivals from West Africa. The East Indians and Chinese came for work and created a new life style and religions.

Common to all of them was emergence in a multicultural and multireligious world, rootedness in the backwardness of life, and suppression by Christians, Whites, and owners. These religions show us the local invention of rites of passage (Platvoet 1995). They show not only an Africanisation of Christianity was launched but also a *creolisation* of religion and religions, even in the Hindu and Muslim frameworks. These peoples also constructed new life styles through code switching and choosing new loyalties by adapting, assimilating, and integrating between old and new, themselves and the others. This experience is captured in the proverb "*Gado no meki ala finga langa wan fasi: ala finga no langa a srefi.*" It is in Sranantongo, the new language of the slaves in Surinam, and it means that "God makes all fingers different with various lengths." Not uniformity but diversity was the principle. Another constitutive proverb is "*Gado sabi fu san a no gi asi tutu*": "only God knows why he did not give horses horns." That means that life is full of mysteries, the Mystery of life.

The Caribbean, as a colonial construction, began with the destructive policies of the owners of Europe. It was a "development project" by European, Christian, white people—the polar opposite of the locals, with their own identity and authenticity, with their worldview, gods and prayers, myths, songs, and proverbs. That world was for them made hard by poverty, the sea, the jungles, the rains, and hurricanes, but also marked the overwhelmingly beautiful flora, the calls of exotic birds and glorious beaches. Thus it was a life tinged forever with a perennial nostalgia.

Traditionally different kinds of religion are distinguished: primal, animistic, particularistic, universalistic, monotheistic, and polytheistic religions. These distinctions are useful but not adequate in the specific situation of the Caribbean. All these kinds are present but another issue is fundamental (Babu 1998; Balutansky-Souriau 1998; Kokot 2004; Maynard 2000). This is the violence of slavery, indentured labour and neo-colonialism introduced structurally or institutionally in combination with religion. The peoples were overwhelmed by European religious power from abroad. Peoples from Africa and Asia came with their own religions into this diasporic situation that shaped them into new phenomena. Some scholars have characterized this encounter by calling it syncretism; others are trying to create new notions, specific for the diasporic and post-colonial situation (Collier-Fleischmann 2003; Gates 1980; Gossai-Murrell 2000). Worth noting here is the theologian of Surinamese Lutheran origin, Sonny Hof, who reflected on the issue of violence and liberation for his inaugural lecture as professor at the Lutheran Seminary in Amsterdam. Later on the *liber amicorum* offered to him at the occasion of his retirement is entitled *Liberation and Freedom*. These concepts are key notions in the Surinamese and Caribbean context, in both the political and the religious and theological fields. In Caribbean history we can recognize the rituals of confrontation and symbiosis, of continuity and discontinuity, in the ups and downs of life, in the togetherness and the feeling of belonging (Wielzen 2005, Platvoet 1999). In the Caribbean creating religions and opting for launching new churches are commonplace. Peoples draw upon their cultural and religious heritages to do this. There are examples such as *Mariannam* (Hindu, South India), *Id ul fitr* or *Bada* (Muslim: Arabic and Javanese, respectively), *Divali* and *Holi Phagwa* (Hindu, India), *kra tafra* (Winti, Surinam), *Epakadono* (Kaliña, Surinam for burial and mourning), *puru blaka* (Sranantongo for ceremonies after a year of mourning), the Asiatic Marriage Law. It is a mixture of religion, politics, strategy, communication, and performance. The same can be found also in the trade unions, the political parties, communications and relationships. The model of unity in diversity is predominant. It is evident in contradictions as the juxtaposition of *cross* and *calabash* in the churches, symbols of Christianity and African religious traditions.

The Terminology of "creolisation"

Andrew Pearse, writing on the cultures and religions of Trinidad in 1956, was one of the first scholars to use the concept of *creolisation* in this way:

> Thus a type of rural life established itself in which law and custom, the African drum and the fiddle, the country doctor and the bush healer, the Catholic liturgy and the cults of Yorubaland and Dahomey, school English and patois, lived side by side in easy accommodation, and a dual acculturative process took its course—creolisation, and accommodation to the institutions and standards of the superstructure (Pearse 1971).

For Pearse *creolisation* is an element of an acculturative reconfiguration, tending to a structural basis. The noun *creolisation* was used in linguistics to denote the various results of the meeting of two or more languages in special circumstances, creating new ways of communication and relationship by new use of words and language. Thus the new language of Sranantongo in Suriname is the creolised product of the meeting or confrontation of languages like some West African languages like Akan, Twi, and Ewe, with European languages such as Dutch, Yiddish, and Portuguese, a process that began with enslavement on the coasts of West Africa and continued onto the plantations in Surinam. This language is completely different from the developments in another Dutch colony in the Caribbean, the Dutch Antilles with Aruba, and Curaçao, where the creolisation of languages resulted in Papiamento. In Surinam the word "Creole" refers to the descendants of the union between the (ex)enslaved Africans and those of European origin. This is in contrast to the "Maroon," a slave who fled from the plantations into the bush in the interior, and who built there a new society and a new people along the rivers. "Creole" has a long tradition dating back to the time of slavery, and originally used for all new things in the colony: pigs, calves, horses, vegetables, as well as human beings. Europeans used the term generally for all peoples other than themselves. "Negerhollands" was the term used in the former Danish islands of the Caribbean (St. Croix, St. John, St. Thomas), although earlier such people were called "Carriols," "Cariolisch," "Criolisch" and finally "Creolisch" (Rossem & Van der Voort 1996). The Surinamese sociologist of religion, Harold Jap a Joe (Moravian) used the concept to *creolise* in his reflection on nationalism and pentecostalism: "Christianity was not accepted in its European form. It was interpreted according to the world-view prevalent in the inter-African syncretism, and became creolised" (Jap A Joe 2001).

The philosophical concept of *creolisation* was extensively promoted when Jean Bernabé, Patrick Chamoiseau and Raphaël Confiant published their *Éloge de la Creolité* (Bernabé et al. 1989). These three writers and scholars from the French West Indies had been embued with the concept of *négritude*, the call for recognition of the black people in the Caribbean and West Africa. Writers and poets such as Aimé Césaire (Martinique), Léopold Sendar Senghor (Senegal), and Léon Gontran Damas (Guyane) were the source of this concept, and many others followed them. The new generation of Bernabé, Chamoiseau and Confiant wanted move beyond the idea of back to Africa and of the Black power movement. They preferred to emphasize the new situation and life construction in the Caribbean, creating in the midst of new—albeit largely negative—life conditions there. For them, the future was more important than the negative past. Moreover, they wished to focus on the localisation of life and on the creativity of people concerning culture, language and religion. They wrote: "Altogether different is the process of Creolization, which is not limited to the American continent" (Bernabé, 1992, p.92). For these writers, the idea of *antillianité* (limited to the Antillian region) was also a forerunner of the concept as was *creoleness* (the consciousness to be a new human being and not only an African descendant), and can be seen as a phase in the development of the concept of *creolisation*.

The Role of Edouard Glissant

The godfather of the new set of ideas was the Martinican philosopher and writer Edouard Glissant. Central to his thought is the concept of relation, especially relation to *tout le monde*, everybody (Glissant). It has to be seen in the context and history of the making of the Caribbean by slavery and the aftermath of slavery and colonialism that so marks the Caribbean. For him, however, *creolisation* has to be a world movement. For Glissant and the group around him, the Caribbean person and all humanity have to seek their identity in diversity. A key concept in Glissant's philosophical work is *diversalité*: the opposite of uniformity and monomy and monotomy, the recognition of the value of diversity

of cultures, colours and history. The experience of the Caribbean with its fragmented, segmented societies makes this idea an appropriate one.

Glissant uses the metaphor of the mangrove: living in water yet looking for
the coast, with roots reaching to the coast. The peoples of the Caribbean came
by ships under bad conditions. The sea is their history and their experience of
the *jahi* system along the way is for them still vivid: people travelling together
on the same ship for months became related for a lifetime, in ways more important and deeper than family blood ties. Glissant, brought up in a French colonial
sphere, pleads for authentic identity for all, against either Euro-centrism or
Afro-centrism. He is looking for a new world like that other Caribbean thinker
Caryl Phillips from St. Kitts, who places a strong emphasis on belonging, the
'high anxiety' of belonging (Phillips).

After a decade of discussion the concept of *creolisation* was expanded to the
entirety Caribbean, to include peoples of Asian descent, among whom the movement of *coolietude*—promoting the culture and religion of the East Indians
(Hindus, Christians, and Muslims) in the French Antilles—had emerged. The
movement of *creolisation* was to be seen as characteristic of a new world order in
the sense of openness and communication leading to continuous transformation,
of people expanding their own boundaries, like the Caribbean people did and continued to do. The movement stipulates the need for universalism in diversity, a life
for everyone everywhere in the world. That means a change in the old world, the
whole world. So the concept of *creolisation* can be both a crowbar and even an
handhold: a political concept for a new order of togetherness. By contrast,
Glissant shows that Europe and also the United States of America are in a process
of archipelagoisation: splitting into regions more focused on their own regional
culture and development. Cross-fertilization is to be the name of the game.

Glissant and the men of *creolité* attest to the fact that words are crucial in
life. The first time those who had been enslaved heard a word was after the
abolition of slavery, a dehumanizing institution. The first word was a word of
liberation. Words could thus be victimized and at the same time be holy. Word
entails relation, the other, and a new world of life. For these writers and philosophers word leads to a creation of a new humankind, whereby they for the first
time live in relation. Relation is revelation of the mystery of life, of God. From
that moment the enslaved created their own world, a new world. Creation
became *creolisation* in that the new man had to deal with a lot of worlds of difference. They started a process, the first of many processes of hermeneutics in
public, with words of recognition. That opens the way to a new epistemology.
Creolisation means for them a new listening and hearing of words and the
Word, a new relation to the diverse world. Everybody is the other, which means
that every relation is a mixture (*métissage*). Words are new worlds of the other
world of men. Languages are worlds of diversity. Crucial to their thinking is
the notion of diversity, *diversalité*. Words in monologue are impossible.

The first words to be heard by the slaves were words of white people, of the churches. The experience of the creative word deepens the memory but also the future. The languages of the colonials are missing the words of the enslaved, are handicapped by the absence of the voice of the minority, the powerless. The promotors of *creolité* (and new notions like *créoliphony, caribbeanitude, mulattitude* and *créolitude*) are promoting an openness to the whole world, *tout le monde*: the other is me. So *creolisation* also means revelation, creation of communication, respect for the otherness of the other, not only in words. Univocity is impossible in that specific framework. Liberation means the liberation of the word, the language, both logistic and the thematic. Words are always words of liberation: words in another sense are nonsense (Chanson 2002).

Creolisation is not only an interesting linguistic issue, but also an anthropological, sociological and theological one as well, avoiding colonial clichés and labels. It means relation, exchange, interaction, cross-fertilisation, and interculturality. Not only those receiving are changing but also those who speak: with two poles, both of them are changing. Diversity is on the way of *creolisation*, a moment of creation of hearing, listening that in the past the world of the enslaved was suppressed.

The Caribbean is more than the history and future of the enslaved. That history created an Indo-Caribbean, an *alakondre* (all countries) people, that includes indigenous spirituality, the Javanese *kejawen* and elements of *inderjaal* of the Hindustanis. This richness is the essential challenge to the *creolisation* of life in specific circumstances. The peoples founded and created for themselves rites of passage. At the same time there is the risk of *creolism*, making *creolisation* into a dogma, an institution. *Creolisation*, by way of contrast, emphasizes the dynamic impact of culture, exchange and the value of otherness.

Theological Appropriation of Creolisation

The champion for doing theology on the basis of these new concepts is the Swiss scholar and pastor Philippe Chanson with an experience of many years in the French Caribbean (Chanson 2003). His starting point for doing theology is his reference to the philosophical ideas of people around the concept of creolisation, *créolité*. He draws a parallel between the creation of God and the creation of new relations between human beings, especially between those who have been enslaved and exploited, as were the peoples of the Caribbean. Chanson recognized the dubious role of the Christian churches in the times of slavery and indentured labour. He understands the conflicts and struggles of writers and scholars with this history and their aversion concerning religion and church. He called the churches to try to understand the mind of the Caribbean man and to act according to this history and future avoiding the hegemony of European Christianity and religious feelings and expressions.

The creation of the new words for a new theology is basic for doing theology according to Philippe Chanson. That means a change of theology and ecclesiogenesis in the Caribbean. Doing theology with these starting points and perspectives has to do with a sort of theology of liberation on both sides: the victims and the transgressors, the Caribbean man and the rest of the world. It means the starting point of theology is the reflection on the life situation of all people of *creolisation*, opening ways of life for all. *Creolisation* is not only the fact that people in the Caribbean combine different sources, but it is also a prospect for the future: people everywhere in this world will increasingly combine and mix. Once again using the metaphor of the mangrove: roots in water to the land, reclaiming land from the sea. That is necessary in the ecological systems of the tropical areas and islands, a little unpredictable, but vivid. So is life, words, relations, liberation and extension.

Global Perspectives

Doing theology in the Caribbean means looking simultaneously through the windscreen and the rear window, forwards and back, and even turning round: constructing rituals and inventing rituals. The process of *creolisation* is not intended only for the South. Neglecting processes of *creolisation* in the North, where so many people of the South now reside, means passing up the possibilities for in-depth growth. Caribbean people are living in the metropolises of USA, Canada, Great Britain, France, the Netherlands, at home all over the world. That is a sign of creation and way of liberation, a strong appeal for reshaping and re-designing humankind and the world, the entirety of God's creation. Concepts of salvation and the like have to be reconsidered. *Creolisation* requires a global vision both in strategy and in content: a new concept and way of doing theology, with everyone participating, everyone speaking and responding. Doing theology will require an overtaking manoeuvre and looking in the driving mirror to reconsider issues such as the nature of humanity, human rights, and holistic creation in a new order. In dialogue, it will involve deconstructing unnameable and unnecessary boundaries. The movement for *creolisation* is asking us to be quite careful with words, the Word, as creating relation, communication, a new world dealing with others. It is a hell of a job, but essential and constitutive.

In this new approach of theology, ecclesiology is as yet barely in focus. Perhaps it is a part of the new road, and only in perspective. Also lacking is the contact with the peoples struggling for survival in their always dependent world as porters and servants to the rich tourists on the sunny beaches and playas, not familiar with the sometimes the new high-brow notions and concepts. A real challenge is to embed the *creolisation* notion in universal theology and especially in pastoral theology and the theology of religions, in the face of the new World, in sight of the Word. The component of recognition is vivid in concepts of the new approach, as is also the fight for identity and authenticity. That is extremely valuable for peoples in the Caribbean, brought together under dehumanising circumstances. It is a glory that they are fighting for life, with new concepts and ideas. We have to appreciate the struggle of Caribbean people, outside the traditional churches, to find new concepts for a better understanding of themselves and others, by way of a philosophy and theology in context and on the local level. Producing religion and also theology means witnessing of the truth. It is honest and proper that theologians of other parts of the world give support and aid. Their presence is long overdue and they owe a debt there. The Caribbean is a seedbed for new thinking, a nursery for peoples all over the world.

References

Augustus, E., Julien, T. & Graham, R. (eds) 1973. *Issues in Caribbean theology*, Port of Spain: Antilles Pastoral Institute.

Balutansky, K. & Souriau, M.-A. (eds) 1998. *Caribbean creolisation: reflections on the cultural dynamics of language, literature, and identity.* Gainesville, FL: University Press.

Bebel-Gisler, D. & Hurbon, L. 1975. *Cultures et pouvoir dans la Caraïbe*. Paris: L'Harmattan.

Bernabé, J., Chamoiseau, P. & Confiant, R. 1989, *Éloge de créolité*. Paris: Gaillimard. (Translated in English *In praise of creoleness*, 1993.)

Bisnauth, D. 1989. *History of religions in the Caribbean*. Kingston: Kingston Publishers.

Caldecott, A. 1970. *The church in the West Indies*. London: Frank Cass & Co. (Reprint of 1898).

Casas, B. de las. 1578. *Brévissima relacion de la destruccion de las Indas occidentales*. In Dutch, *Kort relaas van de verwoesting van de West-Indische landen*. Amsterdam: Arbeiderspers. 1969.

Chanson, P. 1993. From the Creole God to the God of Jesus. *Exchange* (Journal of Missiological and Ecumenical Research) 22(1): p.18–45.

Chanson, P. 1997. *Identité et Diversalité. Complexité anthropologique et complexité christologique. L'apport créole*. Institut œcuménique de Bossey, Céligny.

Chanson, P. 2002. *La Créolité antillaise, avènement de la Parole métisse*. Louvain: Université Catholique de Louvain.

Chanson, P. 2005. Creolite and theology of Creolite in the French West Indies. *Exchange* (Journal of Missiological Research) 34(4): p.291–305.

Collier, Gordon & Ulrich Fleischmann (ed.), 2003, *A Pepper-Pot of Cultures. Aspects of Creolization in the Caribbean*, Matatu, Journal for African Culture and Society.

Dayfoot, A. 1999. *The shaping of the West Indian Church 1492–1962*. Gainesville: University Press of Florida.

Durizot, J.-B. 2001. *Cultures et strategies dans le Caribe*. Paris: L'Harmattan.

Gates, B. 1980. *Afro-Caribbean religions*. London: Ward Lock Educational.

Gregory, H. 1995. *Caribbean theology: preparing for the challenges ahead*. Kingston: United Theological College of the West Indies.

Glissant, E. 1981. *Le discours antillais*.

Glissant, E. 1990. *Poétique de la relation*.

Glissant, E. 1993, *Tout-monde*.

Glissant, E. 1996. *Introduction à une Poétique du Divers*.

Gossai, H. & Murrell, N. 2000. *Religion, culture, and tradition in the Caribbean*. New York: St. Martin's Press.

Hamid, I. 1971. *In search of new perspectives*. Bridgetown: Caribbean Ecumenical Consultation for Development.

Hurbon, L. (ed). 2000. *Le phénomène religieux dans la Caraïbe*. Paris: Karthala.

Jap A Joe, H. 2001. *Nationalism and pentecostalism in Suriname: two sides of the same coin*. Paper, Pretoria, July.

Jenkins, P. 2002. *The next Christendom: the coming of global Christianity*. Oxford: Oxford UP.

Kokot, W., et al. (eds), 2004. *Diaspora, identity and religion*. London: Routledge.

Lampe, A. 1991. *Descubrir a Dios en el Caribe: ensayos sobre la historia de la iglesia*. San José: DEI.

Lampe, A. (ed). 2001. *Christianity in the Caribbean. Essays on Church History*. Kingston: University of the West Indies Press.

Maynard-Reid, P. 2000. *Diverse worship: African-American, Caribbean & Hispanic Perspectives*. Downers Grove, IL: Intervarsity Press.

Pearse, A. 1971. Carnival in nineteenth century Trinidad. (In Horowitz, M. (ed), *Peoples and cultures of the Caribbean: an anthropological reader*. New York: Natural History Press. p. 528–552.)

Phillips, C. 2002. *A new world order*. New York: Vintage.

Phillips, C. 2000. *The Atlantic song*. Dutch translation: *Het Atlantisch lied*. Amsterdam: De Bezige Bij.

Platvoet, J. 1995. *Pluralism and identity: studies in ritual behavior*. Leiden: Brill.

Platvoet, J. 1999. *Defining the pragmatics of defining religion contexts, concepts, and contests*. Leiden: Brill.

Premdas, R. (ed). 1999. *Identity, ethnicity and culture in the Caribbean*. St. Augustine, Trinidad and Tobago: University of the West Indies.

Rossem, C. & Van der Voort, H. (eds). 1996. *Die Creol Taal: 250 years of Negerhollands texts*. Amsterdam: Amsterdam UP.

Sankerali, B. (ed). 1994. *At the crossroads: African Caribbean religion and Christianity*. Trinidad & Tobago: Cariflex.

Smeralda-Amon, J. 2002. *La racisation des relations intergroupes ou la problématique de la couleur: la cas de la Martinique*. Paris: L'Harmattan.

Taylor, P. (ed). 2001. *Nation dance: religion, identity, and cultural difference in the Caribbean*. Bloomington: Indiana UP.

Wielzen, D. 2005. Popular religiosity as an internal dynamic for the local church: the case of Suriname. *Exchange* 34(1): p.2–21.

Williams, L. 1996. *The Caribbean: enculturation, acculturation and the role of the Churches*. Geneva: WCC Publication. Gospel and Cultures, Pamphlet 10.

Henri Gooren

Pentecostal Conversion Careers in Latin America

Jenkins shows that the center of Christianity is shifting from north to south. Pentecostal churches constitute the fastest growing group of churches in Christianity today, already representing a quarter of all Christians worldwide. However, Jenkins tends to equate conversion with recruitment and ignores the huge drop-out rates. Hence, I use the conversion career approach to analyze people's involvement in Pentecostal churches in Latin America. I first deal with the Pentecostal conversion careers in Latin America. Since conversion is often only a temporal phase of affiliation, a subsequent section deals with disaffiliation to Pentecostalism. I end with a conclusion.

The image of Southern Christianity that Jenkins (2002) presents is not always one that Pentecostals in Africa or Latin America will recognize themselves in. Here I aim to present a more balanced picture of Southern Christianity by concentrating on the case of Latin American Pentecostalism. I analyze people's involvement in various Pentecostal churches in Latin America through the use of the *conversion career* approach.[1] The conversion career includes all episodes of higher or lower involvement in one or more religious organizations during a person's lifetime.

In this article the emphasis is on Pentecostal conversion careers in Latin America, based on case studies from Chile, Brazil, Argentina, Nicaragua, Guatemala, Mexico, and Costa Rica. The central question is: *What are the crucial factors that may cause people in Latin America to become active in a Pentecostal church at a certain stage of their lives?* During a person's life, these differing levels of religious activity are influenced by social, cultural, institutional, personality, and contingency factors. A final building block of the conversion careers approach is a careful distinguishing between the five main phases of a person's life cycle: childhood, adolescence, marriage, midlife, and old age. The varying levels of religious involvement during the life cycle of people should be identified and studied systematically in many different cultural contexts.

The structure of this article is as follows. First, I sketch the contours of the conversion careers approach. Next I take a brief look at Pentecostal conversion

---

1   For a detailed elaboration of the conversion career approach, see Droogers *et al.* (2003) and Gooren (2005, 2006a, 2006b).

careers in Latin America. Drop-outs and disaffiliation are often ignored in the literature, or not analyzed systematically. Hence, a section on Pentecostal disaffiliation will prove very helpful here. The conclusion weighs the importance of the types of factors mentioned above by relating the case studies to the different levels of religious participation in the conversion career. What picture arises from these cases of Southern Christianity—in particular Southern Pentecostalism—when compared to Jenkins (2002)?

Jenkins: A New Christendom?

Pentecostal churches constitute the fastest growing group of churches in Christianity today, increasing at the rate of 19 million each year (Jenkins, 2002, p.63). (Neo) Pentecostal churches in all their diversity already represent a quarter of all Christians worldwide (Anderson, 2004, p.1). The vast majority of these Pentecostals live in Africa and Latin America. Philip Jenkins' influential book *The Next Christendom* (2002) convincingly shows that the center of Christianity is shifting from north to south. His book presents a wealth of statistical data on the worldwide growth of Christianity, using as years of reference 1900, 1950, 1975, and 2000, and making bold projections into the years 2015, 2025 and 2050.

From a social science perspective, Jenkins is to be commended for his non-judgmental treatment of the heterogeneous forms of Southern Christianity, including its emphases on personal faith, miracles, spiritual healing, visions, dreams, and prophesying. On the other hand, *The Next Christendom* could also be considered sensationalist and unbalanced. Its use of statistics is exaggerated and its projections into the far future are controversial if not meaningless. There are too many unknown variables to put much faith in extrapolations of current trends into the year 2050—or even 2025. The book is full of sweeping statements and crass generalizations, sometimes making a one-sided use of the available literature. Let me give a few examples.

Jenkins often uses terms like "global Christianity" or "global Islam", which are highly problematic. Each world religion consists of many different currents, which are often engaged in fierce rivalry or competition for members. Even within Latin America, the existing global networks of Pentecostals, whether from the ecumenical CLAI or the neo-Pentecostal mega-churches, are limited to a minority. Pentecostal churches in Latin America and Africa may share some characteristics, but they have little or no contacts between each other.

The book devotes much attention to Pentecostalism, but turns it into a huge essentialized category. Most researchers, however, stress the heterogeneity within Pentecostalism and how it constantly escapes our definitions (Anderson 2004; Martin 2002). Jenkins treats Pentecostalism, together with the African Initiated

Churches, either as a synonym of, or as one big subcategory within, Southern evangelical Christianity.

Perhaps a particular strength of Pentecostalism is its umbrella quality, allowing it to be filled up by multiple local–and locally relevant—churches. But rather than looking at all-encompassing categories, as Jenkins does in his book, it makes more sense to study the wealth and diversity of the myriad local expressions of Pentecostalism. What does it mean to be a poor Pentecostal in Buenos Aires, Lagos, Manila or Guatemala City? What is the relevance of miracles, healings, dreams, visions, and prophesying for them? In fairness, Jenkins also deals with this issue, but he remains too much on the surface and his choice of church cases is not always convincing.[2]

Jenkins' treatment of Pentecostalism in Latin America is oddly unbalanced, with Mexico and Brazil getting most attention. In Brazil, the only church treated extensively (Jenkins, 2002, p.64–67, 206, 208) is the Universal Church of the Kingdom of God (IURD). Many specialists consider this a syncretistic hybrid of folk Catholicism and popular Pentecostalism; some do not even consider it Pentecostal. Persecution of Catholic progressives by Pentecostal dictator Ríos Montt during the Guatemalan civil war is depicted in sensationalist words: "In terms of interdenominational bloodshed, Guatemala in the 1980s looked a little like France or Germany in the 1580s" (Jenkins, 2002, p.157).[3] Few Guatemalans will agree.

Conversion to Christianity is accepted as an unproblematic given throughout the book, although Jenkins (2002, p.39) refers to more sophisticated views of conversion by Hefner (1993) and Rambo (1993). Writing about the millions of Christians in Africa and Latin America, however, Jenkins tends to use conversion simply as a synonym for affiliation. When people join a church, they are "converted" to that church. What happens after that remains a mystery— especially considering that most churches in the South do not keep membership records.[4] Many scholars have demystified the huge Pentecostal growth rates by pointing out the equally huge drop-out rates.[5] Church recruitment is an ongoing process, during which various levels of commitment (affiliation, conversion, etc.) can be discerned.

---

2   Jenkins' new book, *The New Faces of Christianity: Believing the Bible in the Global South*, will go deeper into this issue.

3   Sweeping statements suggesting global religious warfare also abound in Chapter 8 on Islam, entitled "The Next Crusade," which Karel Steenbrink analyzes in this volume.

4   During my recent fieldwork in Nicaragua, for instance, I was surprised to learn that only some of the new Neo-Pentecostal churches and a few of the historical Protestant churches kept membership records.

5   On Pentecostal drop-out rates in Latin America, see, e.g., Bowen (1996), Gómez (1998), and Gooren (forthcoming).

Seeing conversion as a process also helps to understand and analyze the more exotic elements of Southern Christianity: miracles, healings, dreams, visions, and prophesying. These do not always come together as a complete package. People discover them during their recruitment process and make their own emphases from the available repertoire of Pentecostal products. Hence, it makes more sense to speak of people's conversion careers, which is what I shall use as a tool to analyze people's involvement in Pentecostal churches in Latin America.

Conversion Careers: A New Approach to Religious Activity

The *conversion career* is defined as "the member's passage, within his or her social and cultural context, through levels, types and phases of church participation" (Droogers et al., 2003, p.5–6).[6] It represents a systematic attempt to analyze shifts in individual levels of religious activity. Four essential elements of the approach are: the conceptualization of individual dissatisfaction, a five-level typology of religious activity, the need for a life cycle approach, and the many factors influencing changes in individual religious activity.

The conversion career approach will not attempt to locate the basis of conversion at either the level of the individual, the (religious) organization, or society at large—as most sociological approaches have done in the past. Instead, it will identify the factors operating at each of these three meta-levels and pay special attention to their *interconnectedness*. Conversion could be viewed as a way to break out of old social roles and embrace new ones. This never happens in a social or cultural vacuum, of course, and every individual conversion is unique. However, scholars must always attempt to identify both the patterns and the local variations.

Another essential part of the conversion careers approach is to develop a typology of religious activity that includes more dimensions than just disaffiliation and conversion. Based on literature from psychology, social and cultural anthropology, sociology, and theology, I selected five levels of individual religious activity (Gooren 2006a):

Pre-affiliation is the term used here to describe the worldview and social context of potential members of a religious group in their first contacts to assess whether they would like to affiliate themselves on a more formal basis. Some Christian churches use terms like "visitor" or "investigator" instead; sociologists of religion sometimes use the term "seeker."

---

6   My use of conversion career (Gooren 2005, 2006a) is different from Richardson (1978), who coined the term.

Affiliation refers to being a formal member of a religious group. However, group membership does not form a central aspect of one's life or identity.

Conversion used here in the limited sense refers to a (radical) personal change of worldview and identity. It is based both on self-report and on attribution by others: people from the same religious group and also outsiders.

Confession is a term from theology for a core member identity, involving a high level of participation inside the new religious group and a strong "missionary attitude" towards non-members outside of the group.

Disaffiliation refers to a lack of involvement in an organized religious group. This category may include various types. It can refer to an idiosyncratic personal religiosity, e.g., New Age. But it can also stand for an unchurched religious identity: either an apostate rejecting a former membership or an inactive member who still self-identifies as a believer. In the last case, the difference between affiliation and disaffiliation can be very small.

Since changes in the level of religious activity may occur throughout the entire lifespan of people, a life cycle approach obviously becomes necessary. However, most of the literature on religious change (probably ninety percent or more; see Gooren 2006a) deals with conversion during adolescence. Hence it is imperative that a more systematic approach should distinguish the various levels of religious activity during the various phases of people's lives. At the very least, the different aspects and dynamics of five phases of the life cycle should be differentiated: childhood, adolescence, marriage, midlife, and old age. These phases will be operationalized both in terms of age and life phase (e.g., a teenager couple with children would be in the "marriage" stage).

Finally, the many different factors influencing religious change should be identified, operationalized, weighed, and analyzed. I will identify five main groups of factors influencing changes in the individual level of religious activity:

Personality factors, relating to the self and personality traits.

Social factors: e.g., the influence of social networks of relatives, friends or acquaintances on changes in religious activity. Another example is the influence of other church members through socialization and role teaching. This factor is stressed especially in various conversion models by sociologists of religion, together with institutional factors.

Institutional factors deal with dissatisfaction with the current religious group and the impact of the new group. How does it compete with other groups on a religious market by using its attractive elements (e.g., beliefs, doctrine, rules, and organization)? What are the group's recruitment methods? How does it socialize and discipline its new members?

Cultural factors involve the influence on changes in individual religious activity of culture in a broad sense (i.e., including political and economic factors). Social/cultural anthropologists have obviously given special attention to these factors.

Contingency factors: situational events, random meetings with representatives of a certain religious group, an acutely felt crisis, stressful situations, natural disasters, etc.

The next section gives an overview of theories on Pentecostal growth in Latin America. Subsequent sections analyze Pentecostal conversion careers in Latin America in detail, including the phenomenon of disaffiliation or desertion.

Theorizing Pentecostal Growth in Latin America

Only thirty years ago, most countries in Latin America had a population that was 95 to 98 percent Catholic, while Protestants rarely made up more than 2 percent. Nowadays, the population percentage of Catholics is usually in the 70–85 percent range. The percentage of Protestants has increased correspondingly from an average of about 2.5 percent in 1970 to about 12 percent in 2000 (Barrett et al. 2001; Martin 1990; Johnstone & Mandryk 2001). Pentecostals form the overwhelming majority of Protestants in all countries;[7] most people going to church on Sunday are nowadays Pentecostal. Meanwhile, many active Catholics (in some countries even the majority) are nowadays members of the Charismatic Renewal movement, which also emphasizes the Holy Spirit and personal discipline.

Pentecostalism had its first successes in Chile, Brazil, and Peru in the 1960s and (early) 1970s. Panama should be included here, too.[8] Soon after, a Pentecostal boom followed in Guatemala between 1976 and 1986 and in Costa Rica, El Salvador, Honduras, and Nicaragua in the 1980s. In Argentina, the Pentecostal boom started in the 1980s and continued into the 1990s. The latest Pentecostal boom in Latin America started in the 1990s in Venezuela, Paraguay, and Bolivia and seems to continue until today. By contrast, in most of the other countries, Pentecostal growth seems to have leveled off or stagnated.[9] Only a few countries have not experienced a Pentecostal boom at all.[10]

The early literature on Pentecostal growth in Latin America stressed socioeconomic factors like (failing) industrialization and urbanization (cf. Jenkins,

---

7   According to Chesnut (2003, p.8), Pentecostals make up 75 percent of the Protestant population in Latin America.

8   Based on the statistics in Barrett *et al.* (2001) and Johnstone & Mandryk (2001).

9   Barrett *et al.* (2001); Gooren (2001); Johnstone & Mandryk (2001); Steigenga (2001).

10   Barrett *et al.* (2001); Johnstone & Mandryk (2001). For different reasons, Colombia (which remains strongly Roman Catholic) and Mexico (with a clear separation of church and state) remained over 90 percent Catholic. The data on Ecuador and the Dominican Republic are contradictory (ibid.). Uruguay is quite a unique case, with 25–30 percent unchurched people, only 50 percent Catholics, and 5 percent Protestants. For obvious reasons, Cuba is also a special case: 30–35 percent non-religious, 40 percent Catholic, and 5 percent Protestant.

2002, p.72–73), which were supposed to bring urban migrants to Pentecostal churches to find a closely-knit community to ward off Durkheimian anomie (Roberts 1968). Willems (1967) and Kessler (1967) stressed democratic and egalitarian tendencies in Pentecostalism. Lalive (1969) and Bastian (1994), however, saw in authoritarian Pentecostal pastors who dominate submissive members a reflection of the clientelistic power relations of the hacienda. The problem with these structural explanations is that they specify the socio-cultural *context*, but not why people joined specifically the Pentecostal churches (cf. Droogers 2001, Gooren 2001a).

Some authors saw in the growth of Pentecostalism a conspiracy of the Reagan administration and the CIA (Dominguez 1984; Huntington 1984a, 1984b; Valderrey 1985). The so-called "invasion of the sects" was commonly denounced by various Latin American Bishops' Conferences, complaining that North American evangelical groups and Mormons were "buying" members by offering material benefits. This practice is sometimes called *lámina por ánima* (roof plates for souls), but little evidence has been recorded (Cantón 1998; Stoll 1990). Studies show that buying members is only effective for the short term—i.e., until the gifts run out—and that people only stay in a new church when they feel it enriches their lives spiritually. If the church fails to do so, they will simply drop out—as many have done (see the section on disaffiliation below). Hence, the conversion career concept seems more appropriate than seeing conversion as a radical, once-in-a-lifetime change in identity (Droogers *et al.* 2003; Gooren 2006a).

In the 1980s, actor-oriented approaches started to become more common. These stressed that people joined Pentecostal groups because they found something there that was unique and helped them cope with personal and household problems in their daily lives (Brusco 1995; Chesnut 1997; Gooren 1999; Mariz 1994). Only rarely do authors stress the unique religious beliefs and practices that Pentecostalism offers (Droogers *et al.* 2003; Martin 2002; Míguez 1997). Pentecostalism allows for strong participation with room for emotional release. Important attractions are the charismata of the Holy Spirit: speaking in tongues, prophesying, and faith healing. These are not only solutions to personal problems (Jenkins 2002), but also spiritual resources in their own right, giving meaning and relevance to people's lives (Chesnut 2003; Gooren 1999; Míguez 1997).

Pentecostal Conversion Careers in Latin America

With the advent of the actor-oriented approaches, more first-hand conversion stories became available. Still, only a few authors actually write out the full conversion stories of their informants (e.g., Brouwer 2000; Burdick 1993; Cantón 1998; Ireland 1991; Míguez 1997). Other scholars report that they collected conversion stories, but they do not actually write them out or they use only tiny fragments of them (e.g., Brusco 1995; Lalive 1969; Mariz 1994). This is regrettable if one wants to identify degrees of religious participation—in short, the person's conversion career.

The first book on Pentecostalism in Latin America contains excerpts from 27 life history interviews with converts in Brazil and Chile (Willems, 1967, p.125–131). In all cases, the informant's initials, age, occupation, marital status, and religious background are mentioned. The only information missing is at what age the actual conversion took place. Almost forty years later, this material is still very rich and the parallels with conversion stories that were collected decades later are very strong. In fact, many of the stories—right down to the phrasings—are identical to the more recent conversion accounts (see below).

Take, for instance, the conversion story of 'H.A.L.', age 78, a street peddler:

> My wife attended services in the local Methodist temple and invited me to join. I refused because I was drunk almost every night. Once in a dream I saw God who invited me to go to church. I went and accepted Christ. I felt that the Lord had forgiven all my sins. When the services were over I felt relief, satisfaction and *gozo*. I gave up drinking and became a different person. Before my conversion I had a violent temper, but now I live in peace [. .]. I have more self-confidence now, work regularly and make more money (Willems, 1967, p.126).

Another typical story is that of 'E.C.G.', an 18-year-old, single woman (Willems, 1967, p.127):

> Grandmother used to take me to a Pentecostal temple, but I had no energy to resist temptations. Afterwards I returned to church to repent but I always fell back into sin. One day I heard the voice of the Lord who told me that all my sins had been forgiven. My heart filled with *gozo* and I was seized by the Holy Spirit. I danced and heard soft voices singing exquisite melodies. I felt carried away to another place of wondrous beauty. When I recovered I found myself kneeling and praying in front of the altar. Immediately all temptations and anxieties ceased. I gave up painting my lips and curling my hair.[. .] When I was fourteen years old I had ear surgery and became almost deaf. After my conversion I took part in a *cadena de oración* (continuous prayer meeting of seven days). During one of these meetings an *hermano* laid hands on my head and gradually my hearing went back to normal (ibid., p.127).

Willems already concludes in this very early study that all converts shared a strong desire to change their lives and that conversion was often connected to miraculous healings happening in their lives (ibid., p.130–1). This will prove to be a recurring theme in the literature.

In another early study on Pentecostalism in Chile, Lalive d'Epinay gives two quotes from conversion stories. He never specifies the age or occupation of these informants. The first informant was converted at the age of fifteen at an open-air campaign:

> The open-air preaching had an influence on me, and one day I felt an inner need to go to a service . . . I felt something happening in me; I felt repentance and began to weep and to ask Him to forgive my sin and transform my life . . . And at the moment my life changed completely,

to such an extent that when I left the church, I felt that everything had changed, that the streets and trees and houses were different . . . everything was new and transformed (1969, p.48).

Unfortunately, this conversion story stands alone, as there is no information on the life of the informant. It shows that conversion happened at very early age (fifteen), which will also prove to be a recurring theme. At the pre-affiliation level, there was an "inner need" to go to a church service. It is also a rare example of recruitment (i.e., affiliation and a later conversion) through an open-air evangelization campaign, stressing the importance of institutional factors.

Like Willems (1967, p.125–126), Lalive (1969, p.204) noted that conversion through healing is very frequent. The contingency factor illness is thus often an important element of the pre-affiliation situation. The second story is told by a Pentecostal pastor in Chile:

> One night . . . a family came looking for me. The mother was quite paralysed in one leg, and they asked me to take her at once to the hospital . . . I said to them: "I know that we, the Pentecostalists, can cure your mother." They would not hear of it, so then I made a bargain with them: "We will mend the lorry, but while we are doing it, the brothers will come and pray. If by the time we are ready to go your mother is cured, will you all agree to be converted to the Lord?" They agreed . . . When the lorry was ready and we picked up the mother in our arms, she gave a cry and moved her leg. She was cured. Since then that family always comes to our services (ibid, p.204–5).

Again, basic personal data on the converts concerned are lacking. The story is evidence of the fact that conversion through healing takes very concrete forms, but how this fits in with the converts' life histories—their conversion careers—cannot be known.

Daniel Míguez (1997) analyzed, as his subtitle indicates, *The making of a Pentecostal identity in a Buenos Aires suburb*. He collected many rich conversion stories, which contain detailed information on the lives of the informants. The first conversion story is told by Victor:

> I was a true Catholic . . . There were neighbours who were Evangelicals and [my grandmother] sent me there . . . So I already had some respect for Evangelicals, a certain appreciation of them. (Victor was already attracted to evangelical TV programs before his conversion, which happened after a dream): I was always looking for God, and . . . I had a very real dream . . . I kept getting smaller. And I knew I was going to disappear, I felt I was disappearing . . . The only thing I could think of was to say: "Lord, take care of me". . .The desire to find God was so great that I read all the Bible . . . Now the Church holds these house meetings . . . Once there was a meeting near my home and a neighbour . . . invited me. . .Seven years ago I went forward here at church and I made my vow of faith . . . I received Christ in my heart, that's where all our life starts. . .I studied, if there was a need to visit people I visited, then I was designated as leader . . . First I was Visitor . . . I traveled on my bicycle . . . Then I was made Area Leader (Miguez, 1997, p.103–106).

Victor's conversion career can be sketched as following. As a child, he respected his evangelical neighbors. During his adolescence, he liked to watch evangelical

TV programs, because he was "always looking for God." This is the pre-affiliation stage. Then he had a supernatural experience in a dream,[11] which seems to have confronted him with his mortality and insignificance. A neighbor invited him to a house meeting of a local Pentecostal church (a clear institutional factor), where he "received Christ in his heart." He became very active in the church, first as a visitor, then as an area leader. In other words: he went from affiliation to conversion to confession in a relatively short time.

The married coupled Horacio and Elba García, who were around fifty, converted in 1987 after experiencing economic hardships for some time. They were suffering from "extreme anxiety and consequent family disruption." Their son Mario said: "We first went to a *curandero*. But the *curandero* offered us no solution . . . Then some family problems started and we resorted to Umbanda . . . I never believed in them [Catholic priests]." Elba, who was living separately from Horacio at that time, said: "Everything happened through television . . . It was the program of pastor Gimenez, and through that message God touched my heart; things started to change. I had the desire to return home."

After this experience, Elba and Horacio gradually became reunited. At a certain stage, about a month and a half after her conversion, Elba decided to "hand in all the medicines to the pastor" and to trust God for her cure: "It wasn't easy, it was not from one day to the other" (Míguez, 1997, p.107–109).

Miguez writes: "Mario's conversion took longer than that of any other family member: he was then 21 and the moral limits—no smoking, dancing, drinking, flirting—and the fear for peer stigmatisation were major deterrents to his conversion. Mario was unemployed and found his present job through a brother in faith. This was at a time when he still was not resolved to join the church and it contributed to his conversion" (1997, p.110). Horacio and Elba became quite active in Church life as Area Leaders. Even though Mario had gone through a period of withdrawal or at least rare participation, shortly after they re-entered church life they were appointed as Area Leaders.

The conversion careers of Horacio and Elba are quite similar. In their pre-affiliation situation, they suffered economic hardship, anxiety, and a divorce (contingency factors). They experimented with a *curandero* (shaman healer), Umbanda, and a Catholic priest—showing they had a religious problem-solving perspective. Elba was touched by Christ through an evangelical TV program (institutional factor). She went to church and Horacio started going with her. Their conversions contributed to their reconciliation; religion turned out to be part of the solution. Their son Mario converted at a later age, after finding a job through a church member (social networks). He was less active for some

---

11   A dream is either a very original contingency factor or—especially for psychoanalysts—part of the personality of the informant.

time, but he became more involved in church life when he was made an Area Leader. The same happened with his parents. As with Victor, Horacio and Elba went quickly from affiliation to conversion to confession.

Manuela Cantón notes that conversion stories are more or less standardized and fulfill three different functions. The conversion testimonies are socializing, didactic, and proselytizing at the same time. The narratives form the basis of the "new spirituality" (1998, p.134). It thus comes as no surprise that Cantón's book, which is subtitled *Protestants, Conversion Discourses, and Politics in Guatemala (1989–1993)* contains detailed conversion stories.

The book also gives due attention to the time before conversion, or pre-affiliation, in the five-tier typology described above. Cantón's informants mention the importance of their strong dissatisfaction with Catholicism, their extreme suffering, family and alcohol problems, illness, and a general dissatisfaction with their lives (1998, p.148–160). Over half of the informants report that the first contact with the church happened through a spouse, relative, friend, neighbor or acquaintance (Cantón, 1998, p.168). Her study thus confirms the importance of institutional, contingency, and social factors in recruitment.

The first conversion story is told by Carlos, who was 46 at that time. He became an alcoholic at fourteen or fifteen and started using marihuana after he joined the army at eighteen. When he had no money to buy drugs, he engaged in armed robbery on the streets of Antigua and Guatemala City. He said he was in prison forty times and his resentment against society grew stronger each time he was there. He went to a Catholic church in Antigua Guatemala and said:

> 'Lord, I believe that you are the son of God; if you exist, change my life, take away this burden from my soul. Lord, I can't take it anymore!'. . . And you know what happened? Nothing happened, absolutely nothing happened! Witchcraft couldn't change my life; human science couldn't change my life; strong literature like Lenin and Marx couldn't change my life.
>
> Something was happening in my life; I didn't understand all of it . . . For the first time I went to an evangelical congregation . . . I went with long hair and a ring in my ear . . . but something stronger than myself touched my heart, it lifted me up and I walked to the platform . . . I threw myself down on the floor and I started to cry. I started to see my life one by one, step by step, everything that was my earlier life. And I told Him: 'Lord, forgive me, if you are more powerful, if you are stronger than the drugs, change me please, take away what I'm feeling in my heart' . . . nobody could change my life, only His holy and powerful gospel (Cantón, 1998, p.189–196; translation mine)

Carlos' dramatic conversion career went from adolescent alcoholism and drug use to crime and a long prison life; a contingency crisis brought on by a combination of social and personality factors. Carlos was violent and full of resentment against society. He looked for solutions in various places—not all religious. God didn't help him in a Catholic church and neither witchcraft nor socialist authors could change his life. However, God touched his heart when he came forward in an evangelical congregation and his life was finally changed. Unfortunately, Cantón tells us nothing of his life in church after his conversion.

Did he remain an active member? Did he preach and give his testimony? We have no information to ascertain his passage from affiliation to conversion to (perhaps) confession.

The second conversion story comes from Roberto, 36, who certainly had a very different life from Carlos. Roberto is a civil engineer, who was in a Jesuit college for thirteen years and a member of Opus Dei for five years. At 25, he made good money as a professional and had a life of "going out, working, traveling, parties and women." He married at 32 and was unfaithful to his wife various times. Roberto said:

> I was anxious, desperate . . . I went to confess to a priest, who said: 'Pray three Our Fathers and one Hail Mary and it's over.' But the spiritual power kept pressing on me. When I talked to a person, he started to talk about the Lord, he told me an impressive testimony . . . That day . . . I opened my heart to Jesus and the spiritual power left at once . . . a friend invited me to go to the congregation of El Shaddai . . . there they prayed for me to receive the baptism of the Holy Spirit. It impressed me, they prayed for me and I felt a fire, electricity over all of my body and that day I prayed in other tongues (Cantón, 1998, p.198–203; translation mine)

After conversion, his marriage became much better and El Shaddai church members cured his wife's leg, one of which was shorter than the other. He goes on to tell that the Lord blessed them with greater prosperity for the past three years.

In Roberto's conversion career, the initial contingency factor—a crisis— did not come from alcohol or poverty, but from moral lapses. One might speculate whether or not his strong feelings of guilt were influenced by his strict Catholic upbringing. An acquaintance gave his testimony and a friend invited him to come to El Shaddai (social factor). He received much attention there, they prayed for him and he received the Holy Spirit (institutional factor). His wife was cured and they live blessed with prosperity, although it is clear that they were never poor. Again, there is no information about his church commitment following his conversion experience, so his passage among various levels of religious activity is impossible to track. The next section describes and analyzes the phenomenon of Pentecostal disaffiliation.

Pentecostal Disaffiliation

Cantón (1998) provides no information on the informants' church commitment following their conversion. However, it is significant that the Pentecostal informants of Míguez (1997) in Buenos Aires were all designated Area Leaders or Visitors soon after their conversion and subsequent baptism into their church. The fact that these Pentecostals went from affiliation to conversion to confession in a relatively short time appears to have strengthened their church commitment, but it is not entirely clear how this process worked.

There are few studies on religious disaffiliation in Latin America. A 2000 survey of over 2,400 Nicaraguans by the Dutch reverend Henk Minderhoud showed that the total Protestant church disaffiliation (or desertion) was 27 percent of all Protestants. Among these ex-Protestants, 8 percent said they had returned to the Catholic Church and 19 percent reported that they did not belong to any religion anymore.[12]

Gómez (1998) contains even more detailed information on disaffiliation in Costa Rica, based on three big surveys in 1989, 1991, and 1994. The total Protestant "apostasy" was 48 percent in 1989 and 53 percent in 1991. The 1989 survey (Gómez, 1998, p.30) showed that among these ex-Protestants, 62 percent had actually returned to the Catholic Church, a full one-third had completely dropped out of any church and six percent had joined the Jehovah's Witnesses or the Mormon Church. Gómez (1998, p.42) reported that the Catholic desertion among those born into Catholicism was 12.5 percent.

Gómez has a very interesting comparison of the main reasons for entering and leaving Protestant churches, based on the 1994 survey. The main reasons for the original conversion were "the desire to become a new creature in Christ" (50 percent), being born into an evangelical family (11 percent), church recruitment through a friend or relative (10 percent), the attraction of evangelical preaching (7 percent), and being healed (6 percent) (1998, p.58–9). The main reasons for dropping out were: not being able to live up to the evangelical moral standards (29 percent), rejection of bad financial management in the Pentecostal church (13 percent), bad conduct of other members (9 percent) or of the pastor (8 percent) (1998, p.75).

The only monograph on religious disaffiliation is Bowen (1996), who studied Mexican Pentecostals. He concluded that "conversion is often a process of encounter and retreat, which only after some time culminates in conversion. Altogether, 54 percent of converts identified one or another crisis in their lives that significantly affected their conversion decision" (Bowen, 1996, p.95).

Typically, Bowen dedicated more attention to why Mexicans *joined* Pentecostalism than to why they dropped out of it. Consider this story by a woman, 37, who converted after seeing a leaflet advertising a Christian film during a campaign:

> I like films of Christ. The first time I went, there was not a film. I felt deceived . . . The pastor invited people to go forward to give themselves to Christ. I did not go . . . After the film next time, he also made the call. I felt embarrassed, but my sister went up, so, with my children, we went up and delivered ourselves to Christ. I did not know anything of Christ. I did not know

---

12   Source: interview with the Rev. Henk Minderhoud, the Dutch director of INDEF (*Instituto Nicaragüense de Evangelización en Fondo* or Nicaraguan Institute for In-Depth Evangelism). Managua, June 15, 2005.

how to study the Bible. After the campaign we stopped attending, but some brothers came to visit us to teach us (1996, p.99).

It is clear that some people may drift into a Pentecostal church after seeing a film or an evangelical TV program, but their continued commitment would seem to depend on finding a community, on receiving support from like-minded people, and above all on receiving attention by other members (for example, being visited by them).

Bowen noticed that one-third of his informants did not identify any specific experience, crisis, or event that triggered their conversion experience. Two-thirds, however, did report the influence of a turning point or crisis (1996, p.90–96). Not surprisingly, alcohol problems were mentioned by 17 percent of the male informants. For 29 percent of female informants, tensions in the family were the main influence. Finally, illness was a factor in conversion for 20 percent of all informants. This applied to 23 percent of all women and 16 percent of all men. It was also true of 25 percent of all Pentecostals.

However, just like growth rates, the desertion rates were also very high in Mexican Pentecostal churches: "68 percent of those baptized in Evangelical churches in the 1980s had dropped out by the end of the decade" (Bowen, 1996, p.225). The general disaffiliation rate in Pentecostal churches was 47 percent, meaning that only a little less than half of all those who once belonged to a Pentecostal church actually stayed in it.

Bowen identified three major reasons for disaffiliation: 1) There is no clear benchmark for salvation in Pentecostalism, "Anxiety might compel some to ever greater . . . commitment, but . . . others are driven to apathy and despair." 2) Evangelicals' high levels of commitment and their repudiation of so much Mexican tradition have inevitably generated a measure of burn-out. 3) The small size of so many congregations and their intense competition for members made difficult and uncertain their capacity to support a pastor, to survive, and hence to nurture the new members they recruit. This organizational precariousness was then compounded by schisms and nasty internal conflicts (1996, p.225–6).

Bowen concludes that the main reasons for disaffiliation were basically the same reasons that attracted people to affiliate themselves to Pentecostalism in the first place. Salvation sometimes proves to be less secure than people had originally hoped, the high levels of commitment and high standards of conduct are difficult to maintain, and the organization of many Pentecostal churches would seem to stimulate schism rather than control it.

Conclusion

First, some methodological remarks which suggest caution in drawing too general conclusions. The available literature is limited and the conversion stories presented here come from seven countries: Chile, Brazil, Argentina, Nicaragua, Guatemala, Mexico, and Costa Rica. I noticed that essential information on the conversion careers of informants was often missing in the literature reviewed here. Sometimes, the informants' age and job were not even specified. Often, the conversion story ended with the recruitment to the new church, leaving open the matter of continued commitment or disaffiliation in the future. Most informants were again—as in the North American literature on religious conversion—adolescents or people in their twenties and thirties.

I follow the conversion careers approach to analyze the many different stories presented in this article. The approach goes beyond the Pauline idea of conversion as a unique and once-in-a-lifetime experience. Hence, the five different levels of religious participation mentioned in the beginning form the basis of my analysis: pre-affiliation, affiliation, conversion, confession, and disaffiliation. These levels proved very helpful to assess the literature. For each level of religious activity, I discuss and analyze various informants whose conversion stories were described. In doing this, I refer to the factors that the approach identifies as essential in the conversion career: social, institutional, cultural, personality, and contingency factors.

During the *pre-affiliation* situation of the informants, the starting factor most informants mention is a contingency factor: a crisis. However, this crisis can be of many different sorts, although all of these touch upon the informant's personality. In the most extreme cases, the crisis involved drug or alcohol problems, often in combination with crime. These crises were related to the informant's social situation (poverty, child labor, absent fathers) or personality (machismo, insecurity). In other cases, the crisis was less extreme and related to illness, divorce or poverty.[13] In one case, it was related to a dream (Victor). In Roberto's case, the crisis was purely moral, caused by his adultery. Whatever its origin, the crisis always caused anxiety (Horacio and Elba), desperation (Carlos), and dissatisfaction with the current (religious) lifestyle.

Important is also that most informants were at this time still adolescents or in their (early) twenties and that all informants couched the crisis—*and its possible solutions!*—in religious terms. Most informants had a nominal Catholic background. A few were active Catholics; some were seekers, always looking for God (e.g., Victor). When the crisis was at its worst, many experimented with different religious solutions: *curanderos* (shaman healers), Umbanda, Catholicism, doctors, or even utopist socialist authors like Marx and Lenin.

A combination of social and contingency factors is decisive in determining which particular church people will *affiliate* with. It could be a chance meeting with missionaries or the influence of a spouse, friend or neighbor, which serve

---

13   See Jenkins (2002, p.72–78) on poverty and on healing (p.124–130).

to establish the first contact with the new church. In some cases, the influence of evangelical TV programs is mentioned. Here institutional factors are important: the activities a religious group employs to recruit new members, either by sponsoring TV programs or by motivating their members to give their testimonies and bring their family and friends to the church. Not surprisingly, churches which put greater emphasis on this—like most Pentecostal churches—generally achieve higher growth.

Social factors are principally responsible for the question of whether or not the informant will decide to actually affiliate him-/herself with a new church (cf. Rambo 1993). Here, most informants mention the importance of receiving the support of the 'brothers' (and sisters, who are grammatically included in the Spanish word *hermanos*). New members need a lot of attention, nurturing, and counseling; this is mentioned in the conversion careers scheme under 'incorporating, creating, and shaping activities' (Long & Hadden 1983; cf. Jenkins, 2002, p.74–76).

I think that the *conversion* is most often successful when the new church is seen as (contributing to) the solution to the original crisis. This can take many forms: the healing of an illness, giving a new purpose and meaning to one's life, overcoming alcohol problems, giving people peace and tranquility. Even getting a job through another church member is often interpreted as a divine sign that conversion is the right choice. For the believers, there is no such thing as contingency—only divine intervention.

Most of the informants from the literature fit in the highest level of my typology of religious activity: *confession*. In the conversion careers approach, role learning is considered as the basis of church commitment (cf. Bromley & Shupe 1979). A good way to strengthen church commitment is to give the novice a voluntary church assignment. In a great many cases, the informants remained active in church while accepting important leadership or teaching responsibilities. However, there is always the danger that the informant still feels insecure and may feel pressured into accepting a task (s)he is not ready for yet. In that case, disaffiliation may follow.

Disaffiliation also happens when the new members feel rejected or neglected by the other members of the church. Since most Pentecostal congregations are big and its leaders overworked, one can safely assume that many people were never visited and felt neglected. Hence, some dropped out after a while. This applied especially to people who converted very quickly, with only a rudimentary knowledge of the church's doctrine and rules of conduct. The fact that the consequences of conversion are rather limited in so many cases also suggests that many of these 'conversions' are merely a rather superficial form of affiliation and a temporary one at that.

In other cases, however, disaffiliation was caused exactly by the high demands—in discipline, morality, time, and money—of the church in question.

This happened especially in Pentecostal churches. It means that the same factors which were originally responsible for the success of Pentecostalism in Latin America in fact also account for its high drop-out rates. Salvation sometimes proves to be less secure than people had originally hoped, the high levels of commitment and high standards of conduct are difficult to maintain, and the organization of many Pentecostal churches would seem to stimulate schism rather than control it.

The data presented here show that researchers should be wary to simply equate affiliation with conversion, as Jenkins (2002) does. For researchers who wish to understand both the process and effects of conversion, the distinction between conversion and affiliation is critical. To a large degree, this distinction gives us greater insights into the high religious mobility of many individuals in Latin America. In a context of growing religious competition in Latin America, it is all the more important that we: 1) delineate the various levels of religious commitment scholars utilize in their studies of religion; 2) systematize the variables impacting both conversion and disaffiliation; and 3) endeavor to collect the most complete data possible in order to fill in the full model of the conversion career.

Jenkins' main theme, the shift of the center of Christianity from north to south, is beyond dispute. His book is also a good analysis of some essential elements of Christianity in the south, like miracles, healing, dreams, and prophesying. The conversion careers of Pentecostals from various churches presented here provide ample evidence of that. However, they also showed that conversion cannot be treated as an unproblematic subject. Many people in Latin America experimented with certain elements of Pentecostalism at a certain point in their lives, often when they are adolescents or young adults. But in some countries, at least half of all new members dropped out of the Pentecostal church in the first year. It is clear that many Latin Americans are looking for a change of heart, a new identity, but the available evidence shows that this is a lifelong process involving multiple episodes of increasing and decreasing involvement in Pentecostal churches.

References

Anderson, A. 2004. *An introduction to Pentecostalism: global charismatic Christianity*. Cambridge: Cambridge UP.

Barrett, D., Kurian, G. & Johnson T. 2001. *World Christian encyclopedia: a comparative survey of churches and religions in the modern world*. Oxford: Oxford UP.

Bastian, J.-P. 1994. *Protestantismos y modernidad latinoamericana*. Mexico City: Fondo de Cultura Económica.

Bowen, K. 1996. *Evangelism and apostasy: the evolution and impact of evangelicals in Mexico*. Montreal: McGill-Queen's UP.

Bromley, D.G. & Shupe, A.D. 1979. "Just a few years seem like a lifetime": a role theory approach to participation in religious movements. (In Kriesberg, L. (ed). *Research in social movements, conflicts, and change, Volume 2.* Greenwich, CT: JAI Press. p.159–185.)

Brouwer, J. 2000. *Nieuwe scheppingen in Christus: bekeringsverhalen van protestante evangélicos en katholieke carismáticos in Masaya, Nicaragua.* Utrecht: leeronderzoek Cultural Anthropology, Utrecht University.

Brusco, E. 1995. *The reformation of machismo: evangelical conversion and gender in Colombia.* Austin: University of Texas Press.

Burdick, J. 1993. *Looking for God in Brazil.* Berkeley: University of California Press.

Cantón, M. 1998. *Bautizados en fuego: Protestantes, discursos de conversión y política en Guatemala (1989–1993).* Antigua Guatemala/South Woodstock, VT: CIRMA/Plumsock Mesoamerican Studies.

Chesnut, R.A. 1997. *Born again in Brazil.* New Brunswick, NJ: Rutgers UP.

Chesnut, R.A. 2003. *Competitive spirits: Latin America's new religious economy.* Oxford: Oxford UP.

Corten, A. & Marshall-Fratani, R. (eds) 2001. *Between Babel and pentecost: transnational Pentecostalism in Africa and Latin America.* London: Hurst.

Dempster, M., Klaus, B. & Petersen, D. (eds) 1999. *The globalization of Pentecostalism: a religion made to travel.* Oxford: Regnum.

Dominguez, E. 1984. The great commission. *NACLA-report on the Americas* 18(1): p.12–22.

Droogers, A., Gooren, H. & Houtepen, A. 2003. *Conversion careers and culture politics in Pentecostalism: a comparative study in four continents.* Proposal submitted to the thematic program "The Future of the Religious Past" of the Netherlands Organization for Scientific Research (NWO).

Gill, A. 1998. *Rendering unto Caesar: the Catholic church and the state in Latin America.* Chicago: University of Chicago Press.

Gill, L. 1990. "Like a veil to cover them": women and the Pentecostal movement in La Paz. *American ethnologist* 17(4): p.708–721.

Gómez, J.I. 1998. *El crecimiento y la deserción en la iglesia evangélica costarricense.* San José, Costa Rica: IINDEF.

Gooren, H. 1999. *Rich among the poor: church, firm, and household among small-scale entrepreneurs in Guatemala City.* Amsterdam: Thela.

Gooren, H. 2000. Analyzing LDS growth in Guatemala: report from a barrio. *Dialogue* 33(2): p.97–115.

Gooren, H. 2001. Reconsidering Protestant growth in Guatemala, 1900–1995. (In Dow, J.W., Sandstrom, A.R. (eds). *Holy saints and fiery preachers: the anthropology of Protestantism in Mexico and Central America.* Westport, CT: Greenwood/Praeger. p.169–203.)

Gooren, H. 2005. Towards a new model of conversion careers: the impact of personality and situational factors. *Exchange* 34(2): p.149–166.

Gooren, H. 2006a. Towards a new model of religious conversion careers: the impact of social and institutional factors. (In Bekkum, W.J. van Bremmer, J.N. & Molendijk, A. (eds). *Paradigms, poetics and politics of conversion.* Leuven: Peeters. p.25–40.)

Gooren, H. 2006b. The religious market model and conversion: towards a new approach. *Exchange* 35(1): p.39–60.

Gooren, H. Forthcoming, 2007. Conversion careers in Latin America: entering and leaving church among Pentecostals, Catholics, and Mormons. (In Cleary, E.L. & Steigenga, T.J. (eds). *Conversion of a continent: religious identity and change in Latin America.* New Brunswick, NJ: Rutgers UP.

Hefner, R.W. (ed). 1993. *Conversion to Christianity: historical and anthropological perspectives on a great transformation.* Berkeley: University of California Press.

Hoffnagel, J.C. 1978. *The believers: Pentecostalism in a Brazilian city.* PhD dissertation, Indiana University.

Huntington, D. 1984a. The prophet motive. *NACLA-report on the Americas* 18(1): p.2–11.

Huntington, D. 1984b. God's saving plan. *NACLA-report on the Americas* 18(1): p.23–33.

Huntington, S.P. 1994. *The clash of civilizations and the remaking of world order.* New York: Simon & Schuster.

Ireland, R. 1991. *Kingdoms come: religion and politics in Brazil.* Pittsburgh: Pittsburgh UP.

Jenkins, P. 2002. *The next Christendom: the coming of global Christianity.* Oxford: Oxford UP.

Johnstone, P. & Mandryk, J. 2001. *Operation world.* Carlisle, UK: Paternoster Lifestyle.

Kamsteeg, F. 1998. *Prophetic pentecostalism in Chile: a case study on religion and development policy.* Lanham, MD: University Press of America.

Lalive d'Epinay, C. 1969. *Haven of the masses: a study of the Pentecostal movement in Chile.* London: Lutterworth.

Long, T.E. & Hadden, J.K. 1983. Religious conversion and the concept of socialization: integrating the brainwashing and drift models. *Journal for the scientific study of religion* 22(1): p.1–14.

Mariz, C. 1994. *Coping with poverty: Pentecostal churches and Christian base communities in Brazil.* Philadelphia: Temple UP.

Mariz, C. & Campos Machado, M. 1997. Pentecostalism and women in Brazil. (In Cleary, E. & Stewart-Gambino, H. (eds). *Power, politics, and Pentecostals in Latin America.* Boulder, CO: Westview Press. p.41–54.

Martin, D. 1990. *Tongues of fire: the explosion of Protestantism in Latin America.* Oxford: Blackwell.

Martin, D. 2002. *Pentecostalism: the world their parish.* Oxford: Blackwell.

Miguez, D. 1997. *"To help you find God": the making of a Pentecostal identity in a Buenos Aires suburb.* Amsterdam: Vrije Universiteit, PhD Dissertation.

Piedra, A. 1994. El protestantismo costarricense entre la ilusión y la realidad. *Senderos* 16(47): p.77–96.

Rambo, L.R. 1993. *Understanding religious conversion.* New Haven: Yale UP.

Richardson, J.T. (ed). 1978. *Conversion careers: in and out of the new religions.* Beverly Hills, CA: Sage.

Roberts, B.R. 1968. Protestant groups and coping with urban life in Guatemala. *American journal of sociology* 73(6): p.753–767.

Stark, R. & Finke, R. 2000. *Acts of faith: explaining the human side of religion.* Berkeley: University of California Press.

Stoll, D. 1990. *Is Latin America turning Protestant?: the politics of evangelical growth.* Berkeley: University of California Press.

Valderrey, J. 1985. *Las sectas en Centroamérica.* Brussels: Pro Mundi Vita, Boletín no. 100.

Willems, E. 1967. *Followers of the new faith: culture change and the rise of Protestantism in Brazil and Chile.* Nashville: Vanderbilt UP.

Williams, P.J. 1997. The sound of tambourines: the politics of Pentecostal growth in El Salvador. (In Cleary, E. & Stewart-Gambino, H. (eds). *Power, politics, and Pentecostals in Latin America.* Boulder, CO: Westview Press. p.179–200.)

Martha Frederiks

Theologies of Anowa's Daughters: An African women's discourse

Philip Jenkins in his book *The Next Christendom* states that theologies from the South will differ from those from the North. This article presents a case study on African women's theologies to support and illustrate Jenkins' thesis. By studying the topics of cultural hermeneutics, biblical hermeneutics and women's theology of HIV/Aids, the article highlights how African women theologians, like western feminist theologians, focus on gender issues, but "have formulated their own solutions to their own particular problems" and have developed African women's theologies. The article concludes therefore that African women's theologies are not carbon copies of Western feminist theologies but African theologies, which focus on the promotion of life and well-being of men and women in Africa.

In the first chapter of *The Next Christendom* Phillip Jenkins states that if "we want to visualize a 'typical' contemporary Christian we should be thinking of a woman living in a village in Nigeria or in a Brazalian *favela*" (Jenkins, 2002, p.2). Emphasising that this person would be a *young* woman living in Nigeria or Brazil would have made the remark even more to the point, since recent UN statistics avow that half of the world's population is now under 25.[1] Jenkins also observes that due to the phenomenal growth of African Christianity in the last century[2] and the decline of the Christian community in Europe, soon the majority of the Christian community will live in the "South", with Africa and Latin America vying with each other for the title "most Christian continent" (Jenkins, 2002, p.3–3).

Jenkins is by no means the first person to make the observation that Christianity has moved south. Already in the early 1980s Andrew Walls pointed out that centre of gravity of Christianity was shifting and that so-called "Third World Theology" would very soon become "representative" Christian theology (Walls, 2004, p.9). However few scholars seem to have heeded Wall's plea that anyone who wishes to undertake the study of Christianity seriously these days "would need to know something about Africa" (Walls, 2000, p.106). Despite

---

1   http://www.unfpa.org/wpd/ Viewed on 15 Jul 2006.
2   Jenkins, 2002, p.4. Jenkins gives figures of about 10 million Christians in Africa in 1900 and about 360 million in 2000.

the fact that African Christians make up about one-fifth world Christianity, soon becoming a quarter, few curricula include courses on African Christianity or African theology. The same seems true for the study of that other large concentration of Christians, Latin America.

This shift of the centre of gravity of Christianity has major implications for what can be considered typical mainstream Christian theology. Phillips Jenkins warns his readers against too much romanticism about Southern Christianity, which in his opinion is far more conservative than mainline Western Christianity. In Jenkins' view Southern Christianity will neither fulfil the dream of liberation nor the conservative dream of the North, but Christians in South will seek their own solutions to their own particular problems:

> ... some Western Christians have since the 1960s expected that the religion of their Third World brethren would be fervently liberal, activist, and even revolutionary, the model represented by liberation theology ... All too often though, these hopes have proved illusory ... Southern Hemisphere Christians would not avoid political activism, but they would become involved strictly on their own terms.[3]

Jenkins' words resound the passionate appeals made by John Mbiti in the 1970s that African Christianity should be accepted on its own merits and not be judged by Western criteria: "When we speak or write on particular issues about Christianity or other academic matters, we should not be expected to use the vocabulary and approach used in Europe and America: please, allow us to say certain things our own way ... Are we not allowed to become what we wish to become?" (Mbiti, 1970, p.439). It would therefore seem appropriate to avoid categories as "liberal" and "conservative" to describe Southern Christianity. Whatever Southern Christian communities and theologies are like, they are certainly not mere carbon copies of the West.

This article wants to study a group which, according to Jenkins, consists of "typical contemporary Christians", namely African women. More specifically, the article wants to focus on African women theologians and their ideas on women, religion and culture. Gender equality is still a controversial issue in most Southern churches (Jenkins, 2000, p.198ff). Jenkins states:

> African churches still lack the kind of activist women's caucuses that are so commonplace in the United States and Europe. And while believing women are evolving a theology that is both feminist and distinctly African, these ideas have minimal impact when compared with the transformations wrought in the metropolitan countries over the past thirty years or so (Jenkins, 2000, p.199).

---

3   Jenkins, 2002, p.7. Jenkins' terminology of "older" and "newer" churches is confusing. Several Asian and African churches, such as the Mar Thoma Church or the Ethiopian Orthodox Churches, have a longer history than the so-called older Western churches.

Jenkins adds, with a reference to Latin American *mujerista* theology, these theologies on women's issues are generally considered to be export products from the West.[4]

It is undeniably true that theology in Africa is still male-dominated and it is also undeniably true that gender issues are not at the top of the African churches' agendas. Yet Jenkins' verdict that African women's theology is an export product from the West, which has little or no impact in African Christianity, seems a little too rash. One of the leading and most active networks of the women theologians is in Africa: the Circle of Concerned African Women Theologians. It is also the largest theological network in Africa. The Circle consists of several hundreds of women, representing a wide spectrum of denominational and ethnic backgrounds. The group has published more than 31 books since its inception in 1989. Also, more and more joint publications of male and female theologians are appearing. One of the most influential African theological books of the last decade, *The Bible in Africa*, is a co-product of Gerard West and Musa Dube.[5] In francophone Africa, Hélène Yinda and Kä Mana have co-authored several books,[6] and the evangelical *African Bible Commentary* includes contributions by prominent Circle members (Adeyemo 2006). Though Jenkins might be correct in stating that African women have not (yet) had the same impact on church and theology as European or American women have made in their contexts, yet it would seem that African women theologians participate fully in the African theological discourse.

This article wants to look at the development of African women's theologies as they have been represented by the Circle of Concerned African Women Theologians. It wants to show how in their approaches of culture, scripture and HIV/Aids African women theologians have merged the dreams of gender justice and of "mother Africa". Their theologies are syntheses of liberation and inculturation theologies, resulting in unique African women's theologies. They exemplify what Jenkins has called "seeking their own solutions to their own particular problems". Stressing their African-ness, most African women theologians have

---

4   Since Jenkins does not explicitly distance himself from this point of view, it would seem he shares this analysis.

5   Dube, M.W. & West, G.O. (eds). 2001. *The Bible in Africa. Trajections, trajectories and trends.* Leiden: Brill. Many other examples could be given, e.g. Kinoti, H.W. & Walligo, J.M. 1997. *The Bible in African Christianity: Essays in Biblical Theology.* Nairobi: Acton Publishers.

6   Yinda, H. & Mana, K. *Pour la Nouvelle Théologie des Femmes Africaines. Repenser la différence sexuelle promouvoir les droits des femmes et libérer leurs énergies créatives.* Yaoundé: Clé; Yinda, H. & Mana, K. 2004. *Religion, culture et VIH/SIDA: Un hommage au docteur Jaap Breetvelt.* Yaounde: Editions Sherpa; Yinda, H. & Mana, K. 2005. *Manifeste de la femme africaine.* Bafoussam (Cameroun): CIPCRE.

rejected too close a link to Western feminism and have declined the title "feminist" or "womanist". They call themselves "concerned African women theologians"; women who want to solve African gender issues in an African way.

Despite the fairly intense contacts between the various Circle members, one cannot speak about Circle theology in the singular. African women theologians have over the years shown a large diversity in methodology, focus and topics (Kanyoro, 2002a, p.35). As Tinyiku Maluleke once observed, there are "many Ruths and many Africa's" in the pan-African women theologians association (Maluleke, 2002, p.249). Hence, an exposition about the theologies (plural) of Anowa's daughters.

Circle beginnings

Though no specific date can be set for the time in which individual African women theologians started to reflect on women's issues in relation to religion and culture,[7] the beginnings of African women's theology are often pinned down to 1989. In September that year during the Biennial Institute of African Women and Religion in Legon/Ghana, an association for African women theologians was launched: the Circle of Concerned African Women Theologians.[8] The name for the Circle includes the word "concerned", as Isabel Phiri, Circle Co-ordinator since 2002, once emphasised, because "Not all women theologians who are African are concerned with women's issues. Women in the Circle are called *Concerned* African women theologians because they want to get rid of the assumption that concerns over sexism belong to a minority of educated, western women (Phiri, 1997, p.70). Most Circle women prefer to refer to their theology as "women's theology", rather than as feminist or womanist theology. African women theologians decline the name feminist, according Phiri, because "the name itself is enough to cause people to close up and not listen".[9] And though some studies in Third World Theology have treated Afro-American and African female theologians as one and the same strand of theology, African women theologians have also rejected the predicate "womanist" for their theology. As Phiri has pointedly stated, "... while African and African American women theologians may share the same skin colour, the

---

7   The Circle focused and focuses on "women's issues" more than on "gender issues". See Phiri, I.A. 2005. The Circle of Concerned African Women Theologians: Its contribution to ecumenical formation. *Ecumenical Review* 57(1): p.40.

8   Henceforth: the Circle.

9   Phiri, I.A. 2005, p.39. See also Phiri I.A. & Nadar, S. 2006. Treading softly but firmly. (In Phiri, I.A. & Nadar, S. 2006 *Women, Religion and Health: Essays in honour to Mercy Amba Ewudziwa Oduyoye*. Maryknoll: Orbis Books. p.3–8).

contexts within which they do their theology are very different."[10] Phiri acknowledges however that "... a conversation is on-going among ourselves as to who we are. It was noted that Circle members have used different names to describe their work." (Phiri, 2005, p.39).

Kanyoro describes the Circle as "a space for women of Africa to do communal theology" (Kanyoro, 2002a, p.16). This aspect of community and interconnectedness, by which women theologians around the continent try to stimulate and support each other in researching and writing, has been an essential part of the Circle vision (Dube, 2001, p.1). Oduoyoye once phrased the concept of the Circle in a poem:

> A Circle expands forever
> It covers all who wish to hold hands
> And its size depends on each other
> It is a vision of solidarity
> It turns outwards to interact with the outside
> And inward for self critique
> A circle expands forever
> It is a vision of accountability
> It grows as the other is moved to grow
> A circle must have a centre
> But a single dot does not make a Circle
> One tree does not make a forest
> A circle, a vision of co-operation, mutuality and care (Oduyoye, 2001a, p.97).

Meeting on the continent in cycles of about 7 years and on the regional or national level as often as finances permit, the women of the Circle have published a considerable number of books and articles. Thus they have contributed and continue to contribute substantially to the theological debate in Africa.

The Circle however, did not emerge out of the blue. Nyambura Njoroge has identified four major movements that have given voice to African women and thus indirectly have contributed to the vision of the Circle: the missionary movement, the women's movement, the ecumenical movement and the liberation movement. Each of these movements has in its own way raised the awareness

---

10   Phiri, I.A. 1997, p.68. Note: Also the Nigerian theologian Ogbu Kalu seems to presume that African and Afro-American women's theologies are one and the same thing. See Kalu, O. Daughters of Ethiopia. Constructing a Feminist Discourse in Ebony Strokes. (In Phiri, I.A. & Nadar, S. 2006. *African Women, Religion, and Health*. p.261ff.) Also Afro-American women have expressed discomfort at this lumping of African and Afro-American women's theologies: "We must try to avoid setting up those on either side of the cultural divide as antagonist or naively assuming that we can be 'partners' or 'share insights' when our interpretations are rooted in political and cultural realities that have been deeply detrimental to genuine partnership" Bird, P. 2001. A North American Feminist Response. (In Dube, 2002, p.200.)

of women's issues in church, theology or society.[11] Oduyoye, in her article "The Story of a Circle", gives insight in the more direct events leading up to the creation of the Circle (Oduyoye, 2001a, p.97–100). According to Oduyoye the process started in the late 1960s, when during a period of about 10 years she collected the names of African women theologians in order to set up a network. A *kairos* moment was the WCC consultation of Women Theology Students in the mid 1970s. There, during the consultation in Cartigny (Switzerland) a group of 8 African women theologians, among whom Oduyoye, conceived the vision for the Circle.[12] Though within a few years time the first pan-African conference of African women theologians in Ibadan (1980) was organised,[13] it took nearly another decade before the vision of the Circle became reality. This happened in 1989 in Ghana. The Legon convocation, organised with the help of Brigalia Bam (WCC women's desk), John Pobee, (WCC, desk for theological

---

11   Njoroge, N.J. 2002. Reclaiming our Heritage of Power. (In Phiri, I.A., D.B. Govinden, S. Nadar, *Her-stories*. p.42.) An elaborate discussion of the topic can be found on pages 42–54. The missionary movement, according to Njoroge, contributed to an improvement of the position of women by offering female role-models (black and white female missionaries) to African women and by enhancing the self-esteem of women through education and other projects. The feminist and women's movements raised awareness for women's issues by demanding equal rights and equal treatment for women in society. They also exposed societal discrimination against women. These actions indirectly impacted the reflection on the role of women in church and theology. On the international and interdenominational level, ecumenical movements such as the WCC have requested explicit attention for women's issues. The Decade of Churches in Solidarity with Women (1988–1998), often jokingly (and more truthfully) called the Decade of Women in Solidarity with Churches, and the many conferences on women's issues leading up the decade also had their bearing on Africa. These meetings have functioned as stepping-stones, leading up to the Circle. The liberation movement, and more in particular the Ecumenical Association for Third World Theologians, is the fourth and final platform Njoroge identifies. Initially, participants in the liberation movement had little attention for gender issues, and focussed mainly on the struggles of class, race etc. But from 1983 onwards, when the Women's Commission within EATWOT was created, gender became a topic of attention and a strand within liberation theology. Thus, also African women receive an international academic forum to speak about gender injustices. Note: From 1983 onwards EATWOT created a 'Women's Commission' where women from different cultures could share experiences and raise issues. Oduyoye was part of EATWOT's Women's Commission from its inception and she and Virginia Fabella were editors of the first publication of the Women's Commission's: Fabella, V. & Oduyoye, M.A. 1989. *With Passion and Compassion: Third world women doing theology*. Maryknoll: Orbis Books.

12   The exact date is somewhat unclear. Odoyoye gives 1978 as the date (Oduyoye, 2001a, p.98), whilst Njoroge locates the conference in 1976 (Njoroge, N.J. 2001. Talitha Cum! (In Njoroge, N.J. & Dube, M.W. *Talitha Qum! Theologies of African Women*. Pietermaritzburg: Cluster Publications. p.253.)

13   The Ibadan meeting was organised by Oduyoye together with Isabel Johnson (AACC women's desk) and Daisy Obi (Christian Council of Nigeria). (Oduyoye, 2001a, p.98).

education in Africa) and Musimbi Kanyoro (LWF women's desk), became the cradle of the Circle.

Though the various leading members of the Circle stress that the Circle are interreligious, this seems more a principle statement than reflecting an actual reality (Phiri, 2005, p.35; Oduyoye, 2001a, p.99). The majority of the women who are members of the Circle come from a Christian background, though a few Muslim women such as Rabiatu Ammah participate. A group of women from Southern Africa prefers to describe themselves as adherents to African Traditional Religions; only on a secondary plane do they call themselves Christians and Muslims. Yet the explicit statement that the Circle is multi-cultural, multi-religious and multi-racial should be read as an avowal that the Circle is open to African women from all backgrounds.[14]

In the first decade the Circle worked in four study-commissions: women and culture, women in history, biblical and cultural hermeneutics, and ministries and theological formation (Kanyoroy, 2002a, p.29–30). In recent years the importance of the four study commissions seems to decrease and the main emphasis seems to be on the linguistic and regional chapters of the Circle, all working on an overall theme.

Culture: oppression, liberation and the promotion of life

The South African theologian Gerald West once called African women's the-ologies a combination of theologies of bread (with an emphasis on liberation) and theologies of being (with an emphasis on inculturation) (West, 2002, p.35). And indeed the interest of the Circle women seems to be to bring about a dialogue between liberation and inculturation theologies. The aim of this synthesis is the promotion of life and dignity for men and women in Africa and the creation and sustenance of viable communities in church and in society.[15]

The person in whose work this interplay between liberation and incultura-tion is most clearly visible is Mercy Amba Oduyoye. As "queen mother" of the Circle, Oduyoye, as early as the mid 1970s, demanded attention for the pos-ition of African women in church and society.[16] It was time, according to

---

14   Phiri, I.A., 1997, p.70. See also the mission statement at the Circle website: http://www. thecirclecawt.org.

15   ibid.

16   See M. Oduyoye. 1977. *And Women, Where do they come in?* Lagos: Methodist Publications. Or contributions like: Oduyoye, M.A., The Roots of African Feminism. (In Pobee, J.S. et al. *Variations in Christian Theology in Africa.* Nairobi: Uzima); Oduyoy, M. 1979. Women Theologians and the Church in Africa. (In Scott, J. & Wood, B.Y. (eds). *We lis-tened long before we spoke: women theological students talk about theology, ministry, spir-ituality, vocation, mission, theological education and their dreams for the future of the church.* Geneva: WCC 1979.)

Oduyoye, "to break the silence". Possibly due to her own biography, Oduyoye's main focus seems to have been on the topic of African women and culture. Coming from a matrilineal Akan culture and an open-minded Christian home,[17] Oduyoye married a Yoruba man and moved to Nigeria. There she was confronted with the strong patriarchal structures of Yoruba culture. This experience stamped Oduyoye's life's work.

In her publications Oduyoye on the hand analyses African cultures to uncover patriarchy and oppressive rites and structures, while on the other hand she searches African cultures for myths and symbols that can empower women and promote life. Oduyoye has pointed out that culture is neither a neutral nor a solely positive concept. Culture is a complex of structures of an ambiguous nature, often used by those in power: "Women's theology shows a keen awareness of the fact that 'the past' is often misused for the subjugation of women, while traditional values that are advantageous to women ... are overlooked" (Oduyoye, 2001b, p.29). Oduyoye remarks with some humour that "culture is frequently a euphemism to protect actions that require analyses" (Oduyoye, 2001b, p.13). Male inculturation theologians, according to Oduyoye, have tended to be too positive (and naive) about culture, whereas male liberation theologians have presumed that women's liberation was included in the liberation of men (Phiri, 1997, p.68). Oduyoye and others have therefore demanded a more critical evaluation of culture. She cites with affirmation the Nigerian Sister Theresa Okure who stated:

> All serious efforts, aimed at promoting true human development, will demand that we identify and strive after eliminating from our cultures those elements, factors and practices which are inhuman and dehumanising, whether these are found in social culture, political culture, scientific and technological culture, economic culture or even religious and church culture (Oduyoye, 1988, p.367).

Oduyoye and her fellow women theologians have therefore in their early publications paid much attention to traditional harmful practices, such as female circumcision and rites relating to menstruation, widowhood, marriage, etc., and to analyses of patriarchal structures in church and society.[18]

But Oduyoye has also, right from the beginning, searched for elements of culture that can serve as a source of liberation and empowerment. Aware of the

---

17   Oduyoye grew up in a manse. Her father was a Methodist minister who insisted that all his children, girls as well as boys, receive similar education and treatment. For more biographical details see Oduyoye. M.A. 1995. *Daughters of Anowa. African women and patriarchy.* Maryknoll: Orbis Books. p.5–8.

18   Pemberton, 2003, p.70. Compare for example Kanyoro, M.R.A. & Njoroge, N.J. 1996. *Groaning in Faith: African women in the household of God,* Nairobi: Acton Publishers or Phiri, I.A. 2000. *Women, Presbyterianism, and Patriarchy: Religious experiences of Chewa women in Central Malawi.* Blantyre: Christian Literature Association in Malawi.

plurality of African cultures, Oduyoye often takes her own Akan and her husband's Yoruba culture as starting points for her deliberations (Oduyoye, 2001b,
p.13) In publications like *Daughters of Anowa*, she uses Asante and Yoruba
myths as empowering resources for her theology (Oduyoye, 1995, p.19–76). A
key symbol in Oduoyoye's theology of empowerment and life is the prophetess
Anowa, a mythical figure that features in the novel of Ayi Kwei Armah. The
writer sketches Anowa as a mythical woman, representing Africa, whose people
"were characterised by a communal instinct ... and more by peace than clamor
for heroic action". Anowa is also seen as a figure that in the past opposed
(European/Arab) slavery and slave-trade. Thus she is portrayed as a symbol of
liberation. Oduyoye adopts this liberative reading of Anowa and makes the
Anowa figure a key concept in her empowerment theology.[19] She calls upon
women to accept Anowa as ancestor for the whole of Africa; an icon symbolis-
ing peace, community and the promotion of life. And she invites women to
join Anowa in her fight for life and viable, peaceful communities, despite the
forces that endeavour to domesticate Anowa and her daughters. Thus, Oduoyoye
transcends the meaning of a mythical Akan figure to the continental level and
uses cultural symbols and myths as liberative instruments to uplift and
empower women and to promote life in the community.[20]

Another crucial African concept that Oduyoye uses in her theology, is the
notion of motherhood. According to Oduyoye, motherhood is not (just) something biological but stands for the nurture, the protection and the promotion of
life in the wider context of the community. By urging women to assume their

---

19   Oduyoye, M.A., 1995, p.6–7. NB. Oduyoye in the same pages also mentions a novel on
Anowa by Ama Ata Anoo. In this book Anowa is a priestess who, after a fierce fight for liberation, has to succumb to pressures of patriarchy. Occasionally Oduyoye also uses this
interpretation of Anowa.

20   For a critical reflection on Oduyoye's use of Anowa, see Pemberton, 2003, p.75 ff. Another
Akan figure that features regularly in Oduyoye's work is Eke: "The ancients tells us that as
the Akan, the Children of Anowa, progressed south from northern Africa towards the savan-
nah and the Atlantic, they became thirsty and there was no water for miles around. With
them was a priestess named Eku who had a dog. They came upon a lake, but were frightened
to drink the water lest it was poisonous. Eku let her dog drink of the water. Nothing happened to the dog. Then Eku herself, as leader, tried to prove to the people that the water was
drinkable. She drank and nothing happened to her. Whereupon all the people shouted "*Eku
aso*?" (Eku has tasted) and they ran forward to drink. The place where the incident happened
is known to this day as Eku-Aso. Most migration stories of the Akan do put women at the
centre, with women leading the community to freedom and prosperity" (Oduyoye, 1995,
p.8). A similar attempt to use culture as a positive and life-giving well, can be found in a
joint article of Oduyoye and Elisabeth Amoah, *The Christ for African Women*. Oduyoye,
M.A. & Amoah, E. 1993. (In Fabella, F. & Oduyoye, M.A. *With Passion and Compassion:
Third World women doing theology.* Maryknoll: Orbis Books.

motherhood Oduyoye encourages women to be(come) guardians of life and people who build and sustain the community. It is clear, according to Oduyoye, that this concept is ambiguous because the promotion of life will demand sacrifices. But, and here she makes a link to Christology, sacrifice is the way of Christ, who gave his life so that others might have life. This brings Oduyoye to speak about "messianic feminism". Women, according to Oduyoye, have to calling to save the community and sacrifice themselves for the sake and the life of others even where they don't (always) have the power to implement structural changes (Hoedemaker, 1997, p.225, 229).

It is undeniable that motherhood plays a crucial role in African cultures. Also the notion of life, the promotion of life and life in abundance is a thoroughly African concept. As such Oduoyoye uses notions that are important to African cultures. But Western feminists, such as Carry Pemberton, have sternly criticised Oduyoye for using metaphors that confirm the traditional female role models and again push women in their sacrificial, nurturing and mothering role (Pemberton, 2003, p.88). It would indeed seem that with the concept of "motherhood" Oduyoye seeks to promote life *within* the patriarchal role models rather than to call upon women to opt for the subversion of patriarchy. No doubt this should be read again the background that most African women theologians, including Oduyoye, see women's liberation as a joint project of women and men. Oduoyoye speaks about wanting "to engage in a critical discussion without violating one another" (Oduyoye, 2001b, p.127). Or, as she once phrased it in her early years:

> Feminism emphasizes the *wholeness* of the community as made up of male and female beings. It seeks to express what is not so obvious, that is, that male-humanity is a partner with female-humanity and that both expressions of humanity are needed to shape a balanced-community within which each will experience a fullness of Be-ing (Oduyoye, 1986, p.121).

Oduyoye, by using metaphors like Anowa and motherhood, brings together the strands of liberation and inculturation theologies. For her, liberation is not just liberation *from* something, for example liberation from oppressive structures and cultural practices. But liberation is also liberation *to* something, a task, a calling. People are liberated so that they themselves can become guardians and promoters of life in Africa.

Other Circle theologians, like Elisabeth Amoah and Theresa Okure, theologise in similar ways. On the one hand they criticise religion and culture for their oppressive structures and on the other hand they study the traditional African cultures and their oral traditions to find empowering and liberating concepts and role-models to further women's issues. Thus, Circle women, as daughters of Anowa, integrate the methodologies and ideals of 'the theologies of bread and the theologies of being' in order to promote life for men and women, life in abundance in Africa.

Hermeneutics

The bi-focal lens of liberation and inculturation can also be found in the area of hermeneutics, an important field of research for African women theologians.[21] African women theologians hold the same ambiguity towards religiously authoritative texts as they hold towards cultures. Both individual women and the Circle as an organisation have therefore published extensively on the interpretation of religious texts. A joint Circle project on hermeneutics for example led to publication of *Other Ways of Reading: African women and the Bible* (Dube 2001). The Setwana Biblical scholar Musa Dube is known for her numerous articles on African women's hermeneutics whilst the Kenyan theologian Musimbi Kanyoro in 2002 published a monograph on hermeneutics, called *Introducing Feminist Cultural Hermeneutics: an African perspective*.

Justin Ukpong, in the opening article of *The Bible in Africa* sums up the contributions of African women theologians to the field of hermeneutics as 'feminist hermeneutics'. He distinguishes five different feminist approaches within African hermeneutics (Ukpong, 2001, p.21ff). The first approach, according to Ukpong, challenges the fact that the Bible and the history of Christianity are interpreted in male, androcentric terms: "Feminist theologians refer to such hermeneutics as the imprisonment of God in maleness." This is for example reflected in the overall use male nouns and pronouns for God. Rose Teteki Abbey in *Rediscovering Ataa Naa Nyonmo—The Father Mother God* tries to address this issue by underscoring feminine images of God in the Bible and by feeding into the Bible the gender inclusive Ga image of God as Ataa Naa Nyonmo, meaning father-mother God. Thus she stresses the maleness as well femaleness of God (Abbey, 2001, p.14–158). Nearly all women, however, have opted to work within the framework of the Bible, despite its male-centeredness. The South African feminist theologian Christina Landman is one of the few Circle women who draws the ultimate consequences from the fact that the Bible is seen to be a male book. Landman proposes to discard of the Bible as a religious text and pleads to accept alternative documents as an authoritative canon, such as the Nag Hamadi texts (Landman, 2003, p.83–93).

The second strand of feminist hermeneutics, according to Ukpong, tries critiquing and/or reinterpreting texts that are oppressive for women. Okure's article on Eve can serve as an example of this approach (Okure, 1985, p.82–92). The third strand of hermeneutics focuses mainly on positive approaches and texts relating to women in the Bible,[22] whilst the fourth seeks

---

21 The Commission for Cultural and Biblical Hermeneutics exemplifies this.
22 Compare for example Mbuy-Beya, B. 1998. *Woman, who are you: A challenge.* Nairobi: Pauline Pubications Africa; Tappa, L. 2002. Celle par qui le scandale arrive ou la cote d'Adam. Les mensonges d'une lecture patriarchale de la Bible. (In Yinda, H. (ed). 2002. *Femmes Africaines. Le pouvoir de transformer le monde.* Yaounde: Editions Sherpa. p.53–60.)

to find an overall, basic biblical concept that can serve as hermeneutical tool to interpret both negative and positive texts. Oduyoye for example very clearly opts for the hermeneutical lens of liberation and life-enhancement to interpret texts (and cultures).[23] But also Theresa Okure states that "the liberative elements in the Bible with respect to women stem from the divine perspective, the oppressive ones from the human perspective" (Okure, 1989, p.52). Kanyoro in *Introducing Feminist Cultural Hermeneutics* goes even one step further and pleads for an engendered cultural hermeneutics, 'an analysis and interpretation of how culture conditions people's understanding of reality at a particular time and location'. Kanyoro sees this engendered cultural hermeneutics as a prerequisite for Biblical hermeneutics (Kanyoro, 2002b, p.9–10).

The final approach of African feminist hermeneutics, according to Ukpong 'seeks to interpret biblical texts from the perspective of women's experience.'[24] Nyambura Njoroge's article, "Woman, why are you weeping," exemplifies this (Njoroge 1997). In her article Njoroge links the stories of African women, distressed, confused and hurting to the story of the women at the empty grave. The opening sentences of the article read:

> Before African women theologians began to speak out for themselves, there was unnamed hidden pain, a cry for help, no response, long silence, more pain until we could bear it no more. . . . In tears, we are searching for our Redeemer, who affirmed our dignity and humanity as persons created in the image of God. Yet, the African church is taking too long to learn to ask the question which the two angels and the risen Christ directed to Mary Magdalene: 'Woman, why are you weeping?' (Njoroge, 1997, p.427).

A similar re-reading of a biblical story from the perspective of African women can be found in Njoroge's moving article on 2 Samuel 21:9–14. Called "A Spirituality of Resistance and Transformation," Njoroge re-reads the story of Saul's wife Rispah to call upon African women to imitate Rispah's non-violent resistance to King David, thus demanding justice to be done to her family (Njoroge, 2001, p.66–83).

African women's hermeneutics however, as was already evident in Rose Teteki Abbey's article on Ataa Naa Nyonmo, goes beyond liberative—feminist—hermeneutics and combines liberation and inculturation hermeneutics. Dorothy Akoto's article on the re-reading of Ps. 23 can serve as an example of how these two strands merge. In "The Mother of the Ewe and Firstborn Daughter as the 'Good Shepherd' in the Cultural Context of the Ewe Peoples,"

---

23   Oduyoye, M.A. 1996. *Peace and Justice: A theological hermeneutic through an African woman's eyes*. Amsterdam: Free University Publications. p.10: "what gives life and is life-giving and life-sustaining is the yardstick for measuring worthiness".

24   Ukpong. J., 2001, p.21–2. An example of this approach can be found in Nasimiyu-Wasiki, A. 1992. Polygamy: A feminist critic. (In Oduyoye, M.A. & Kanyoro, M. *The Will to arise. Women, tradition and the church in Africa*. Maryknoll: Orbis Books. p.101–118.)

Akoto re-reads Psalm 23 in a way which is both liberative for women and uses concepts from the Ewe culture (Akoto 2001). She contextualises the metaphor of the Good Shepherd by inculturating the qualities of the shepherd rather than the metaphor itself. Thus, she opts for the new metaphor of the "mother" and "the firstborn daughter". These have in Ewe culture all the nurturing, guiding and life-giving qualities that the metaphor 'Good Shepherd' seeks to transmit. Her rephrasing of Ps. 23 is as follows:

> My Mother, my shepherd,
> Because of your industry as an economist, trading and toiling endlessly
> I never know want; your dependants and more are provided for
> You jealously guard law and order in the community as a politician
> Ensuring that they provide for the welfare of all and sundry
> When the community is sick and waywardness is rising
> Your instructions lead and direct towards the right ways of living
> The health of the community is restored
> Even when life becomes tempestuous, the future unknown and scary
> When the situations are threatening and trying, there is no cause for alarm
> For your teachings, your instructions, are always there to guide
> Your words of chastening are a source of purification and encouragement
> You jealously guard the good because you are 'nyornu' (maker of good things)
> Your eyes are always fixed on the prize
> Your words of praise, comfort and encouragement make you an educator
> For they nullify feelings of bitterness and hatred and restore peace and calm.
> My Mother, my shepherd, the good and rightful paths in which you offer training
> Your tender love and care will always abide
> As long as I live, I will continue to bask in your amazing motherliness
> Surely, your guidance, your council, your industry will be appropriated for ever and ever
> (Akoto, 2001, p.266–7).

Later in the article she re-read the passage of John 10 on the Good Shepherd by using the metaphor of "the firstborn daughter". This recast is again based on Ewe culture, where the first born is said to have opened the door of the womb for other children to come and where the older daughters act as substitute mothers for the younger children (Akoto, 2001, p.272ff). Mmadipoana Masenya makes a similar re-reading of the story of Esther, by using myths for Lesotho (Masenya, 2001, p.27–50).

Musa Dube takes the exercise of integrating liberation and inculturation yet another step further by combining feminist liberation and inculturation with post-colonialism. In her essay, "Fifty Years of Bleeding," she interweaves the story of the woman with an issue of blood (Mark 5:24–43) with an African oral saga and the tale of Africa's history over the last fifty years, with Mother Africa posing as the bleeding woman.[25] This same theme of Mother Africa

---

25   Dube, M.W. Fifty Years of Bleeding: A storytelling feminist reading of Mark 5:24–43. (In Dube, 2001, p.50–60.)

returns in her article, "The Five Husbands at the Well of Living Water," where the rejected Mother Africa (the Samaritan woman) is visited by her former husbands: Mzilikazi, David Livingston, Cecil Rhodes, Ian Smith and Canaan Banana.[26] Even more radical is Musa Dube's experiment of divining the text of Ruth. Following a practice of pastors in African Independent Churches, Dube, in "Divining Ruth for International Relations," proposes to see the Bible as a divination set. This hermeneutical method sees the text as instrument of divination, which can give clarity and guidance in certain situations. Dube in her article applies this divining reading of the text of Ruth to the international relationships of Southern Africa.[27] In these articles however, the emphasis seems to be more on post-colonialism than on women's issues, though the texts Dube uses always seem to feature women.

Different from what Ukpong seems to suggest, African women theologians have hardly ever focussed on liberative feminist hermeneutics per se. Though they agree with the general feminist critique that the Bible is full of oppressive texts and pre-dominantly male images in and though they have emphasised the need for alternative forms of theology, such as a narrative theology,[28] they have hardly ever left it at that. Rather, they have used African concepts and African methodologies such as story-telling and divination to contextualise both the form and the content of hermeneutics. The hermeneutical methods of African women theologians again show how theologies of liberation and theologies of inculturation can be integrated into one holistic approach.

Women, theology and HIV/Aids

Tinyiku Maluleke once challenged the Circle women to put to rest their dreams of changing African women into African Ruths and to theologise in the context of 'ruthless Africa'.[29] The HIV/Aids pandemic, the third major field of

---

26   Dube, M.W. John 4:1–42—Five Husbands at the Well of Living Water: The Samaritan woman and African women. (In Njoroge, N.J. & Dube, M.W. *Talitha Cum! Theologies of African Women.* p.40–66.)

27   Dube, M.W. 2001. Divining Ruth for International Relations. (In Dube, 2001, p.179–199.) For more details and comments see Frederiks, M.T. 2003. Miss Jairus Speaks. *Exchange.* 32(1): p.79–80.

28   Women theologians have pleaded for other forms of theology such as story-telling, song and dance. See Oduyoye, M.A. 2001b; Moyo, F.L. 2002. Singing and Dancing Women's Liberation: My story of faith. (In Phiri, I.A., Govinden, D.B. & Nadar, S. 2002. *Her-stories.* p.389–409.)

29   Maluleke, 2001, p.249: "Stop the cult that wishes to see positive and successful role models everywhere. African women's theological hermeneutics will be the better for it. Why must role models be successful anyway? Many African Ruths are not 'successful'. Patriarchy, culture and globalization will not let them succeed." Maluleke also observes that "The Ruths of Africa are not roaring successes."

research of the Circle is certainly an example of how ruthless life in Africa can be. The HIV/Aids epidemic has left very few African countries and families untouched, making tens of thousands of victims. There are no words to describe the personal grief and the societal disruption the epidemic has caused and is still causing. Few families in Southern Africa are not affected by the epidemic and societal structures are falling apart. All this poses major challenges to the society at large, and to the churches and theology in Africa. What to say in the face of HIV/Aids? In what way have churches and their theologies contributed to the spread and the stigma of HIV/Aids? And how can churches respond in a more constructive way to the HIV/Aids crisis? These are just a few of the many questions arising from the pandemic.

HIV/Aids as a theological theme has come to the agenda of the Circle only recently. Faced with the enormous impact of HIV/Aids on the society and aware of the intricate relationship between HIV/Aids, gender roles, cultural practices and poverty, the Circle decided to change the topic for its continental Circle meeting in 2002 (August 4–8). In Addis Ababa the Circle women met to discuss the theme "Sex, stigma and HIV/Aids: African women challenging religion, culture and social practices". Papers were presented on topics as diverse as the theodicy question, HIV as a weapon in the civil war in Congo, cultural practices (such as dry sex and levirate marriage) that enhance the spread of HIV/Aids and the role of African churches in the epidemic.

Meanwhile, several of these papers have been published. In 2004 a book was published on the role of the churches in the pandemic, called *African Women, HIV/Aids and Faith communities* (Phiri et al 2004). The articles vary distinctly in theme and approach. Some emphasise how the churches can and do play a positive role in the epidemic through liturgy and pastoral care and give practical resources for pastors in the form of prayers and litanies.[30] Others, like Masenya's article "Trapped between Two 'Canons'" and Chauke's "Theological Challenges and Ecclesiological Responses to Women Experiencing HIV/Aids" are much more critical towards the churches.[31] In a number of heart-rending case studies Chauke shows how traditional practices like levirate marriage, coalesced with a church morality of obedience to husbands and parents, have enhance the vulnerability of women to HIV/Aids. She concludes on the rather stern note that the "church, along with its leaders, are reluctant to involve themselves in a

---

30   Landman, C. Spiritual Care-giving to Women Affected by HIV/Aids. (In Phiri et al, 2004, p.189–209); Govinden, D.B. This is My Body Broken for You. (In Phiri et al, 2004 p.259–288.)

31   Masenya, M. Trapped between Two 'Canons': African South African Christian Women in the HIV/Aids Era. (In Phiri et al, 2004, p.113–128); Chauke, E.. Theological Challenges and Ecclesiological Responses to Women Experiencing HIV/Aids: A South Eastern Zimbabwe context. (In Phiri et al, 2004, p.128–148.)

meaningful way to help the people who are infected, because some church leaders think that HIV/Aids is God's punishment for sin."[32] Thus, according to Masenya and Chauke the church is an accessory to the spread of HIV/Aids.

In 2005 yet another volume, *Grant Me Justice: HIV/Aids and Gender Readings of the Bible*, appeared (Kanyoro & Dube, 2005). This book is a collection of articles on biblical passages, read in the context of HIV/Aids. The aim of the book is to empower women with the help of biblical stories to resist injustices that make them more vulnerable for HIV/Aids and to demand that justice be done. In an article on Job, the reader is taken to meditate on suffering in the context of HIV/Aids, whilst with the stories of Tamar and the Canaanite woman, women are called upon to break the silence on HIV/Aids and lament over the evil that has struck Africa.[33] Kanyoro, one of the editors of *Grant me justice*, writes in the preface: "Bible stories . . . model for us forms of resistance, sometimes needed in order to bring change. Resistance and challenging culture and cultural practices is one of our most urgent tasks in the face of HIV/Aids" (Kanyoro & Dube, 2005, xi). The two books differ somewhat from earlier Circle publications. The central focus of the publications has shifted from women's issues to HIV/Aids. Though both books still pay special attention to the plight of women in the HIV/Aids epidemic, the matters discussed are much more general and pertain to men and women. More than liberation or inculturation theologies or a combination of the two, these books can be qualified as contextual theologies. They propose theologies that endeavour to make sense of the many questions arising from the context of the HIV/Aids epidemic (in particular matters affecting to women) and seek ways towards viable communities in a context of death and dying. While the topic of gender justice is still interwoven with the theme of HIV/Aids, the topic of inculturation appears to have (temporarily) vanished into the background of the Circle agenda. But, considering that the first Circle publications on HIV/Aids only appeared three years ago, it is still very early to draw any definite conclusion on the approach of the Circle towards the pandemic.[34]

---

32   Chauke, E, 2004, p.147.

33   Nadar. S. 'Barak God and Die!' Women, HIV and a Theology of Suffering; Ackermann, D.M. Tamar's Cry: Re-reading an ancient text in the midst of an HIV and Aids pandemic; Boniface-Malle, A. Allow Me to Cry Out: Reading Matthew 15:21–28 in the context of HIV/Aids in Tanzania. (In Kanyoro & Dube, 2005, p.60–80; 27–60; and 169–186 respectively.)

34   The Circle continues to publish on HIV/Aids. Two more books seem to have been published in 2005, but I have not been able to find any copies or references to the books on the websites of publishers that these books have indeed already been published. The books are: Hinga, T. Kubai, A. & Mwaura, P. 2005. *HIV/Aids, Women and Religion in Africa*. Pietermaritzburg: Cluster Publications; Akintunde, D.O., Amoah, E. & Akoto, D.B.E.A. (eds). 2005. *Cultural Practices and HIV/Aids: African Women's Voices*, Accra: Sam Wood. The Circle has also announced a French book under the editorship of Helene Yinda and a Portuguese publication edited by Victoria Pereira and Felicidade Cherinda.

One of the few examples of an integrated approach of liberation and inculturation to combat HIV/Aids has been Isabel Phiri's article on virginity testing (Phiri 2003). In the essay she proposes to adopt the Zulu practice of virginity testing as a way to guide and mentor girls in the violent context of South Africa. Other women theologians however, among whom Beverley Haddad, have strongly rejected virginity testing in the fight against HIV/Aids. Haddad emphasises that virginity testing encourages alternative forms sex, such oral and anal sex, which contribute to spread of HIV/Aids, while virginity testing as a practice is humiliating to women, as women's virginity can be tested, while men's cannot (Haddad 2005).

It seems fair to state, that among African theologians, the women have taken up the challenge to theologise in the context of "ruthless Africa". More than their male colleagues they have researched and published on theology in the context of HIV/Aids. But, according to Isabel Phiri, the HIV/Aids crisis has also challenged African women theologians in another way. It has also challenged women to get practically involved. Nowadays women theologians participate in creating educational (video) material, partake in advocacy and lobby work, and have produced a curriculum for HIV/Aids education in theological institutions.[35] For some women, this is a way to do something concrete and constructive, in situation where otherwise silence seems to be the only option. Beverley Haddad, a South African pastor/theologian who has many people living HIV/Aids in her parish, sums up the difficulty of theologising in context of so much despair and death. In a recent article interview she says to share much of the confusion of her parishioners: "We have few answers and much silence. My efforts have turned to lobbying and advocating a swift rollout of anti-retroviral treatment."[36] Isabel Phiri has captured this shift in the work of the Circle with the words:

> With our growing influence comes increased responsibility. People now look to the Circle for more in-depth and practical involvement in the life of communities. The Circle women are being challenged not only to respond to the dearth of theological literature from African women but also to play a significant role in helping to create and sustain viable communities of women and men in the church and in society in Africa.[37]

The context of HIV/Aids seems to have compelled the Circle women not just to write about liberation and the promotion of life for men and women in

---

35   E.g. Dube, M. (ed.). 2003. *HIV/Aids and the Curriculum. Methods of integrating HIV/Aids in theological programmes*. Geneva: WCC Publications.

36   Interview with Adriaan van Klinken with Beverley Hadad, February 22 2006, Pietermaritzburg. Van Klinken does research into the relation between gender, theology and HIV/Aids with three female African theologians: Beverley Hadad, Isabel Phiri and Fulata Moyo. The Master thesis, called *Theologising life in the face of death* will become available in August 2006. B. Haddad, "We Pray but We Cannot Heal: Theological Challenges Posed by the HIV/AIDS Crisis," a not yet published article (still in progress).

37   http://www.thecirclecawt.org. Viewed 18 May 2006.

Africa, but also to live it out and work towards it in concrete action. Many women, either in their churches or in the society, have therefore become activists advocating free anti-retroviral medication, demanding a de-stigmatisation of HIV/Aids and sex, combating poverty and striving for justice and liveable communities for men and women alike. The Mission Statement of the Circle nowadays emphasises that the Circle women pledge to do more than research and publication alone. They commit themselves, in the words of the Mission Statement in writing and action to "not only affirm the need for justice and human dignity for all women and all people but also, more importantly, to be lead agents in creating such justice."[38] Daughters of Anowa indeed.

Conclusion

Phillip Jenkins in *The Next Christendom* indicated that theologies from the South will probably differ from those of the North. He posited that they will neither fulfil the revolutionary dreams of liberal theologians nor the ambitions of conservative North, but rather will "develop a wider theological spectrum than at present" (Jenkins, 2002, p.9). His observations are proven correct, at least in the case of African women's theologies.

In this article we have presented African women's theologies as a case-study of a group of theologians who have formulated "their own solutions to their own particular problems". African women's theologies focus on the issues of women, religion and gender, but do so in an inclusive and African way. In their work they merge liberation and inculturation theologies into contextual African women's theologies. The Nigerian theologian Ogbu Kalu underlined this explicit African character of the Circle theologies in a recent article, when he designated the theologies as "feminist discourses in ebony strokes".[39] It may be clear by now that African women theologians reject the term 'feminist' for their work. The term is perceived to be too antagonistic, too aggressive and too Western. African women theologians perceive gender liberation and gender equality as a joint project, undertaken together with men and aimed at promoting life for women *and* men in Africa. In striving for gender justice, the women have opted for African concepts such as nurture, motherhood and life-giving to express their dignity. African women theologians consider African cultures to be sources of oppression and patriarchy, as well as resources for liberation and dignity. The same ambiguity African women theologians

---

38   http://www.thecirclecawt.org. May 18 2006.
39   Kalu, O. 2006. Daughters of Ethiopia. Constructing a feminist discourse in ebony strokes. p.261ff.

display to culture, they also exhibit in the field of hermeneutics: for nearly all African women theologians the Bible is and remains a source of inspiration and dignity, despite its overall male character and strong patriarchal character. At times, the women have used African myths, symbols and stories in an attempt to reinterpret the texts in a more women-friendly and empowering way.

More, recently African women seem to have abandoned their exclusive focus on gender issues all-together and have ventured in the wider field of social issues, with particular attention for the HIV/Aids epidemic. Though the work of Circle women still shows a bias towards women's issues—the crisis seems to have hit the already vulnerable women and girls even more fierce than men—the theological concepts, liturgies and models they develop are applicable and beneficial to the wider community. This shift in focus ties in with—and is a natural consequence of—the overall aim of African women's theology: to develop a contextual theology, which sustains and promotes life for both men and women and which facilitates the establishment viable communities in Africa.

Western feminist have expressed their doubts about the enterprise of African women theologians have undertaken. Some have questioned whether a joint project of men and women in this area of gender justice is feasible.[40] Others, such as Pemberton, have criticized African women for choosing traditional female values such as nurture and sacrifice to express their dignity (Pemberton, 2003, p.88). Again others, like Phyllis Bird, have indicated that in their opinion few African women theologians are willing to draw the ultimate conclusions from their observations that the Bible is patriarchal document.[41] No doubt, there is some truth in these critiques. Seen from the point of view of Western feminist theologians African women theologians do not seem to go "all the way"; African women's theology is different, less radical, less confrontational. But why use Western standards to evaluate African women's theology? To quote John Mbiti again: Are we not allowed to become what we wish to become?

African women's theologians seek for meaningful and contextual ways to convey their theologies. They express their theologies in concepts of life-giving, caring, motherhood and nurture, merging liberation and inculturation theologies. Whether these contextual theologies, that are liberative and empowering in the African context, are applicable and inspiring to women (and men) of other contexts, has never been issue for African women theologians. After all, they are African women, daughters of Anowa, theologising in the context of Africa.

---

40   Russell, L.M. & Oduyoye, M.A. Wise woman bearing gifts. (In Phiri, I.A. & Nadar, S. *African Women, Religion, and Health.* p.51.)

41   Bird, P.A North American Feminist Response. (In Dube, 2001, p.206.)

References

Abbey, R.T. 2001. Rediscovering Ataa Naa Nyonmo: the father mother God. (In Njoroge, N.J. & Dube, M.W. 2001. *Talitha cum! theologies of African women.* Pietermaritzburg: Cluster Publications.)

Adeyemo, T. 2006. *Africa Bible commentary: a one-volume commentary written by 70 African scholars.* Nairobi: World Alive Publishers.

Akoto, D.B.E.A. 2001. The mother of the Ewe and Firstborn daughter as the 'Good Shepherd' in the cultural context of the Ewe peoples: a liberating approach. (In West, G.O. & Dube, M.W. *The Bible in Africa.* p.260–278.)

Dube, M. (ed.) 2001. *Other ways of reading: African women and the Bible.* Atlanta: Society of Biblical Literature.

Haddad, B. 2005. Reflections on the Church and HIV/AIDS: South Africa. *Theology today.* 62: p.35. Interview by Van Klinken with Haddad, 22 Feb 2006.

Hoedemaker, L.A. 1997. *Theologiseren in context.* Kampen: Kok.

Jenkins, P. 2002. *The next Christendom: the coming of global Christianity.* Oxford: Oxford UP.

Kanyoro, M.R.A. 2002a. Beads and strands: threading more beads in the story of the Circle. (In Phiri, I.A. Govinden, D.B. & Nadar, S. (eds). *Her-stories: hidden histories of women of faith in Africa.* Pietermaritzburg: Cluster Publications. p.35.)

Kanyoro, M.R. 2002b. *Introducing feminist cultural hermeneutics: an African perspective.* Sheffield: Sheffield Academic Press.

Kanyoro, M.R.A. & Dube, M. 2005. Grant me justice: HIV/Aids and gender readings of the Bible. Pietermaritzburg: Cluster Publications.

Landman, C. 2001. The implementation of biblical hermeneutics. (In Njoroge, N.J. & Dube, M.W. 2001. *Talitha cum! theologies of African women.* Pietermaritzburg: Cluster Publications. p.83–93.)

Maluleke, T.S. 2001. African "Ruths", ruthless Africa: reflections of an African Mordecai. (In Dube, M.W. (ed). 2001. *Other Ways of Reading.* Geneva: WCC publications. p.249.)

Masenya, M. 2001. Esther and Northern Soto Stories. An African-South African woman's commentary. (In Dube, M.W. *Other Ways of Reading.* p.27–50.)

Mbiti, J.S. 1970. Christianity and traditional religions in Africa. *International review of mission.* 59: p.439.

Njoroge, N.J. 1997. Woman, why are you weeping? *Ecumenical review.* 49(4): p.427–438.

Njoroge, N.J. 2001. A spirituality of resistance and transformation. (In Njoroge, N.J., Dube, M.W. 2001. *Talitha cum! theologies of African women.* Pietermaritzburg: Cluster Publications p.66–83.)

Njoroge, N.J. 2002. Reclaiming our heritage of power. (In Phiri, I.A., Govinden, D.B. & Nadar, S. (eds). *Her-stories: hidden histories of women of faith in Africa.* Pietermaritzburg: Cluster Publications.)

Oduyoye, M.A. 1986. *Hearing and knowing: theological reflections on Christianity in Africa.* Maryknoll: Orbis Books.

Oduyoye, M.A. 1988. African women hermeneutics. (In Maimela, S., König, A. (eds). *Initiation into theology: the rich variety of theology and hermeneutics.* Pretoria: J.L. van Schaik Publications. p.367.)

Oduyoye, M.A. 1995. *Daughters of Anowa: African women and patriarchy.* Maryknoll: Orbis.

Oduyoye, M.A. 2001a. The story of a circle. *Ecumenical review.* 53(1): p.97.

Oduyoye, M.A. 2001b. *Introducing African women's theology.* Sheffield: Sheffield Academic Press.

Okure, T. 1985. Biblical perspectives on women: Eve the mother of all the living (Gen. 3:20). *Voices from the third world.* 8(2): p.82–92.

Okure, T. 1989. Women in the Bible. (In Fabella, V. & Oduyoye, M.A. 189. *With passion and compassion.* p.52.)

Pemberton, C. 2003. *Circle thinking: African women theologians in dialogue with the West.* Leiden: Brill Academic Publishers.

Phiri, I.A. 1997. Doing theology in community: the case of African women theologians in the 1990s. *Journal of theology for Southern African* 99: p.70.

Phiri, I.A. 2003. Virginity testing? African women seeking resources to combat HIV/Aids. *Journal of constructive theology.* 9(1): p.63–78.

Phiri, I.A. 2005. The circle of concerned African women theologians

Phiri, I.A., Haddad, B. & Masenya, M. 2004. *African women, HIV/Aids and faith communities.* Pietermaritzburg: Cluster Publications.

Ukpong, J. 2001. Developments in biblical interpretation in Africa. (In West, G.O. & Dube, M.W. *The Bible in Africa.*)

Walls, A. 2000. Eusebius tries again. *International bulletin of missionary research.* 24(3): 106.

Walls, A. 2004. The gospel as liberator and prisoner of culture. (In Walls, A. *The missionary movement in Christian history.* London: T&T Clarke)

West, G.O. 2001. Mapping African biblical interpretation: a tentative sketch. (In Dube, M.W. & West, G.O. (eds). *The Bible in Africa.* p.35.)

Gemma Cruz-Chia

Filipina Domestic Workers in Hong Kong

This paper explores the role and significance of migration in relation to Christendom as explicated by Philip Jenkins in his book *The Next Christendom: The
Coming of Global Christianity.* It explores, in particular, the experience of
the Filipina domestic workers in Hong Kong vis-a-vis Jenkins' position that the
Southern churches will fulfill neither the Liberation Dream of the South nor the
Conservative Dream of the North, but will seek their own solutions to their particular problems. The paper begins with a brief exposition of the context, feature,
and character of the migration of Filipinas to Hong Kong as domestic workers.
This is followed by an examination of how religion serves as both comfort and
challenge or as a source of oppression and, at the same time, a means in the struggle for survival and liberation of the Filipina domestic workers in Hong Kong.
Having discussed all of the above, the paper then concludes with some theological challenges posed by migrant Christianity to Christian theology based on the
experience of religion by the Filipina domestic workers in Hong Kong.

How could we sing the Lord's song in a strange and alien land?

-Psalm 137:4

Migration is a phenomenon that is as old as humankind. Today, however, its
density, velocity, multi-directionality, and consequent complexity are radically
redefining human geography. The United Nation's 2002 International Migration
Report, for instance, says that there are roughly 175 million migrants, 105 million or 60% of whom are in developed countries. Of these, 56 million are in
Europe, 50 million in Asia, and 41 million in North America. Indeed, the volume of migration in the last decades is such that it is believed to be responsible
for two-thirds of the population growth in industrial countries, according to
Migration News ("Global Trends," April 2003).

Today, almost 10% of the Filipino population is outside the country and
around 70% is affected by migration. Filipino migrant workers are in 193 out
of the 224 UN-registered countries in the world. Such is the intensity of contemporary Filipino labor migration that it has captured the imagination of the
international community, which has started to refer to the Filipino migrants'
community as a diasporic community. Today also, this Filipino labor migration
is getting more and more concentrated in Asian destinations and experiencing
intense feminization. From Hong Kong to Singapore . . . Saudi Arabia to
Malaysia . . . Taiwan to Japan … Filipino women are migrating in tens of thousands to work mainly in the service sector, particularly as domestic workers.

There is, however, another aspect in the life of Overseas Filipino Workers (OFWs), especially women OFWs, that is capturing the attention of those who take some time to be with them. Noted Filipino sociologist Randy David, based mainly on his experience with Filipina migrants in Hong Kong, Singapore, and Japan, asserts that in the midst of "the loneliness that grips [them] . . . the terror and insecurity that they must deal with on a day-to-day basis as unprotected guest workers in foreign lands . . . the resilience of *Pinoy* OCWs (overseas contract workers) is legendary.[1] Their joys and celebrations are louder than their distress. Only in rare instances do they crack; they gently bend with the wind" (David, 1998, p.50–52). This, according to David, is due to their spirituality or religion.

In his book *The Next Christendom: The Coming of Global Christianity*, Philip Jenkins also draws attention to the significance of contemporary migration, especially in terms of how it is re-shaping and re-defining not just human geography but also the religious features and landscape, particularly of Christianity. Jenkins sharply observes how, over the past half century, the center of gravity of the Christian world has moved decisively to the global South. He also boldly points at how within a few decades European and Euro-American Christians will have become a small fragment of world Christianity primarily because of southern-derived immigrant communities. Indeed, the impact of the face of (the Christian) religion in the context of migration is a basic strand in Jenkins' vision of the next Christendom. He posits, for example, that the Southern churches will fulfill neither the Liberation Dream nor the Conservative Dream of the North, but will seek their own solutions to their particular problems. With the same first world context, albeit in an Asian setting, the case of the Filipina domestic workers in Hong Kong, I believe, eloquently illustrates Jenkins' contentions.

The Filipina Domestic Workers in Hong Kong

The Filipina domestic helpers (or DHs as they are popularly called) in Hong Kong, who number approximately 150,000, account for the second largest population of Filipina domestic workers in out-migration.[2] Based on the records of the Hong Kong Immigration Department, the earliest documented migration of Filipinas as domestic workers in Hong Kong was in 1973. Driven by the economic instability in the Philippines, many of them, mostly between the ages of twenty and forty, married and (mostly) unmarried, left the country to

---

1   *Pinoy* is a popular shortened name or reference for Filipinos. OCWs or Overseas Contract Workers is the former term for OFWs or Overseas Filipino Workers.

2   For the purposes of brevity the Filipina domestic helpers in Hong Kong will hereafter be referred to as "DHs".

work as maids for expatriates in the former British colony. Most of the early batches that went to Hong Kong have a high level of education. They are young and single educated women, mostly in their twenties to thirties, and with rural origin or background. They were mainly from Luzon and came from extended families which belong to simple town folk.

When the British government liberalised the entry of female foreign domestic workers mainly from the Philippines, their number rose significantly and steadily. From the early 1970s to the 1990s Hong Kong is the consistent destination of Filipina DHs in the same way as Filipina DHs have been Hong Kong employers' consistent favorite because of their relatively better facility with the English language. Today, the Filipina DHs make up the majority of Hong Kong's 240,000 foreign house help and make up the largest ethnic migrant group.

But despite all the seeming advantages, life for Hong Kong's modern-day "*amah*" is in itself a saga riddled with drama. It is a saga born in the constricting mold of gendered Filipino socialization, forged in the gendered economy of globalization, and sealed by the anti-migrant domestic worker policies of Hong Kong.[3] But then again, their life is not just about marginalization and exclusion. It is equally about their strategies for survival which offer us windows into human liberation.[4]

Religion as a Source of Oppression

Despite all the re-creations of home and the availability of Filipino food, music, games, etc. many of the DHs still feel homesick. And when the other forms of oppression, e.g. socio-economic, political and cultural oppression, add on to their homesickness they survive by turning to a pervasive influence in their lives: the Christian religion. This, however, also contributes to their oppression. For one, Hong Kong, unlike the Philippines, is not a predominantly Christian country. Moreover, within the Filipino Christian and even the Catholic community there is a wide array of confusion and oppression—indifference if not oppression—reinforcing religious groups. Charismatic groups that peddle a "prosperity gospel" fall into this category.

Class issues also make the other Filipina migrant Christian communities and the local Christian community dissociate with a Filipina migrant DH church. On the part of the local community, this is affirmed by the following excerpt

---

3   See Chang & Ling, 2003, p.27–43; Constable 1997; Asian Migrant Center 2000; Vasquez 1995; Boase 1991; Mission for Filipino Migrant Workers 1983.
4   See references to this in Cruz 2003; Contable 1997; Youngs, 2000, p.44–58.

from the national report on Hong Kong presented at the FABC-sponsored Symposium on Filipino Migrant Workers in Asia:

> As we appreciate the contribution of our Filipino brethren to the Church of Hong Kong, we also recognize the difficulties in establishing a Church that is both Filipino and Chinese. We are aware that we still need to inculcate among our Chinese people that the Church is universal and that two cultures can proclaim the same faith in the same Church, in different ways and languages. The Diocese of Hong Kong would like to see the Chinese and the Filipinos join one another at Mass and gatherings, as equals and as friends. We may still be a long way from the reality of our dream but we hold this reality as our best dream and with the cooperation of the jolly and forgiving Filipinos, this will surely come true in God's own time (*Asian Migrant,* p.7)

Nevertheless, as Filipinos who come from the first Christian and still predominantly Christian country in Asia known for religiosity, DHs immediately find the nearest church and join a religious group as soon as they can (ECMI-CBCP, *Character Formation Program on Migration*, p.69).[5] Eliseo Tellez Jr. alleges that the strong reliance on religion for comfort also lays them open to another problem with the local people, who frown at the crowds they create on church grounds and consider their presence a "nuisance." He describes further this religion-based oppression of the Filipina DHs:

> …the church is a sanctuary to them. . . . Anyone who utters the name of Jesus is their friend. This makes them easy prey for charismatic groups which do not ordinarily concern themselves with things mundane like the migrants' almost slave-like conditions. The growing number of commercialized charismatic groups is one of the current challenges to the churches in Hong Kong (Tellez, 1991, p.82).

Fr. Pidgeon, a Redemptorist (C.SS.R.) priest, says "the indifference of the local church at the grassroots level leads to the proliferation of myriad and assorted [religious] groups", many of whom "do their members more damage than good." He also pointed out how the migrants' hunger for religion or deep desire to experience the comfort of religion are taken advantage of by religious groups, which do not have sound leadership and are un-Catholic in their teaching (Pidgeon, 1999, p.6–7). The Tracer study reports one concrete case of how unscrupulous "religious" leaders and groups worsen their oppression. It exposed a case shared by a representative from the Philippine consulate in Hong Kong where they traced the insanity of a few migrant workers to their membership in a church group. Although the group's name was not revealed, the informant from the consulate elaborated that "allegedly, the group placed too much pressure on their members causing the unfortunate events" (Vasquez, 1995, p.68).

The oppressive experiences they get out of this strong tendency to draw upon their Christian, especially Catholic, religion, is not only external but also

---

5   ECMI-CBCP stands for Episcopal Commission for Migrants and Itinerant People-Catholic Bishops Conference of the Philippines.

internal. As admitted by another Filipino religious minister in Hong Kong, their oppression is rooted in a situation of "centuries of the misuse of religion . . . [which] has created a people that are susceptible to blackmail." "Filipino Christianity," he says is "a brand of Christianity that is more enslaving rather than liberating" ("Ministry Alongside Migrant Workers" 2003). That is why many of them also become captive victims of charismatic groups which emphasize non-liberating concepts of the Divine.

This is not surprising since *Pinoy* DHs, like most Filipinos, have a strong association with religion. All the more so when they are in a foreign land. In the case of the *Pinay* DHs, it is in fact heavily woven into their submission as a racial or ethnic group. This predilection has strong roots in patriarchal Spanish socialization. Jane Corpuz-Brock in her article *Gospel, Cultures, and Filipina Migrant Workers*, sheds light on how this came about in the Spanish era:

> . . . Her [Filipina] freedom of choice in important aspects of her life was curtailed by the imposition of new laws and mores. Confined in her area of action, the woman poured all her innate sensibility and energy into the activities allowed her, developing a religious fervor which would verge on fanaticism. She was constantly reminded of her innate danger to men as the seductive Eve and was relentlessly exhorted to follow an impossible model—the Virgin Mother. She could venerate her but her efforts to emulate her brought her into scrupulous frustrated efforts which ended up giving her an abiding guilt complex which added to her timidity and lack of self-confidence and, in many cases, reducing her to frigidity . . . patriarchal society succeeded in alienating her [Filipina] from public life, public decisions and public significance. She should henceforth be a delicate ornament of the home or the victim soul of the convent (Mananzan, 1991, p.34–35).

Indeed, "the church and state were responsible for the imposition of religious and sexual purity on the Filipina" (Mananzan, 1991, p.30–31). Today, this preoccupation with religion persists among Filipinas, most especially among Filipina migrant workers. To them, religion is a cogent and authoritative tool in understanding and behaving in light of their oppression. Whether superficial or deep, exploitative or responsive, religion is *a*, and oftentimes *the,* norm to view and confront personal and social oppression. Not surprisingly, religion is used to, at best, cushion the impact and, at worst, to rationalize or justify their multifarious oppression. To be sure, religion is often invoked as a source of life orientation. This is evident especially in their writings in the print media. DH writers in *Tinig Filipino*, for instance, often couch their advice to fellow DHs in religious language. Lanie Jose in an article entitled "Because of Love" encourages her fellow DHs to learn to love their employers no matter how bad they may be. She criticized and even blamed the DHs:

> If you only came here to work and you're just after money and never winning your employer's trust and confidence, then, *there's something wrong with you*...They may be the meanest boss, very inconsiderate, too meticulous, fault-finder, and strict but then, we have to learn to dance with them. . . . My secret in winning their confidence? Simple! I always have a ready smile. . . . I maintain my patience and above all, *I always seek the Lord's guidance* (emphases mine) (Jose, 1992, p.8).

Many of them rationalize their oppression by seeing it from the perspective of religious based notions of dependence on God and suffering. They become more submissive, however, when the latter is linked with sacrifice and becomes "redemptive suffering." They reckon that it is acceptable, even good, to suffer if it will mean redeeming someone. Like Jesus, the dutiful Son, they just consider their submission to the oppressive situation as an act of a dutiful daughter, wife, mother, and a Filipino citizen.

Positive or romanticized religious notions of sacrifice as a means of viewing and enduring their oppression are common among them. Melanie Romero in a letter to *TNT* (*TNT* stands for "tago nang tago", keeps on hiding) entitled "Rewarding Sacrifice" shares how "strong faith," "grace of perseverance," and "prayer" are keys to finishing a troublesome contract. In relation to this, she rationalizes that one just has to bear the difficulties because blessings will come afterwards (Romero, 1999, p.22). Tina Bautista, however, puts it succinctly: "Central to every Christian's respect for life is the hope that sadness will always give way to joy. As we reach the end of our journey, climbing ever nearer the summit of Calvary, we are assured that death gives way to resurrection and everlasting life" (Bautista, 1999, p.27).

Most of them, indeed, make sense of, accept, and even embrace their oppression by viewing it from a religious perspective, most especially in terms of "the sufferings and death of Jesus", which "remain at the very heart of their [Filipinos'] spirituality" (Pidgeon, 1996, p.30). Camille Policarpio acknowledges this glorification of suffering inherent in the Christian heritage of the Filipina as the root of her capacity to endure suffering. Her question: "Do you simply cry at night and pray that God will punish the wicked and save the oppressed?" is a telling indication of how this religious notion becomes a means to deal with their oppression (Policarpio, 1996, p.4). At the same time, the questioning stance with which she approaches it seems a critique of the prevalent attitude. Still, this spiritualization and valorization of suffering is evident in many DHs' reflections on their experiences of injustice:

> We find ourselves wondering about these unpleasant situations and often bow our heads in despair. There are times when we shed tears and question God for abandoning us . . . Instead of becoming bitter, why not thank the Lord for the troubles that helps us recognize our spiritual needs. When we take these burdens a challenge for us, we come to . . . understand clearly that it brings us humility, contentment, and spiritual health. These difficulties we face supply us with spiritual growth if we accept them as a test of our faith in God (Becasen, 1999, p.14).

The Bible is also used to justify suffering and as a ticket to heaven. Erlinda Layosa, for example, quotes a biblical passage which says, "You servants must submit to your masters and show them complete respect. . . . If you endure suffering even when you have done right, God will bless you for it" (Layosa, 1990, p.15). Obviously, the Bible plays a major role in the life of the DHs especially when it comes to dealing with their oppressive life in Hong Kong. Even the widely-read magazine *Tinig Filipino* was not able to displace it in terms of popularity. All publications, which cater to the DHs, like all the publications for OFWs, have columns or articles on religion especially on the Bible. *TNT*, for example, has a "*Pag-aralan ang Biblia*" (Bible Study) column. Others like *Tinig Filipino* have religion columns which significantly uses the Bible in relation to the DHs' situation. Mommie Jingco, a regular columnist on religion in *TF* utilizes and even quotes from the Bible to make her fellow Filipina DHs feel good and accept their role as "servants" as well as make them understand why it is alright for them to be submissive to their "masters":

> What is wrong with being a domestic helper anyway, or shall I use the word servant or *muchacha*? From Christ's point of view these are the people who will become great because they humble themselves to serve others. It was [Christ who] promoted servanthood.
>
> . . . . Here are some tips to remember from the Scriptures: ". . . . Servants be obedient to those who are masters according to the flesh, with fear and trembling as to Christ; not with eye service, as men pleasers, but as bond servants of Christ doing the will of God from the heart, with goodwill doing service, as to the Lord, and not to men, and knowing that whatever anyone does, he will receive the same from the Lord, whether he is slave or free" (Ephesians 6:5–7) (Jingco, 1991, p.24).

Kimberly Chang's analyses based on her 1992–1997 field work on the Filipina DHs, are by far the most comprehensive and perceptive on the DHs' utilization of faith to redefine service which, in their case, have been heavily imposed with sexual overtones. Chang notes, for instance, how some DHs "define themselves as servants of the Lord rather than the physical world of men" and "describe this service to God and Church as cleansing, filling them with a sense of 'righteousness' and 'completeness'" (Chang & Ling, 2003, p.38–8). She cites here, Layosa's "love letter" supposedly written by God to Filipina overseas workers who are described as the "Chosen People to be Helpers of the World." In the said letter, Layosa said that God urges Filipina domestic workers to embrace their work as servants, bringing to it their "true Christian values, your resilient, cheerful, persevering, and helpful qualities and humble ways" (Layosa, 1994, p.6). Chang and Julian Groves, with whom she did the fieldwork, claim that statements like this cleanse the notion of the Filipina DHs' service of its sexual overtones and turn it into "an almost sacred activity, giving the women a sense of moral identity and purpose" (Chang & Groves, 2000, p.73–87).

Religion as a Means in the Struggle for Survival and Liberation

Turning to religion is another strategy by the Filipina DHs to oppose their oppression. Like other Filipino migrants who live up to the renowned Catholic image of the Philippines, the church is not just the principal site of celebration for *Pinoy* identity and community for the Filipina DHs. It is also the central source for dealing with and combating their multi-dimensional oppression. It is their refuge in times of crisis and their home when they want to shout for joy. As a Filipino priest said in one of his sermons: "The Filipinas have only one day a week of freedom, so they maximize it by liberating the Filipino spirit. That spirit includes communing with God."

Sunday, the day of freedom and the most favored off day, would not be complete without them going to Mass. In Hong Kong, it is common knowledge that it is the Filipinas who fill up the churches on Sundays. Hundreds of them flock to the ten Catholic and nine Protestant churches as well as the five charismatic services (four for JIL and one for *El Shaddai*) which have English and *Tagalog* Mass or service.[6] Saint Joseph's Church, the most popular Catholic Church, has countless of them flocking to it not only because a number of the Masses are said in *Tagalog* but also because it has Mass almost every hour from morning till dusk on Sundays. And the sight of Saint Joseph's Catholic Church on a Sunday is indeed extraordinary. How often do you find a church where crowds fall in line just to get inside? How often do you find a church that has people lining up to get in both from the front and the back? How often do you find a church that has to close its doors to people because it is already filled to capacity? Lastly, how often do you find a church that is truly a women-church? This is Saint Joseph's Church on a Sunday. At the Protestant church (Saint John's Cathedral) nearby, the sight is almost the same. A handful of men [including the priest] and a sea of women.

For the Filipina DHs, the Mass is a non-negotiable weekly event or ritual in their sojourn in Hong Kong. Amidst the confusion and isolation wrought by their marginalization, the Eucharistic celebration is a powerful means for defying their feelings of negation. For a number of them, it does not even matter which church they go to. The important thing is they see a church building, a cross, or Filipinas in a religious gathering. That is enough to draw them. In fact, there are some who officially belong to one denomination but go for the Eucharistic celebration or religious gathering of another denomination. The young DH I met on the grounds of Saint John's Cathedral goes to Mass there even though she is a Catholic. What matters to her is she has been to Mass.

Even the lack of actual church buildings is not a problem for them. If there is no church building available for them, the Filipinas find places, create, and build their own "church" out of parks, gyms, and auditoriums. Eliseo Tellez Jr. says that Filipino NGOs in Hong Kong even establish and forge links with them by "visiting churches and hanging around church grounds" since the church is where the Filipina DHs meet. Even "the physical structure of a church is

---

6   The strong religious inclination of its migrants is an acknowledged reality in Hong Kong that the SCMP even publishes every Sunday a list of churches and religious organizations which offer services.

sometimes enough to assure them that things will improve" (Tellez, p.82). It is also where they socialize. Indeed, the establishment of literally "Filipina churches" provides what could be the single most important source of continuity in their world that has changed in so many ways. Religion is a basic value among Filipinos and their "church," or the "Filipina DHs' church", represents the continuation of this most important institution in their lives. The church is both a religious and a social center—the place where they hold meaningful rituals and forge ties with their fellow Filipina DHs. Randy David describes one such experience of this power of religion in the DHs' life in Hong Kong:

> I recently sat through a Sunday service in one such gym in Hong Kong, and wondered what it was that drew in the participants. It could not have been the long high-pitched and thoroughly uninspiring lecture-sermon of the *pastora*, who certainly did not deserve her audience's reverential attentiveness. I am more certain now that it was the community, and the bonding and the comfort they derived from each other's sheer presence, that made them come . . . For when it was time to sing . . . the gym came alive. A band started to play a rousing tune, and costumed dancers with ribbons and tambourines took center court. I thought for a while it was a prelude to a basketball tournament. Three thousand Pinoys, almost all of them women, stood up. With eyes closed and arms raised, they swayed their bodies to the rhythm of a prayer. They cheered, they clapped and they shouted God's name; and in that anonymous collective drone, they cried out their individual pain (David, 1998, p.50–1).

Shu-Ju Ada Cheng, in her comparative study of migrant women domestic workers in Hong Kong, Singapore, and Taiwan, singles out this practice of the Filipina DHs in Hong Kong as a factor that explains "their ability to break the isolation and engender (the) visibility." She specifically extols Church attendance as one factor that "provides an important opportunity and space for Filipino women to establish their support system and networking, which is essential for breaking the isolation of the household" (Cheng1996, p.119). Indeed, many admit to a feeling of "homecoming" whenever they join other DHs for a Eucharistic celebration. Wherever it is held, "it's another home" where they can "forget [the] misgivings induced by being a stranger in another country" (Yeung, 1983, p.66). They do not care whether they have to stand instead of sit, kneel on a rough floor, or put up with the noise and the stares of curious passersby. For them, "it is the spirit in which one attends the Mass that counts" (Yeung, 1983, p.66).

In their church or in their religious institutions, Filipina DHs look for "Pastor", "Father" or "Sister": church people whom Filipinos have a high regard for. Not surprisingly, these religious leaders figure significantly in the DHs' religious strategy. For one, priests can give them confession: a sacrament that is very much sought by Filipinas in Hong Kong. It is where they expunge themselves of all their guilt—a deeply ingrained and easily imbibed religious feeling among Filipino Christians. This may be guilt from leaving and not even saying goodbye properly to their children; guilt from leaving their husbands all their domestic responsibilities; guilt from being an "absentee mother"; guilt from not sending money or enough money; or simply the guilt of falling short of religious obligations like not going to Mass or confession. It is where they ask for forgiveness from all their sins which heavily weigh on them as a result of a Spanish Christian heritage that puts a lot of emphasis on human beings' weakness, sinfulness, and consequent unworthiness. So many of the Catholic DHs avail themselves of this sacrament to remove the religious burden of guilt that one of the difficulties a Filipino missionary priest identified in his 1998 apostolate report is "giving confession to thousands of *El Shaddai* members."

Hong Kong has numerous temptations and many of the Filipina DHs give in to these "sinful" situations, e.g. prostitution, pre-marital sex, extra-marital affairs, etc. All these, in one way or another, compound their oppression and they look at confession as the only way through religion that this can be dealt with. "What fun would sin be without guilt? Jesus Christ is firmly planted on Philippine soil" is the accompanying caption in the *TNT* item on Catholicism as one of the 20 best things about being *Pinoy*. This, for me, captures how confession plays a crucial role to the predominant religious feelings of guilt among Filipino Christians (More 20 Best Things, 1999, p.20–1). For women, the need to eradicate their guilt on sexuality—related misdemeanors in the light of restrictive (Filipino) Christian teachings and notions, makes the sacrament of Confession all the more important.

For a number of DHs the time in and for the church does not end with the Mass or Confession. A lot of them practically spend their one and only day-off in the parish. Some even engage in pastoral work or outreach activities every Sunday by caring for sick people, visiting the needy, and performing other charitable activities (*Pilgrims of Progress,* 1994, p.15). In Saint Joseph's Church, where I went for a Mass one Sunday in July 2003, many stay and eat in the church grounds with their friends. Most linger for a chat on the latest stories or news in their friends' lives or for news about the Philippines. Some peruse or buy books from the makeshift booth of religious items by the Daughters of Saint Paul. Others return the books they borrowed or borrow books from the "Borrow A Book" program of the parish. Borrowing and reading a book is obviously one Church-initiated means that Filipina DHs take advantage of to negate their problems and resist *pagpurol ng utak* (dulling of the mind because of lack of use). But even without the book lending, most of them gravitate to the church primarily as a way of resisting the loneliness and isolation of migration. Hence, the church also becomes a focal point in their life for social reasons. Isabel Escoda, in her portrait of the *amah* as Filipina says how "she starts to feel at home, especially after she has met some congenial fellow Filipinas at the Catholic Church where she attends Mass each Sunday" (Escoda, 1989, p.49–50).

But it is also in church, particularly during their church activities or during their fellowships, that many Filipina DHs who are at the forefront of the struggle for justice got their inspiration and started their "mission." Connie Bragas-Regalado witnesses to this:

> When I first came to Hong Kong, my first Sunday's off was at the Church of All Nations in Repulse Bay. An old friend who was already involved with the Filipino Fellowship of the said church fetched me. It all started with Bible Studies and Choir service . . . I volunteered to be part of the Church Board of Social Ministry. Then the group decided to request a paralegal training, which was conducted by the Mission for Filipino Migrant Workers. Then I learned about the Mission and UNIFIL . . . their work (Bragas-Regalado, 2000, p.24–5).

The rest is herstory for Connie. From working as a DH in Singapore and then in Hong Kong, she went on to join UNIFIL in 1994 and served as one its key people as well as in other Asian migrant worker associations in Hong Kong. Today, UNIFIL is widely-respected within the Filipino community and within the Hong Kong community.

To further eradicate their feelings of loneliness and isolation, Filipina DHs also turn to the church by forming or joining choir groups, fellowships, and having Bible study sessions. It is also in their churches where they hold their regular prayer meetings; come and informally share their troubles and "adventures" with their friends; engage in their usual devotions and comply with their Christian obligations; and run to "Pastor", "Father," or "Sister" who in the Filipino Christian (especially Catholic) mentality is not only a figure of authority but also their "savior" in a lot of ways. They run to these religious leaders not only for their religious needs but even for their political and economic needs. The following excerpt from the letter to a priest by a DH illustrates this:

> ". . . if you have received my letter which I mailed last October 2 because until now I haven't received any reply regarding the extension of my visa . . . I have no money at hand if only I knew that I'm going to pay I should have sacrifice to borrow . . . All this was done too late. Is there any remedy for this father? I cry for self-pity. I spend all my money, sacrifices and efforts just for this but I'm frustrated so I call again for your help father on what I will do to extend my visa (Mission for Filipino, 1983, p.98).

Aside from giving religious services, churches provide well-organized and extensive means to help them. The Catholics, for example, have the Diocesan Pastoral Center for Filipinos (DPCF), while the Protestants have the Mission for Filipino Migrant Workers (MFMW). These two Church-based institutions have a variety of strategic activities designed to resist the Filipina DHs' multiple oppression. They organize the DHs into groups and create group activities. Both have hotlines and shelters for DHs in distress. They give counseling, help in pursuing cases, and offer religious formation programs, e.g. Theology classes, and livelihood courses which a lot of the DHs avail of especially those designed for reintegration.

Other church-based or religious activities help Filipina DHs resist as well. These include religious talks or seminars like catechism, retreats, and recollections as well as lay leadership training. During Holy Week, they also engage in a number of activities like Way of the Cross and reflection on the Seven Last Words. Occasional gatherings which simultaneously tackle legal and spiritual matters are also attended by them.[7] A number of Filipina DHs, meanwhile, join the programs of some churches that set up special joint savings accounts in which Filipina DHs may place a portion of their earnings for later withdrawal to pay for education or travel expenses. This is their way to make sure that they will be able to save even just a little since most of them are not usually able to save money for themselves.

Prayer also plays a major role in contesting their difficulties. Their resolute propensity for praying or calling on God is confirmed in the Tracer study. The study also pointed out that this finding actually confirms the findings of other two studies.[8] One interesting phenomenon among the DHs in their sojourn in Hong Kong is the emergence of the image of God as a foreigner and other related images like God as a host or God as God of strangers. These are not common God images in the Philippines, but Filipina DHs are discovering and embracing them in order to resist their oppression as migrants. They resort to imaging God as a foreigner or a God of foreigners/ strangers and everyone (including their supposed-to-be Chinese hosts) as God's guests in an apparent resistance to how their host community treats them as migrants. One of their songs in a Eucharistic celebration I attended in July 2003 picks up this theme by depicting God as a gracious host:

The Lord is my shepherd, He is Lord
And I'm His guest.
Fresh and green are the pastures
Where He leads me to my rest.
Near peaceful waters He leads me
To cheer up my cheerless heart
He guides me on the safe path
He will always do His part.

Without doubt, Filipina DHs' recourse to Christian-related means and resources is strongly facilitated by the desire to fight the difficulties, especially the injustices, born out of their status as Filipino women migrant domestic workers. But when their exposure to the multiple religious traditions in Hong Kong

---

7   At the start of the year 2003, for example, the International Christian Assembly held an activity aimed at serving the temporal, e.g., legal, and spiritual needs of the Filipina DHs. See "Legal at espiritwal", *The Sun* (January 2003).

8   Noel Vazquez et al ... refer here to the study done by M. Ramirez, *the Socio-cultural Presuppositions of Filipino Outmigration* (Melbourne: Mass Media Scalabrinian Fathers) and E. Samonte, "Filipino Migrant Workers in Japan: In Search of a Better Life and the Price of a Dream," *UP Journal of Industrial Relations*, p.24.

seeps in and the stifling Filipino Christian traditions and norms weigh heavily on them, Filipina DHs take another religion-related means to resist their oppression—religious conversion. Most conversions occur within denominations or within the same religious tradition, particularly the Christian tradition.

Moreover, the change is often from the established Roman Catholic and Protestant denominations to the charismatic groups. Across religious traditions, however, a significant number of conversions to Islam are also happening. Sithi Hawwa in the article *Religious Conversion of Filipina Domestic Helpers in Hong Kong* says that in Hong Kong, Filipina DHs make up 70% of the 60–70 annual average of conversions to Islam (Hawwa, 1990, p.10). This is significant, considering the fact that Muslims and Christians in the Philippines have a deep-seated historical conflict. In any case, Hawwa says that Filipina DHs are primarily brought and converted to Islam through their Pakistani boyfriends and Sr. Madiha, a Filipina DH convert whose similar background and good relationship with them have led to the conversion of 300 of them in just a matter of 5–6 years.

Apparently, their formation of social networks to resist their discrimination is the primary means by which they come into close contact with the Pakistani men. A lot of these Pakistani men become their boyfriends and even husbands; this creates good conditions for possible conversion. Aside from romantic involvement and inter-marriage with the Pakistani men, factors such as prior contact with Muslims (like Sr. Madiha), previous work experience in the Middle East, influence from converted family members, employers or co-workers, dissatisfaction with their former religion, mere curiosity, or a desire for enlightenment also account for their conversion. It is also interesting to note that most conversions are fueled by a desire for "greater autonomy and liberation", especially from stifling marriage-related policies of Christian Philippines. Hawwa (1990) names these marriage-related policies in the Philippines that the Filipina DHs find delimiting: the ban on divorce and abortion and the severe restrictions on birth control methods.

Obviously, the Filipina DHs feel that Christianity adds to their oppression and to halt this they choose religious conversion. This becomes the easier and preferred option, especially in the face of their immersion to the more liberal views, practices, and other religious traditions in Hong Kong. Given the factors for the conversion, it not also surprising then that a lot of converts revert back to their religion when Islam becomes repressive or less able to contribute to the mitigation of their oppression. The reasons for the reversion to their old religion that Hawwa enumerates attest to this: "inability of Mosque to fund sisters in terms of financial crises, the absence of a physical space for converts with terminated contracts, the unwillingness of fellow Muslims to employ them. . . . and the dissatisfactory behavior of Muslim men" (Hawwa, 1990, p.10).

Having said all of the above one can say that there is, indeed, some truth to Jenkins' contention that Southern churches will fulfill neither the Liberation Dream nor the Conservative Dream of the North, but will seek their own solutions to their particular problems. At a closer scrutiny, however, I reckon that the theme of liberation still figures strongly in migrant religion and one cannot just dismiss it. I dare say it is embedded in the migrants' very search for solutions to their problems and/or in their struggle for a better way of life, if not more humane conditions. Moreover, I think the liberation motif also forms part of the very challenge that migrant religion has brought to the consciousness of institutional religion and Christian theology, insofar as respectful and adequate consideration of these challenges could lead to a more life-giving Christian religion.

From Christendom to *Kin*dom[9]

Religion has, arguably, never gone through so much significance, dynamism, expansion, transformation, and even revolution as in the context of contempo- rary migration (Jenkins 2002). One can see this in how it features significantly in the lives of the DHs in Hong Kong. Away from their home country and in search of company, pleasure, and intimacy, religion, particularly the Christian religion, becomes a formidable anchor in their lives. Even historians and soci- ologists point out the salience of religion in the lives of migrants and contend that any study of migrants that ignores the role of religion will most likely be incomplete and skewed. In 1978, for instance, sociologist Timothy Smith went so far as to say that immigration itself is a "theologizing experience", since immigrants often make sense of the alienation that is inherent in migration in religious terms.[10] Hence, it would be a tragedy if Christian theology does not put this phenomenon under closer scrutiny.

---

9   I take "kindom" from Ada Maria Isasi-Diaz who uses it instead of the usual word "kingdom" for two reasons: first, she argues "kingdom" is a sexist word; second, she reckons that today the concept of kingdom—as in the word "reign"—is both hierarchical and elitist. Kindom, on the other hand, makes it clear that when the fullness of God becomes day-to-day reality in the world at large, we will be sisters and brothers—kin to each other—and will indeed be the family of God. See endnote in Ada Maria Isasi-Diaz, "Solidarity: Love of Neighbor in the 21st Century, in *Lift Every Voice: Constructing Christian Theologies from the Underside,* eds. Susan Brooks Thislewaite and Mary Potter Engel (New York: Orbis, 2004, p.306).

10   As early as 1960 Will Herberg pointed out how the early U.S. immigrant would "sooner or later…give up virtually everything he had brought with him and the 'old country'—his lan- guage, his nationality, his manner of life—and will adopt the ways of his new home" except his religion for "it was largely in and through his religion that he, or rather his children and grandchildren, found an identifiable place in American life." See Will Herberg, *Protestant- Catholic-Jew: An Essay in American Religious Sociology* (Garden City, NY: Doubleday, 1960) as quoted in Helen Rose Ebaugh and Janet Salzman Chafetz, *Religion and the New Immigrants: Continuities and Adaptation in Immigrant Congregations* (Walnut Creek, CA: Altamira Press, 2000), p.7.

So, what are the theological implications of migrant religion, given the experience of the DHs in H.K.? What is the face of a Christian theology that takes into account the new or more pronounced issues and questions put forward by migrants' experience and practice of religion? Lastly, what are the areas in Christian theology that need re-elaboration, re-definition, and re-orientation if it is to dialogue with migrant religion?

Religion obviously plays a crucial role in the identity negotiation, particularly ethnic identity, of the DHs. It is so bound up with the reproduction and maintenance of their ethnicity, that one can say their experience also falls under the perception that migrant religion is "ethnoreligion." Yet religious conversion cannot also be denied as a phenomenon in the DHs' lives. Based on the DHs' experience these heavily religious aspects of their struggle largely have to do with the dislocation and the lack of recognition for cultural and religious pluralism within and across religious traditions.

Key to attending to the challenges of migrant religion and/or religious identities in the context of migration, then, is the articulation of a Christian theology of religious pluralism (both intra or internal and inter or external) in dialogue with cultural pluralism. Based on the experience of the DHs and, as illustrated in the report of the diocese of H.K., cultural pluralism and (in the case of the DHs) plural class identities have significant effects among worshipping Christian communities. Both local and migrant congregations face formidable challenges in finding a way to worship together. There is also the issue of active evangelization and conversion across Christian denominations, which Catholic leaders in H.K. tend to view negatively. I believe these issues can be addressed by a Christian theology of religious pluralism. The same is true with the question of external pluralism or the reality of religious plurality, in most migrant-receiving countries, which has implications on migrants' religious identities. As the DHs' struggle shows, exposure to or immersion in other religious traditions, particularly in the context of labor out-migration, may not only pose limitations in practicing one's religion but opens up more strongly the possibility of conversion. A Christian theology of religious pluralism, which recognizes and respects the integrity of other religious traditions, can respond to such changes and situations.

Such changes also challenge Christian theology to explore more deeply the catholic character of the Church and/or Christianity itself in articulating a Christian theology of religious pluralism. Catholicity is "the ability to hold things together in tension with one another" (Dulles 1985). As a heuristic means, it can help in situating ethnicity in the context of the radical universality that is humanity's call and deepest identity. As it is about "wholeness and fullness through exchange and communication" catholicity can address the questions raised and/or experienced by migrant religion in view of internal and external pluralism (Wiedenhofer 1992). By focusing on wholeness as the physical extension of the Church, catholicity strikes at the exclusivity that could arise as a response, either wittingly or unwittingly, among migrants and between migrants and the local people, whether they share each other's religion or not. By speaking about fullness as orthodoxy in faith it (catholicity) allows more room for doctrinal re-appropriation or re-interpretation as particular traditions of a religion inter-act with one another hence addressing the problems or difficulties posed by internal pluralism. Lastly, and most importantly, catholicity as "exchange and communication"[11] provides a theological framework for dealing with the inter-action or relations among the members of a multi-ethnic church or congrega-tion. Authentic Christian catholicity calls us not only towards openness to social diversity, but also towards embracing it. As Miroslav Volf writes, a catholic per-sonality is "a personality enriched by otherness, a personality which avoids exclusivism and, at the same time, transcends indifferent relativism. It does not simply affirm the otherness, as otherness, but seeks to be enriched by it" (Volf, 1996, p.51).

This becomes especially urgent since, as Paul Schotsmans says, catholicity is not often the case in Christianity, especially in Roman Catholicism. In his article *Ethnocentry and Racism: Does Christianity have a Share in the Responsibi-lity?*, Schotsmans says church language itself prompts intolerance towards other views of faith and those who put these views into practice (Schotsmans, 1993, p.88). Roman Catholicism's harassment and even excommunication of its own theologians attest to this (Chia, 2003, p.29–52). According to Schotsmans, this tendency for "totalizing religious dogmatism" encourages ethnocentrism even more.[12] This theoretical and practical stance cannot hold, not only because of the changes presented by a globalizing world, but most especially because it negates the very character of the church as catholic and as the people of God.

The migrant congregations' dynamic spirituality, particularly in terms of wor-ship, also presents a challenge to Christian theology in terms of its reflections on the liturgy. Best depicted in Randy David's quote on his experience of a mostly-DHs' religious service, migrant churches' vitality and dynamism in their faith

---

11   Robert J. Schreiter, *The New Catholicity*, p.128, says this needs to be strengthened, espe-cially in terms of intercultural communication and its meaning for culture itself, in the face of global integration. The transnational character of migrant religion as illustrated by Jehu J. Hanciles, "Migration and Mission: Some Implications for the Twenty-first Century Church," *International Bulletin of Missionary Research* 27:4, p.150–52 in the case of migrant Pente-costal churches bolsters this. In the said article, Hancile reveals how migrant Pentecostal churches make use of their transnational networks to facilitate migrant movement and recruit so much that churches initiated by them often become veritable centers of trans-migration and transnationalism.

12   Schotsmans cites as an example a research comparing the behavioral patterns of Catholics, Protestants, Jews, and non-believers, where Catholics have been found to react in a more ethnocentric or racist way than the other groups (Schotsmans, 1993, p.87–89).

celebrations stand in stark contrast to the boring rituals of organized or institutional religion. In a globalizing world where the need to communicate and connect in an embodied way is sought for in religion by migrants and (almost always) with their fellow migrants, the less-participatory and clergy-centered Roman Catholic liturgy, for instance, can be alienating for migrants. Migrants "need that sense of family in order to survive in an alien world; they need to celebrate God's future in the midst of an oppressive and alienating present"[13] and liturgical celebrations are one of the ways in which they seek and/or express these.

In relation to this, the fact that religion, as experienced by the DHs in Hong Kong, serves as both comfort and challenge also has theological implications, especially in terms of how Christian theology deals with popular religion. This is because migrant religion, especially the DHs' Catholicism, is steeped in popular religion. Undoubtedly, this is a tricky task for Christian theology.[14] For a long time "popular religion" has been associated with the unlettered masses, magic, superstition, and religious ignorance which had somehow not been "christianised." Today, although there is a theological re-evaluation of this phenomenon by looking at it as a source not only of oppression[15] but, possibly, also of liberation,[16] this line of thinking has yet to be more deeply and openly articulated.

Popular religion tends to be the religion of the vanquished, the religion of the oppressed. This seems to hold true among migrants too. In the first place it is usually the marginalized from the sending country, e.g. poor or (poor) women,

---

13   These are the words of Justo Gonzalez, "Hispanic Worship: An Introduction," in *Alabadle! Hispanic Christian Worship,* ed. Justo L. Gonzalez (Nashville: Abingdon Press, 1996), p.20–2, quoted in Aida Besancon Spencer, "God the Stranger: An Intercultural Hispanic American Perspective," in *The Global God: Multicultural and Evangelical Views of God,* eds. Aida B. Spencer and William Davis Spencer (Grand Rapids, MI: Bridge Point Books, 1998), p.96, to describe and explain the *fiesta* spirit of Latino worship.

14   Ernest Henau, "Popular Religiosity and Christian Faith," *Concilium* 186 (1986): p.79, says this has to do with the fact that as a religion that is lived and experienced, not expressed in formulae, and transmitted by means of other forms, popular religiosity leads to insights and intuitions which cannot be adequately contained within the framework of formulated logic. It can, therefore, be easily dismissed as subjective and emotive—attributes that are downplayed in mainstream theology, which is highly rational and logical.

15   Because it is subject to socio-historical conditions, popular religion can be ambivalent. Moreover, because it is tied up with individual and collective identity it can also be the cause of the most profound alienation and oppression. It can hold people in the grip of irreversible regression and can have pathological and destructive effects. As such, Christian theology must grapple with it by judging it on its own merits. It must expose and point out the various mechanisms of oppression, in Church and society, which have penetrated it and critically distinguish the various ways of dealing with it so that its liberating potential can be surfaced. Puebla 450 quoted in Norbert Greinacher and Norbert Mette, "Editorial," *Concilium* 186 (1986), ix–x.

16   See, for instance, Enrique Dussel, "Popular Religion as Oppression and Liberation: The Chilean Example," *Concilium* 186 (1986), p.82–94 and Ada Maria Isasi Diaz, *En La Lucha: Elaborating a mujerista theology* (Minneapolis: Fortress Press, 1993), p.34–61.

who migrate and bring with them their icons, novenas, devotions, etc. They literally carry with them many symbols of popular religions, which become their
"weapons" to make sense of their oppression and assert their identity in their
host society. The Puebla document contends that popular religion "can give
coherence and a sense of direction to life; it is a central factor in creating and
maintaining individual and collective identity and could even be an expression
of discipleship" (Greinacher & Mette, 1986, ix). It could serve as a protest against
the official (read dominant or institutional) culture and religion and at the same
time contribute to the symbolic resolution of real-life contradictions (Parker,
1986, p.28–35). Through it unsatisfied longings of hope or people's deepest
hopes and aspirations find expression, making it a means of comfort and, at
the same time, a means of protest or resistance.

There is also the gender issue. Traditionally, women are stereotyped as the
"keepers" of religion and this is still in place among migrants. In fact, in their
study of migrant congregations, Helen Rose Ebaugh and Janet Saltzman Chafetz
points out that while there are "conditions under which [migrant] religious congregation promotes an improvement in the status of women," situations that
legitimate their traditional subordinated status persist. For instance, they often do
traditional women's work in their churches like preparing food, teaching Sunday
school classes, and performing music and social services (Ebaugh & Chafetz
2000). While this definitely needs some looking into, it is also noteworthy to
look at how this somehow becomes a strategy for survival for migrant women.

Aside from being oppressed people, migrants are also uprooted people and
religion helps them a lot to deal with the ruptures and discontinuities in their
lives. For many Filipino migrant women, like the DHs, turning to religion is one
important means to resist their oppression. Religion is a basic value among
Filipinos and their "church" or the "Filipina DHs' church" represent the continuation of this most important institution in the DHs' lives.

The fellowships or meals that usually follow the DHs' Mass/service, prayer
meetings, or any religious gathering also give us a glimpse of the rich possibilities
that Filipino migrant women's faith expressions, in the context of migration,
can offer for theological reflections, particularly feminist-theological reflections.
First of all the women usually go to great lengths to procure the necessary
ingredients for the ethnic viands which are usually the staple food whenever
they gather. They exert so much energy and creativity just so they can come up
with the real or, at least, close to the real recipe.[17] Hence, one could imagine

---

17   Ebaugh and Chafetz, (2000, p.90–2) argue that the collective consumption of traditional
      foods, together with the use of native language, plays a central role in how migrant groups
      define cultural boundaries and reproduce ethnic identities and to the extent that women
      monopolize this role, they constitute a critical linchpin in the reproduction of ethnicity
      within migrant congregations.

the joy of a migrant woman, not only at seeing compatriots, especially fellow women, but also at seeing, smelling, and eating "home" food as well.

I for one remember how delighted and, at the same time, amazed I was at seeing and eating Philippine viands like *adobo* and native delicacies like *bibingka* on a table in a house in The Netherlands on the third Sunday of my first month in my former host country. And the women-dominated Filipino migrant community in the Dutch city where I used to live does this once a month, like all the other Filipino-Dutch communities in the Netherlands, most of whom are led and sustained by women. I have been to a number of gatherings of some of these women-run Filipino communities in The Netherlands and I am very much inclined to say that like the DHs' the *salo-salo* (shared meal) after the Mass could actually be the real Eucharist. Seeing one is indeed like witnessing the Gospel at table. The spirit of joy, the atmosphere of warmth and affection, and the sense of community are such that the experience itself becomes a God-experience. It is like seeing "the substance of religion and more . . . the strength that comes from valuing the intangibles, the meanings that are continually created and understood, when human beings come together to share their lives and their fears, their meals and their memories" (David, 1998, p.52). It is the Eucharist in the flesh, rooted in the resiliency, tenacity, and beauty of woman-spirit. This reminds us that Christian life is not just about individual salvation but also about collective liberation. It teaches us that Christian spirituality must not just be about fasting, but also about celebrating; it must not just be about families, but also about communities. Most of all, it reminds us that spirituality must never be confined to prayer or any other religious activity, but to anything and everything that celebrates our humanity.

References

Asian Migrant Center. 2000. *Baseline research on racial and gender discrimination towards Filipino, Indonesian and Thai domestic helpers in Hong Kong*. Hong Kong: AMC.

Bautista, T. 1999. Pro-life corner. *TNT Hong Kong*. 5 (4): p.27.

Becasen, M. 1999. Are you dealing with agonizing burdens? *TNT Hong Kong*. 5 (4): p.14.

Boase, M. 1991. The two weeks rule in the context of the legal position of foreign domestic helpers (FDHs). (In Christian Conference on Asia's *Serving one another: the report of the consultation on the mission and ministry to Filipino migrant workers in Hong Kong*. Kowloon. Hong Kong: CCA Urban Rural Mission.)

Chang, K. & Groves, J. 2000. Neither 'saints' nor 'prostitutes': sexual discourse in the Filipina domestic worker community in Hong Kong. *Women's studies international forum*. 23 (1): p.73–87.

Chang, K. & Ling, L.H. 2003. Globalization and its intimate other: Filipina domestic workers in Hong Kong. (In Marchand, M. & Runyan, A. (eds), *Gender and global structuring: sightings, sites, and resistances*. London: Routledge. p.27–43.)

Cheng, S. 1996. Migrant women domestic workers in Hong Kong, Singapore, and Taiwan: a comparative analysis. (In Battistela, G. & Paganoni, A. (eds), *Asian women in migration*. Quezon City, Philippines: SMC. p.119.)

Chia, E. 2003. *Towards a theology of dialogue: Schilebeeckx's method as bridge between Vatican's dominus Iesus and Asia's FABC theology.* Unpublished dissertation, Katholieke Universiteit Nijmegen. 19 Nov 2003.

Constable, N. 1997. *Maid to order in Hong Kong: stories of Filipina workers.* Ithaca, NY: Cornell UP.

Cruz, G. 2003. No strangers in this church. *National Catholic reporter.* 3 Dec 2003.

David, R. 1998. *Public lives: essays on selfhood and social solidarity.* Pasig City, Philippines: Anvil.

Dulles, A. 1985. *The catholicity of the church.* Oxford: The Clarendon Press.

Ebaugh, H. & Chafetz, J. 2000. *Religion and the new immigrants: continuities and adaptations in immigrant congregations.* Walnut Creek, CA: Altamira Press.

ECMI-CBCP, *Character Formation Program on Migration.* Makati City, Phils: St. Pauls Publications, 2002.

Escoda, I. 1989. *Letters from Hong Kong: viewing the colony through Philippine eyes.* Manila: Bookmark.

Greinacher, N. & Mette, N. 1986. Editorial. *Concilium* 186: p.ix.

Hawwa, S. 1999. Religious conversion of Filipina domestic helpers in Hong Kong. *ISM Newsletter* 4: p.10.

Jenkins, P. 2002. *The next christendom.* Oxford, Oxford UP.

Jingco, M. 1991. Lowly yet fulfilling. *Tinig Filipino* Oct 1991: p.24.

Jose, L. 1992. Because of love. *Tinig Filipino* Feb 1992: p.8.

Layosa, E. 1990. Don't find fault . . . find a remedy. *Tinig Filipino* Jul 1990: p.15.

Layosa, E. 1994. Into thy hands. *Tinig Filipino* Apr 1994: p.6.

Mananzan, M. 1991. The Filipino women: before and after the Spanish conquest of the Philippines. (In *Essays on women.* Manila: Institute of Women's Studies. p.34–5.)

Ministry alongside migrant workers. *Migrant's Focus Magazine.* Issue 1. Viewed 12 Feb 2003. <http://www.migrants.net/resources/magazine/issue1/profiles6.htm>

Mission for Filipino migrant workers. 1983. *The Filipino maids in Hong Kong: MFMW documentation series No. 1.*

More 20 best things about being pinoy. *TNT Hong Kong.* 5 (4): p.20–1.

Parker, C. 1986. Popular religion and protest against oppression: the Chilean example. *Concilum* 186: p.28–35.

Pidgeon, F.J. 1996. Pag-aralan ang biblia. *TNT Hong Kong.* 2 (2): p.30.

Pidgeon, F.J. 1999. Challenging the Christian community. *TNT Hong Kong.* 5 (4): p.6–7.

Pilgrims of progress: a primer of Filipino migrant workers in Asia. 1994. Manila: FABC-OHD.

Policarpio, C. 1996. Mga dapat malaman. *TNT Hong Kong* 2 (3): p.4.

Romero, M. 1999. Up close and personal. *TNT Hong Kong* 5 (4): p.22.

Schotsmans, P. 1993. Ethnocentricity and racism: does Christianity have a share in the responsibility? *Concilium* 4: p.88.

Talks with Connie Bragas-Regalado. 2000. *Migrant Focus Magazine.* 1 (2): p.24–5.

Tellez Jr. E. 1991. An overview of Filipino migrant workers in Hong Kong. (In Christian Conference on Asia's *Serving one another: the report of the consultation on the mission and ministry to Filipino migrant workers in Hong Kong.* Kowloon. Hong Kong: CCA Urban Rural Mission. p.82.)

Vasquez, N. et al. 1995. *Tracer study on Filipina domestic workers abroad: the socio-economic condition of Filipina domestic workers from pre-departure until the end of their first two-year contract in Hong Kong.* Geneva: International Organization for Migration.

Volf, M. 1996. *Exclusion and embrace: a theological exploration of identity, otherness and reconciliation.* Nashville: Abingdon Press.

Wiedenhofer, S. 1992. *Das katholische kirchenverstaendnis.* Graz: Verlag Styria.

Yeung, C. 1983. A building that serves both God and mammon. *SCMP* 27 Jun.

Youngs, G. 2000. Breaking patriarchal bonds: demythologizing the public and the private. (In Marchand, M. & Runyan, A. (eds), *Gender and global structuring: sightings, sites, and resistances.* London: Routledge. p.44–58.)

Robert Schreiter

Epilogue

Philip Jenkins' book *The Next Christendom: The Coming of Global Christianity* has set off lively discussions in academic and missiological circles. To be sure, Jenkins is not the first author to raise questions about the shifting demographic center of Christianity and its consequences; Frans Verstraelen enumerates a number of earlier works on the same topic in the opening of his chapter in this book. Indeed, the kinds of things Jenkins was pointing to have been raised since the 1970s. Nonetheless, his voice came as an unexpected one, since he was known most recently for his focus on U.S. cultural patterns and other issues in U.S. history. His name was not a familiar one to those who have been working in the area of global Christianity. As someone relatively new to this field, a number of reviewers have noted that his views have at times lacked the nuance that long-term researchers would expect. (His views have received more of that nuance, especially regarding Africa and Asia, in his 2006 sequel, *The New Faces of Christianity: Believing the Bible in the Global South*.) But by bringing a fresh eye and perhaps some new perspectives, he has caused even seasoned thinkers to reconsider some of their views.

In this epilogue to the papers collected in this volume, I would like to look at three areas that will continue to remain contested as we look to the future of global Christianity. While the general outline of the issues may seem to be clear, we simply do not yet know just how to think about them. The first of these areas has to do with the general frameworks we use to help us understand the potential shifts that are going on as the center of Christianity moves South. The second has to do with the variety of Christianities we are now finding in any part of the world, North or South. The third will explore a variety of other factors that will impinge upon the development of global Christianity as a whole. All of these areas are filled with contested claims. Not all of these claims can be analyzed or even fully presented here. But these areas all represent sites that will need to receive further investigation if we are to find our way amidst the varieties of Christianity in the world of the twenty-first century.

The General Frameworks for Interpreting Global Christianity

One of Jenkins' conclusions about the future of global Christianity is that Christianity in the Global South will not end up looking like that of the Global North; rather, the Christianities in the South will take their own form and direction. A number of things stand behind this conclusion. Perhaps most prominent of these is the demise in the 1990s of the secularization hypothesis as the guiding engine of future developments in religion.

On this view, the development of secularization in Europe was seen as the vanguard of what was to come for the rest of the world. As countries reached levels of economic and political development similar to Europe's (and North America's), religious belief and practice would come to look more and more like the diminished form or salience of religion that had come about in those two regions. Religious belief would be articulated more in light of reason as it had come to be understood in the European Enlightenment, thereby relegating its claim to authority to what could be expressed and explained rationally. The practice of religion would become increasingly a private matter and, in some places, disappear altogether.

This hypothesis had its origins in the work of Max Weber at the beginning of the twentieth century, and had served as the master narrative of modernity regarding the future of religion for nine decades. However, the assurance with which this had been accepted began falling apart in the mid-1990s, as a worldwide resurgence of religious sentiment became more evident. The Global South has not followed in the secularizing footsteps of the Global North: the South was becoming more religious rather than less so.

Jenkins' conclusion in *The Next Christendom* about how Christianity in the Global South would be different from that of the Global North takes us up to that point of departure from the secularization hypothesis: Christianity in the Global South would fulfill neither the Liberationist Hope nor the Conservative Dream of those of the Global North. It would meet neither utopian expectations of the left nor the restorationist aspirations of the right. Instead it would somehow go its own way. But saying what the New Christendom would *not* be provides little guidance into the future. If the secularization master narrative could not describe where Christianity was going, what could? As a number of contributors to this volume have pointed out (Ustorf, Knighton, Chesworth, and Steenbrink among them), the shadow of Huntington's *Clash of Civilizations* haunts the accounts of the future that are being proffered here. Huntington's 1993 *Foreign Affairs* essay, later expanded into a book, has been one of the most pervasive if not contested paradigms for understanding the current state of the world. In this proposal, the ideologies that gave shape to the Cold War era have been replaced by civilizational units that are often driven by religion. Huntington's proposal tries to account for the resurgence of religion and the redrawing of the maps of conflict. While his proposal has been roundly criticized (see for example Menzel 1998), it continues to enjoy a certain cachet. At first glance it seems to offer helpful explanatory categories, but it also quickly breaks down when faced with particular situations. As Olivier Roy (1994) pointed out already more than a decade ago, political Islam would never likely find the internal coherence to function as the kind of civilizational unit that

Huntington envisioned. The years since Roy's prediction have substantiated his claim. Some of the contributors in this volume note a whiff of U.S. imperialism emerging through Jenkins' proposal: Huntington's view of the world is certainly from a U.S. perspective.

A larger problem, however, is the lack of useful models for understanding the role of religion in the world today. Since the middle of the 1990s, those who study international relations have noted repeatedly that all of the models now available are thoroughly secular, leaving no room for religious players, except perhaps as extremist actors on the fringe of the stage (Johnston & Sampson 1994). Efforts are now under way to develop models that find more comprehensive ways of including religion in international relations, but there is still a long way to go (Petito & Hatzopoulos 2003; Fox & Sandler 2004; Thomas 2005).

So what should be done in the meantime? The "Clash of Civilizations" paradigm is, at best, a very blunt instrument and, at worst, a legitimation for U.S. neoconservative foreign policy. Scott Thomas' cultural-linguistic model (Thomas 2005), that mirrors the work of theologians such as George Lindbeck (1984), may explain the integrity of distinctive religious communities (and variants within them), but does not help in the larger question of how these communities may interact with one another and with other actors in both conflictual and peaceful ways. Global Christianity exhibits a spectrum of polities, from the transnational, centralized coherence of the Roman Catholic Church on one end, to the myriad independent Pentecostal churches on the other, with a host of variations in between.

So any grand or master narrative eludes us at this point. What David Held and others (1999) have called a "medieval model" (i.e., a congeries of multiple, often tiny principalities held together by an overarching though not always effective imperium), may be as close as we can come at this point.

Jenkins' most recent book on this topic (Jenkins 2006) provides considerably more detail, at least on Africa and Asia. But there is still no overarching model that might provide a way of understanding what future directions might be anticipated. Given the new-found importance of religion in international and intrastate affairs—either as a driving force or a convenient legitimation of politics that were going to happen anyhow—we are badly in need of some frameworks that will help us think through these things.

The Varieties of Christianity

Jenkins readily admits that he paints in broad strokes. In many ways, the sequel *The New Faces of Christianity* is intended to fill in some of the details. A number of essays in this volume take that a step further, looking at distinct formations in the Caribbean (Vernooij)—an area that does not fall within the purview of

Jenkins' work—as well as Latin American Pentecostalism (Gooren), Northern Europe (Verstraelen), of women in Africa (Frederiks) and in South Asia (Cruz-Chia). If anything, the current state of the study of Global Christianity gives pride of place to these formations, trying to overcome the dichotomies of early postcolonial thinking, and the generalizations that often marked the treatment of the "other" from a European or North American point of view.

What can emerge from this more closely studied perspective on groups of Christians? For one (as is often the case), the generalizations do not hold very firmly. For another, they may not be very instructive. One sees this in the two contributions that focus on women. Frederiks shows how the Circle of Concerned Women Theologians in Africa has set its own agenda rather than simply following the feminist or womanist agenda from elsewhere. In some ways, these views of African women look more like the thinking of the youngest generation of feminists coming of age in the Global North who mothers were feminists: they can allow for a more complex image than those needed a generation earlier to demarcate territory for women. Cruz-Chia, in looking at Filipina domestic workers in Hong Kong, shows that their response to oppression is more complex either than the Liberationist or the Conservative Dream, yet contains elements of both.

That generalization will not get us far is especially clear in the case of Pentecostal and Charismatic forms of Christianity, which may now account for a quarter of all Christians in the world. In the 2006 survey of ten nations on four continents by the Pew Forum on Religion and Public Life (2006), one begins to see the sheer complexity and diversity of these renewalist populations on virtually every topic. In Latin America, Pentecostals are now the majority of the Protestant population in Brazil, Chile and Guatemala. David Martin (2001, 2005) has been perhaps the keenest student of Pentecostalism and of its interaction with secularization. In many ways the shapes that Pentecostalism has taken in the Global South seems to have learned how to travel globally, just as has secularization among elites (as Verstraelen points out in regarding Africa). It is, as Pentecostal scholars themselves have indicated, "a religion made to travel" (Dempster, Klaus & Petersen 1999).

Moreover, forms of Christianity thought to have taken on firm form continue to metamorphose in a changing world. Several decades ago, a great deal of attention was given to the AICs, or African Instituted Churches. They were seen to be indigenous reactions to missionary Christianity, and more representative of a truly contextual form of Christian faith in Africa. In some places, the AICs have been superseded by Pentecostal and Neo-Pentecostal churches. Even more interesting is the migration of AICs to Europe and North America, where they have become thriving congregations in major cities, attracting African immigrants and non-Africans as well. There seems to be no end to the variety of forms that Christianity is taking on as it encounters new and changing situations.

Other Factors Impinging Upon the Future

A number of authors in this volume point also to other factors that will impinge on the character of global Christianity beyond its numerical growth and demographic shifts. Sebastian Kim, for example, points out that numbers—impressive though they may be—are by no means everything. Access to power, to communications, and to other resources also shapes the profile of what Christianity is and may become. Africa may soon be the most populous continent for Christianity, but will African Christianity then become decisive for the global faith? The rapid growth of Christianity in China, at a time when that country is undergoing a tremendous economic transformation, may yield yet another picture. Although Christianity has its roots there in missionary faith, the growth of the last half century has all been internal and Chinese-led.

Where Pope Benedict XVI intends to take the Roman Catholic Church in the coming years is another example. His focus appears to be very much on Europe and the decline of faith there. His early attempts at engaging Islam appear not to be particularly sensitive or effective. Will he try to create a Catholic Christianity as a bulwark against the corrosive powers of modernity? Will he find allies in the Global South, or will they brush his efforts aside as they themselves seek to reap the benefits of modernization?

Steenbrink and Chesworth note especially the contestations going on between Christianity and Islam in two countries important for the future of both of those faiths, Indonesia and Nigeria, respectively. Indonesia is the largest Muslim country in the world that represents a generally moderate form of Sunni tradition. Nigeria finds the two faiths rather evenly positioned over against each other, with a conflicted colonial past and an uncertain political future. Jenkins has made much of the stance of the Anglican Province of Nigeria, as the largest in the Anglican Communion, and most clearly opposed to practices of that Communion in the United Kingdom and the United States. How will the two largest and fastest growing forms of religious belief confront and interact with each other in the coming decades? No one can give a clear picture of this, but nearly everyone would agree that the outcome of these contestations will do much to shape the world picture in the coming decades.

Philip Jenkins' book has done much to stir up a simmering discussion that has gone on for some years now. As globalization quickens the pace of life in many parts of the world, as migration keeps shifting the face of individual regions, and as conflicts continue to erupt at different places, the unmistakable face of religion—and it largest single form, Christianity—will continue to make its mark. The questions that are now being raised, and have been touched upon here, will be following us for the coming decades. Finding adequate models to express and perhaps explain what is happening, attending to the varieties of Christianity forming and reshaping, and charting the other variable in the mix will continue to be a significant task for those interested in global Christianity.

References

Dempster, M., Klaus, B. & Petersen, D. (eds) 1999. *The globalization of Pentecostalism: a religion made to travel*. Oxford: Regnum.

Fox, J. & Sandler, S. 2004. *Bringing religion into international relations*. New York: Palgrave Macmillan.

Held, D., McGrew, A., Goldblatt, D. & Perraton, J. 1999. *Global transformations: politics, economics and culture*. Cambridge: Polity.

Huntington, S.P. 1996. *The clash of civilizations and the remaking of world order*. New York: Simon and Schuster.

Jenkins, P. 2002. *The next Christendom: the coming of global Christianity*. New York: Oxford UP.

Jenkins, P. 2006. *The new faces of Christianity: believing the Bible in the global South*. Oxford: Oxford UP.

Johnston, D. & Sampson, C. (eds) 1994. *Religion, the missing dimension of statecraft*. New York: Oxford UP.

Lindbeck, G. 1984. *The nature of doctrine: religion and theology in a postliberal age*. Philadelphia: Westminster.

Martin, D. 2001. *The world their parish: Pentecostalism as cultural revolution and global option*. Oxford: Basil Blackwell.

Martin, D. 2005. *On secularization: towards a revised general theory*. Aldershot: Ashgate.

Menzel, U. 1998. *Globalisierung versus Fragmentierung*. Frankfurt: Suhrkamp.

Petito, F. & Hatzopoulos, P. (eds) 2003. *Religion in international relations: the return from exile*. New York: Palgrave Macmillan.

Pew Forum on Religion and Public Life. 2006. Spirit and power: a 10-country survey of Pentecostals. http://pewforum.org/surveys/pentecostal.

Roy, O. 1994. *The failure of political Islam*. London: I.B. Tauris.

Thomas, S. 2005. *The global resurgence of religion and the transformation of international relations*. New York: Palgrave Macmillan.

Contributors

John Chesworth is Programme Director for Post-Graduate Courses in Islam and Christian-Muslim Relations at St. Paul's United Theological College, Limuru, Kenya.

Gemma Cruz-Chia is an Assistant Professor in the Department of Theology of Saint Ambrose University in the U.S.A. Her area of specialization is immigration and feminist ethics.

Martha Frederiks is a lecturer at the Centre for Intercultural Theology, Interreligious Dialogue, Missiological and Ecumenical Studies at Utrecht University, The Netherlands. Among her publications is *We Have Toiled All Night: Christianity in the Gambia: 1456–2000* (2003).

Henri Gooren is a cultural anthropologist working at the Centre for Intercultural Theology, Interreligious Dialogue, Missiological and Ecumenical Studies at Utrecht University, The Netherlands.

Philip Jenkins is Distinguished Professor of History and Religious Studies at Pennsylvania State University, U.S.A. He has published widely on contemporary religious phenomena. His most recent book is *The New Faces of Christianity: Believing in the Global South* (2006).

Sebastian Kim is Professor of Theology and Public Life at York St. John University in the UK. He previously served on the Cambridge University faculty of divinity as the Director of Christianity in Asia. He is the author of *In Search of Identity: Debates on Religious Conversion in India* (2003).

Ben Knighton is Ph.D. Programme Leader at the Oxford Centre for Mission Studies in the UK. He has written *The Vitality of Karamojong Religion: Dying Tradition or Living Faith?* (2003).

Robert Schreiter is Vatican Council II Professor at Catholic Theological Union, USA. From 2000 to 2006 he was also Professor of Theology and Culture at the Radboud University Nijmegen, The Netherlands. Among his books is *The New Catholicity: Theology between the Global and the Local* (1997).

Karel Steenbrink is Professor of Intercultural Theology at Utrecht University. From 1981 to1989 he taught at the State Academy for Islamic Studies of Jakarta and Yogyakarta, Indonesia. His most recent books are *De Jezusverzen in de Koran* (2006) and *Catholics in Indonesia, vol I: 1808–1902* (2003).

Werner Ustorf is Professor of Missiology at the University of Birmingham, UK. Among his many works are *Sailing on the Next Tide: Missions, Missiology, and the Third Reich* (2000), and (with Hugh McLeod), *The Decline of Christendom in Western Europe: 1750–2000* (2003).

Joop Vernooij is Associate Professor Emeritus of Missiology at the Radboud University Nijmegen, The Netherlands. He worked for many years in Surinam and has published extensively on Christianity in that country. Among his works is *De Rooms-Katholieke gemeente in Suriname: Handboek van de geschiedenis van de Rooms-Katholieke Kerk in Suriname* (1998).

Frans J. Verstraelen is Professor of Religious Studies at the University of Zimbabwe, Harare. Among his many publications is *Christianity in a New Key: New Voices and Vistas through Intercontinental Communication* (1996).

Frans Wijsen is Professor of World Christianity and Interreligious Relations, and Director of the Nijmegen Institute for Mission Studies at Radboud University Nijmegen, The Netherlands. His latest publication is *Seeds of Conflict in a Haven of Peace: From Religious Studies to Interreligious Studies in Africa* (2007).

Index of names

Note: P. Jenkins is not listed in the Author index as his name appears 335 times in the text.